Nightwood Theatre

CANADIAN PLAYS
Series Editor: Anne Nothof

The *Canadian Plays* series features a broad range of new Canadian plays with an emphasis on Alberta works and theatre professionals. Publications will include single full-length plays and thematic collections by single or multiple playwrights, as well as theatre history and criticism. The target audience comprises theatre lovers, actors and playwrights, directors and producers, teachers, students, and librarians.

SERIES TITLES

Hot Thespian Action: Ten Premiere Plays from Walterdale Playhouse
Edited by Robin C. Whittaker

Nightwood Theatre: A Woman's Work Is Always Done
by Shelley Scott

Nightwood Theatre

A Woman's Work Is Always Done

SHELLEY SCOTT, PH.D.

AU PRESS

© 2010 Shelley Scott

Published by AU Press, Athabasca University
1200, 10011–109 Street
Edmonton, AB T5J 3S8

Library and Archives Canada Cataloguing in Publication

Scott, Shelley
    Nightwood Theatre : a woman's work is always done / Shelley Scott.

(Canadian plays series, ISSN 1917-5086)
Includes bibliographical references and index.
Issued also in electronic format (978-1-897425-56-5).
ISBN 978-1-897425-55-8

    1. Nightwood Theatre--History. 2. Feminist theater--Canada--History.
3. Women in the theater--Canada--History. 4. Feminism and theater--
Canada--History. I. Title. II. Series: Canadian plays series

PS8169.F45S36 2010   792.09713'541   C2009-907004-9

Cover design by Honey Mae Caffin, intertextual.ca
Book design by Natalie Olsen.
Printed and bound in Canada by Marquis Book Printing.

Alberta Foundation for the Arts

This project was funded in part by the Alberta Foundation for the Arts.

A volume in the Canadian Plays series:
ISSN 1917-5086 (Print)
ISSN 1917-5094 (Online)

Contents

Acknowledgements

This book began as my doctoral dissertation at the Graduate Centre for Study of Drama, University of Toronto. I extend my deepest gratitude to my thesis supervisor, Michael J. Sidnell, and to Richard Plant, Ann Saddlemyer, and Ann Wilson for their guidance. Twelve years after its completion, my dissertation has become a book, thanks to everyone at Athabasca University Press, especially Anne Nothof and Erna Dominey, who have been wonderfully supportive.

Some of the material from the introduction has been previously published in the journal *Canadian Theatre Review*; other material from the introduction has appeared in *Theatre Research in Canada/Recherches théâtrales au Canada* vol. 18 no. 2 (Fall 1997) and was reprinted in *Feminist Theatre and Performance: Critical Perspectives on Canadian Theatre in English*, Volume 4, edited by Susan Bennett (Toronto: Playwrights Canada Press, 2006). Some material in chapter two has appeared in *Resources for Feminist Research* vol. 31 no. 3/4 (Fall 2005) and other material from this chapter appeared in the *British Journal of Canadian Studies*. My thanks to the editors of these journals for first publishing my articles on Nightwood.

Thanks to the cast and crew of the productions of *Goodnight Desdemona (Good Morning Juliet)* and *This is For You, Anna* that I directed at the University of Lethbridge, and to all of my colleagues at the U of L who facilitated and responded to those shows. I have published articles about these productions in *CTR* and *Resources for Feminist Research*. I acknowledge with gratitude the University of Lethbridge Research Fund award I received in the spring of 2006. Thanks as well for their assistance and support to my copy editor, Paula Ayer, and indexer, Adrian Mather, and to Jamie Dunsdon, Denis Salter, and my many friends and colleagues at the Canadian Association for Theatre Research. And finally, very special thanks to all of the people who have worked with Nightwood Theatre over the years, and particularly to the women I have interviewed.

This book is dedicated to my husband, Bill Tice.

Preface

The first time I heard about Nightwood Theatre was in 1989, in Richard Plant's Canadian Theatre course at the Graduate Centre for Study of Drama at the University of Toronto. I was in the first year of my two-year MA program, and had come back to academia after three years working for the Alberta Status of Women Action Committee — first as a volunteer, then as the paid coordinator of the provincial office in Edmonton. I had determined that being a professional lobbyist was not the career path for me; I missed being in school, and I missed being involved in theatre even more. After completing the MA, I continued into a PhD program at the same university, and when the time came to select a dissertation topic, Nightwood jumped out at me. It represented the perfect point of intersection between my newfound commitment to Canadian theatre and my long-term connection to feminism.

I spent some time as a volunteer in the Nightwood office, located at that time on Adelaide Street — helping to construct a database, stuffing envelopes, working front of house, and selling tickets to the "Five Minute Feminist Cabaret." The women I had the most contact with were Leslie Lester and Soraya Peerbaye, and the place I spent most of my time was in their office closet, digging through the theatre's collected archives. It was a hot, dark closet and the archives were largely unorganized — just file folders in boxes, which I would drag out and sort through one by one, making an inventory and photocopying items of particular interest. Those materials are now in the University of Guelph Theatre Archives, but back in the early 1990s, I felt like I was the only one who knew the wealth of history in those boxes.

In addition to excavating the archives, I conducted interviews with people at Nightwood over the years. I began by interviewing Cynthia Grant and Kim Renders, the two founding members of Nightwood still living in Toronto (by then, Maureen White had moved to Ireland and Mary Vingoe was busy running Ship's Company in Nova Scotia). Cynthia had her own personal archive and was eager to share articles from Nightwood's earliest period. Kim later became a colleague when we taught in the same semester at the University of Guelph. In 1996, the Canadian Association for Theatre Research (at that time known as the Association for Canadian Theatre Research) bestowed honorary membership on all four founding members of Nightwood. I was thrilled that Nightwood was being recognized, and I remember being especially pleased that Kim was able to attend the awards banquet in St. Catharines to accept on behalf of the founders.

I went on to interview all the other women who had been leaders at Nightwood: Kate Lushington (who actually stored her boxes of archival material in my basement for a time); and Leslie Lester, Alisa Palmer, and Diane Roberts, who were extraordinarily welcoming and warm. I completed the dissertation and graduated in 1997. Although I moved away from Toronto afterward, I was determined to keep my research focused on Nightwood. I interviewed Kelly Thornton on 28 May 2002, just after she took over the company as artistic director, and then interviewed her again in 2006 along with Monica Esteves, Nightwood's producer.

Despite these significant connections to Nightwood, my intention has never been to claim an insider's status, to relay personal anecdotes, or to settle debates. My research has always been focused on materials in the public domain: the productions and play scripts, the media coverage and journal articles, the programs and posters. In addition to the plays and productions, I am interested in the ways Nightwood has presented itself to the public through the media and on its own website, and in how Nightwood interacts with its supporters through vehicles such as the newsletter. I am concerned with how Nightwood has communicated its feminist mandate: for example, what kinds of terms are used in a press release? How does a program blurb convey the company's history in a quick paragraph, or how is a play described in a newspaper interview to convey what its director thinks about its feminist message? What I have discovered is that, over the years, the definition of feminism has continually changed and that, as a women's theatre company, Nightwood has had to respond and adapt to changing attitudes — including the prevalent attitude that feminism has ceased to be relevant.

While this book has come a very long way from its origins as a dissertation, my overarching focus has remained on contextualizing Nightwood in terms of feminist theory and history; if anything, that focus has broadened. I had never intended to write only a straightforward history of Nightwood, although the compilation and maintenance of the chronology has been a paramount undertaking. Rather, I wanted to explore how feminist theory has changed since Nightwood's founding in 1979, and how Nightwood as a women's theatre has changed to reflect developments in feminist philosophy. This is a complex matter, for there is a great difference between feminist activism — as it is practiced by an advocacy and lobbying organization like the Alberta Status of Women Action Committee, for example — and the scholarship of feminist academia. Adding to the complication is the fact that a Canadian theatre company is an intensely busy place, influenced by the many people who come and go, marking the work with their own political and creative visions.

I have considered Nightwood in three distinct contexts: first, of contemporary conceptions of feminist theory; second, of other feminist theatre companies in Canada and beyond that grew up in the same time period; and third, of collective creation and its place in Canadian theatre history. Nightwood's significance is most clearly understood when considered within these frames of reference.

For most people, the point of contact with any theatre company is through viewing or reading its plays. While I have seen a good number of Nightwood plays, many others were produced before I arrived in or after I left Toronto, and my access to them is only through the published texts and other production records. I have also directed university productions of two plays that originated at Nightwood: *Goodnight Desdemona (Good Morning Juliet)* and *This is For You, Anna*. It may well be impossible to determine how audiences perceive a theatre company based on a performance they have viewed; after all, an idea that seems like "old news" to one spectator may be a revelation for another. But it is possible to look at which plays a company has chosen to devise, produce, and market, and, by closely examining the politics and aesthetics of those plays, to comment on the relationship between a theatre and the discourse in which it chooses to engage.

So my focus remains on Nightwood and how it communicates to the world — primarily through its plays, but also through articles in journals and newspapers, for example. Of course, the world communicates back to Nightwood too, through reviews, grants, and even box-office returns, but these have been of secondary importance for me, partly because they are skewed by so many variables. Funding cuts in Canada have more to do with what party is in government and how much it values the arts, or how the economy is doing, than with any factor specific to a feminist company. All small companies struggle. I am more interested in how Nightwood responds by marketing itself — how it tries to persuade the public of its worth and value, the tools and language by which it engages in self-definition and self-determination, and how all this is coloured by the dominant feminist and other political discourse of the day. For example, in Nightwood's most recent mandate statements and website copy, the term "theatre ecology" has been used for the first time. It is an evocative phrase that clearly reflects contemporary preoccupations about the environment, perhaps even suggesting an alliance with ecofeminism.[1]

Throughout its history, Nightwood's decisions have been governed by what I describe as a dialectic of accident and intention. Over the years, there have been shifts in policy; various aspects of programming have been emphasized over others; and conflicts and controversies have flared up. There is little value in passing judgment in retrospect, in trying to assess who was right or if mistakes were made. Theatre, like feminism, is always in motion. The debate over whether Nightwood was really a collective in its earliest years serves as a good example of how differing perspectives and memories make it hard to write a definitive version of history. Debates such as this one will surely never be resolved, since they concern personal recollections and perceptions, and different conclusions can remain equally "true" for different individuals. What is more interesting to me is the way Nightwood's founders have chosen to write about this question in the public forum; how subsequent artistic directors rewrote, reacted to, or rebelled against the same question; and how little any of it influences the critical response to the productions, or the business of appealing to ticket-buyers in the twenty-first century.

Feminism and theatre were my first areas of interest, and they remain my twin companions throughout the book. My personal identification has been mostly with materialist feminism, at least until the term Third Wave caught my attention a few years ago. Third Wave feminism is most often associated with a younger generation of feminist activism, an interest in popular culture and sexual agency, and an acceptance of pluralism and contradiction. Although the Third Wave has been notoriously hard to define, I associate it with many of the topics most interesting to me, such as the complications of gendered identity. In my first book (*The Violent Woman as a New Theatrical Character Type: Cases from Canadian Drama*, Edwin Mellen Press, 2007), I argued that Western culture has ignored or misrepresented acts of violence and aggression by women in order to maintain an ideal of maternal femininity. That book was a Third Wave project, because it took the position that in order for women to claim their full humanity, the whole, unvarnished range of their experiences must be acknowledged—not just those depictions that are flattering or politically convenient. I am most interested in feminism, and theatre, that embraces contradiction and explores complicity. Feminism is a strategy and theatre is one of its many tools, but it is a strategy that reinvents itself again and again. Theatre is an art form, a business, and a medium for many practitioners. Theatre is a set of practices and a profession. Writing about both, I am guided by my own preferences and readings, but what I have produced here is a history that engages with the faces and functions that Nightwood has chosen to show us all.

In 1993, Rita Much wrote, "By nurturing an entire generation of women theatre artists for the past thirteen years — writers, designers, directors, actors — and by emphasizing a non-naturalistic style, Nightwood Theatre has made a permanent impression on the nature and scope of contemporary Canadian theatre, its politics and its aesthetic, as well as the conditions in which this theatre is created."[2] We are now sixteen years further into Nightwood's history, and Nightwood has influenced more than one generation of women theatre artists. With youth programs like Write From the Hip and Busting Out! and support for festivals such as "Hysteria," that influence will continue well into the future. Nightwood's fervent commitment to women artists is perhaps best characterized by former artistic director Alisa Palmer, who threw down the gauntlet in the Spring 1997 Nightwood newsletter: "Artists and audiences, feminists and thespians alike, are hankering for women's art that laughs like a maniacal harlot in the pallid and even-featured face of the Disneyfied, sanitized Mega-theatre culture." Palmer vowed that Nightwood, in solidarity with other struggling companies, would "keep the theatre doors open, the art outspoken, and the strategies for survival boisterous and ingenious."[3]

Introduction
Context, Creativity, Collectivity

Nightwood Theatre was founded as a Toronto collective in 1979, and can usefully be considered in the context of other women's theatre companies of the period. In *Contemporary Feminist Theatres: To Each Her Own*, Lizbeth Goodman has discussed the origins of British and American feminist theatre in the countercultural movements of the late 1960s. She suggests that by 1968, the feminist movement was recognizing that public demonstrations were more effective than private group discussion sessions, and that this realization led to some of the early feminist theatres. The existence of a diverse fringe theatre movement also allowed for the development of splinter groups concentrating on women's issues.[1] Each decade since then has produced a new group of women playwrights, championed by women's companies and producing collectives, and complemented by women directors. In England alone, Women's Theatre Group was founded in 1974; Monstrous Regiment in 1975; and the lesbian-centred Siren in 1979. Mention must also be made of the highly influential Sistren Jamaican Women's Collective, founded in 1977.

But the theatres that can be most closely compared with Nightwood remain within North America. Dinah Luise Leavitt identifies four companies as American feminist pioneers: New Feminist Theatre (founded in 1969), It's All Right to Be Woman (1970), the Westbeth Playwright's Feminist Collective (1970), and the Washington Area Feminist Theatre (1972). According to Charlotte Canning, New York's New Feminist Theatre toured to Canada in 1974 and reported that women actually joined the company along the way.[2] Leavitt claims that the New Feminist Theatre was mainly interested in reaching as many people as possible with its feminist message, so they "sought the establishment theatre's audience."[3] She contrasts this with a group like It's All Right to Be Woman, an all-woman collective of eleven members that sometimes went so far as to exclude men from the audience for their performances.

It's All Right to Be Woman had the primary goal of empowering its female audience; the company was run and all of its shows were created in an entirely collective manner, with the work developed through a lengthy process of sharing personal material, consciousness raising, and acting exercises.[4] Canning cites It's All Right to Be Woman, along with another company called Womansong Theater, as examples of the most extreme form of collectivity; company members even refused to list their individual names on programs or in interviews.[5]

The earliest American company that might be closely compared to Nightwood is At the Foot of the Mountain. From an earlier incarnation, ATFOTM emerged as an all-woman collective in Minneapolis in 1976. Although the company folded in 1991, it was until that point hailed as the longest-running feminist theatre in the U.S. Its core members resembled Nightwood's early members in their level of university education, involvement with outside companies, and extensive experience in theatre. Their mandate from 1976 read in part, "We struggle to relinquish traditions such as linear plays, proscenium theatre, nonparticipatory ritual and seek to reveal theatre that is circular, intuitive, personal, involving."[6] The company was determined to create a different kind of theatre through an alternative method of working, emphasizing process, ritual, and what they defined as matriarchal power structures. At the Foot of the Mountain was similar to Nightwood in its emphasis on creating theatre that was also political, rather than on agitprop or street theatre activities. Both companies reached out to their audiences by mailing out brochures and newsletters, holding open workshops, and inviting the community to view works in progress.[7] While At the Foot of the Mountain encouraged discussions after all its performances, Nightwood has tended to do this only in fairly controlled ways—for example, through feedback forms at "Groundswell," its annual festival of new play development, or at panel discussions with a moderator and guest speakers. Only recently, in its 2006/2007 season, has Nightwood started having "talkback" sessions after Tuesday night performances. The two companies were also similar in having a relatively large and active staff and receiving government funding through arts council grants. There is one marked difference between the two companies, however: Leavitt writes that when ATFOTM was invited to perform at "the prestigious 'Alternative Theatre Festival' in 1977, they declined because they suspected they would be a hit and that this kind of success would inhibit the work they want to do." While they received good reviews and grants, At the Foot of the Mountain members were said to "reject most traditional success indicators."[8] This has never been the case at Nightwood, which has actively pursued as much of a profile as it has been able to afford.

Martha Boesing of At the Foot of the Mountain was one of the women who attended "The Next Stage: Women Transforming the Theatre," a two-day conference held as part of the first "Festival de Théâtre des Amériques" in Montreal in May of 1985. Cynthia Grant was the panellist representing Nightwood. Other Canadian participants included Rina Fraticelli, Kate Lushington, and Pol Pelletier, and participants from the U.S. included Joan Schenkar, Maria Irene Fornes, Judith Malina, and JoAnne Akalaitis. Honor Ford-Smith attended, representing Sistren. On her panel, Martha Boesing argued that women's theatre is experimental and should therefore not censor itself on aesthetic grounds by imposing standards of excellence that are traditional and patriarchal. Aesthetic criticism, Boesing said, is "based on a language not our own." Instead, she believed, women should develop a new form of criticism, one that could transcend race, class, and nationality, and by which the transformative nature of women's theatre could be understood. Part of her suggestion was to invite the audience in to provide feedback at every stage of the work, not just for the finished product.[9]

Another American company that invites a close comparison with Nightwood is The Women's Theatre Project, which, unlike At the Foot of the Mountain, is still going strong; it is the largest and oldest theatre company in the U.S. devoted to producing the work of female playwrights. The company was founded by Julia Miles, who, while working with new playwrights at The American Place Theatre from 1964 to 1978, was disturbed by how few plays by women were produced on the mainstage. In the late 1970s, a group called Action for Women in Theatre issued a report on the status of women in American theatre (which paralleled the 1982 Canadian study by Rina Fraticelli discussed later in this introduction). Miles learned "that only 7 per cent of the playwrights and 6 per cent of the directors in funded non-profit theatres during 1969–1975 were women."[10] She was also aware that only ten percent of the plays submitted to The American Place Theatre were by women. Miles concluded that a special environment was needed to "welcome women in a professional embrace" by providing role models as well as all the tools required — designers, a theatre space, and an audience.[11] With an $80,000 grant from the Ford Foundation, The Women's Project at The American Place Theatre was founded in 1978. Julia Miles still serves on the board as artistic director emeritus.

The Women's Project began with a developmental process to take scripts through a rehearsed reading, directed by women and including a taped audience discussion. Scripts went on to secondary development work, and then to studio productions. A director's unit was also established, which began collecting statistics on the employment of women directors.[12] In only the second season, two of the Studio Production plays also made it onto The American Place mainstage, and Julia Miles began publishing volumes of the plays coming out of The Women's Project. In a volume of plays published in 1989, Miles commented in her introduction that, since the statistics were released in 1978, the number of plays by women being produced at non-profits had tripled to about 20 percent. "Not enough," Miles insists. "Statistically 20,000 people see a Broadway play each night. Only 1,000 of those see a play written by a woman — Wendy Wasserstein's *Heidi Chronicles*. Not enough."[13]

Today The Women's Theatre Project operates three ongoing programs. Since its first production, in 1978 — *Choices*, by Patricia Bosworth — the company has continued to produce women's plays and cultivate women theatre artists. The Project maintains the Julia Miles Theater in Manhattan, as well as a separate rehearsal space. In the Lab Series, which runs programs for playwrights, directors, and (as of 2006) producers, eight to ten members participate in a two-year development program. Participants meet monthly for developmental work sessions with industry professionals and workshop plays in progress.

Perhaps the most ambitious undertaking of The Women's Theatre Project is Ten Centuries of Women Playwrights, an arts education program in New York high schools. A Women's Project teaching artist, along with guest playwrights, actors, and directors, works alongside classroom teachers to introduce students to plays by women. The students improve their reading, writing, listening, and speaking skills through vocabulary, creative writing, and historical research assignments. The students then begin writing and preparing their own scenes, culminating in a public performance at the Julia Miles Theater.

The commitment of The Women's Theatre Project to produce plays by women is obviously shared by Nightwood, and its determination to nurture writers is paralleled by Nightwood programs such as "Groundswell," Write From the Hip (a development program for younger playwrights), and the recent Emerging Actors Program, which matches young theatre school graduates with professional actors to work on "Groundswell" shows. And while Nightwood cannot boast anything quite as ambitious as Ten Centuries of Women Playwrights, the intention to inspire young women is certainly present in its program for teenage girls, called Busting Out!

In Canada, Cynthia Zimmerman has argued that women's theatre arose from the nationalist movement in theatre, and from a general environment conducive to the exploration of issues and social change. "In the early seventies in Canada," she writes, "it was the nationalist movement that was the proud parent."[14] Both Lizbeth Goodman and Zimmerman recognize that women's performance, whether in Canada or beyond, developed within the context of broader social forces. The British playwright and historian Michelene Wandor has claimed that whenever there is a movement toward social change and greater freedom, women will seize the window of opportunity to create new forms of resistance.[15] Canadian Yvonne Hodkinson has charted a similar evolution in her discussion of women in theatre. In her introduction to *Female Parts: The Art and Politics of Women Playwrights*, Hodkinson laments that after women won the right to vote in 1920, the women's movement seemed to lose its impetus.[16] Women did not start confronting social and psychological patterns of oppression in an organized way until the 1960s—a period marked by the publication of landmark American studies such as *The Feminine Mystique* (1963) and *Sexual Politics* (1970). In Canada during this period, playwrights such as Beverley Simons, Aviva Ravel, and Patricia Joudry began integrating a feminist sensibility into their work and using it to explore female psychology. Groundbreaking plays such as *The Fairies are Thirsty* (*Les fées ont soif*) by Denise Boucher and *Jennie's Story* by Betty Lambert portrayed women's oppression by patriarchal institutions, particularly the Catholic Church. Hodkinson notes that many female Canadian playwrights, such as Diane Grant, Wendy Lill, and Carol Bolt, began their exploration of feminist themes by looking back at women's history; she finds it revealing that so many feminist plays deal with historical settings and figures, describing this phenomenon as one of "unravelling women's past as a first step to understanding present day Canadian women."[17] Hodkinson articulates an important feminist principle: autonomy means being born into a world where one has a meaningful past and can therefore make choices for the future.

How Far Have We Come?

In 1982, Rina Fraticelli, artistic director of the Playwright's Workshop in Montreal, was commissioned by Status of Women Canada to conduct a study on the status of women in Canadian theatre. Although her report was solicited by the federal government, it was not published in full, nor was it ever acted upon at a government level. However, Fraticelli's findings did serve as a wake-up call to Canadian women theatre-makers. Some of her statistics were published in arts-related and feminist journals; they were used to particular effect by the Toronto director Kate Lushington to illustrate her article "Fear of Feminism," published in *Canadian Theatre Review* in 1985.[18]

Although Nightwood Theatre had existed since 1979, and had not initially promoted itself as a women's theatre company, the release of the Fraticelli report was a catalyst toward a clearly feminist mandate. In their applications for government funding, press releases and advertising brochures, and programming, the women of Nightwood Theatre drew upon the awareness sparked by Rina Fraticelli's statistics to articulate a new vision — one in which they could play a major role in addressing the gender imbalance in Canadian theatre. In a 1984 funding application to the charitable Laidlaw Foundation, Nightwood's artistic coordinator, Mary Vingoe, stressed the urgent need for developmental contexts for women playwrights, directors, and performers by observing, "Our theatre increasingly finds itself viewed as a central resource and potential producer for women artists in the city."[19] Nightwood's commitment to producing work by women took on an urgency that has carried the company forward for thirty years.

In 2006, updated statistics on the status of women in Canadian theatre were released, this time as part of a national campaign called Equity in Canadian Theatre: The Women's Initiative, spearheaded by Nightwood in partnership with the Playwright's Guild of Canada Women's Caucus and the Professional Association of Canadian Theatres (PACT). In addition to hosting a series of public debates and presentations on the issue of gender inequity in the theatre world, The Women's Initiative conducted a survey of

273 professional theatres in Canada to determine how many were headed by women, what percentage of plays produced were written and directed by women, and other related statistics. Although only 128 of the 273 companies responded, the information gathered revealed that there had been little significant change since Rina Fraticelli's report was prepared in 1982. In terms of budgets, the survey found that the mean average of total revenues for companies headed by male artistic directors in 2004/2005 was $1,923,493, while the equivalent figure for companies headed by women was $1,165,275. The companies directed by males had average earned revenues of $1,270,065, while the "female companies" earned $695,998 on average. There was a tremendous gap in revenues from fundraising, and a smaller one for government revenues.

Furthermore, female-led companies were less likely to be incorporated or to have charitable status, and were less likely to be full members of PACT. While 49 percent of companies that responded to the survey reported having a regular performance space, 67 percent of these companies were male-led and only 33 percent were female-led. Clearly, even by 2006, gender equity in Canadian theatre had not yet been achieved.[20]

While the findings of chief researcher Rebecca Burton are still being analyzed, Kelly Thornton, the current artistic director of Nightwood, hopes that their dissemination in 2006 will have the same kind of ripple effect that Fraticelli's report had in the early eighties. Once Fraticelli's report brought the issue of gender equity into public consciousness, it became something for artistic directors to consider in their hiring practices and programming decisions. But over the years, awareness of the issue seems to have faded, and some might even assume that equality has already been achieved. However, as Kelly Thornton and the other women of the Initiative point out, it only takes a quick consideration of playbills from theatres across the country to observe the continued dominance of men as artistic directors, directors, and playwrights — especially at the larger, better-funded regional theatres. Rebecca Burton has also interpreted the negative responses the Initiative encountered — questions about why such a survey was needed, or why a company should spend time filling it out — as further evidence that the theatre sector is reluctant to confront discrimination within itself.[21] In this climate, Nightwood — a company where women's work is always done — remains relevant.

WHAT ARE WE LOOKING AT?

This book focuses on Nightwood as the pre-eminent women's theatre company in Canada. Because of its unique status as a Canadian women's theatre company spanning the period from 1979 to the present, Nightwood can be examined as something of a microcosm, or a case study, of developments in feminist theatre and the production of women's work. Over the years, the company has presented itself as a producer of new works by Canadian women; as a provider of opportunities for women theatre artists; as an inclusive theatre company committed to producing work by women of colour; and as the "home company" for some of the most celebrated names in Canadian theatre. Ann-Marie MacDonald is probably the best example of a "big name," since her 1988 comedy *Goodnight Desdemona (Good Morning Juliet)*, winner of the Chalmers and Governor General's awards, is one of the most frequently produced of all Canadian plays. But many women theatre artists from across the country have had some connection with Nightwood, whether through its annual "Groundswell Festival" of new work, its playwright-in-residence and various play development programs, or its sponsorship of the annual "Five Minute Feminist Cabaret" fundraiser, a revue-style evening of entertainment with intense community involvement. Since Nightwood's founding by Mary Vingoe, Kim Renders, Maureen White, and Cynthia Grant, the company has gone through numerous changes in leadership, produced both collective creations and plays by single authors, mounted tours, collaborated with other companies, and sought out many ways to encourage new work by women.

The role and development of Nightwood within the feminist and theatrical communities of Toronto leads to larger questions about aesthetics, process, and representation. For example, Nightwood's work can be considered in the context of the company's history and mandate, but also in the larger context of international feminism. It is illuminating to consider Nightwood's actual practice and to compare it with that of other companies that existed in the time period when Nightwood was first starting out, and with theatres that exist now. Nightwood can also be considered in terms of feminist theory, by considering what critics have written about the intersection of theatre and feminist philosophy as both have evolved from the 1970s to the twenty-first century.

The chronology at the end of the book can be considered in a number of ways. It lists all of Nightwood's productions and many of the people who have contributed to the company. The involvement of certain individuals or the development of ongoing projects can be traced through various stages, from an appearance at a "Groundswell Festival" to a later production. Many familiar names in Canadian theatre, including Judith Thompson, Anne Anglin, and Sarah Stanley, are evident, as are numerous collaborations with other companies that place Nightwood within the community of Toronto theatre. There are also names from the international theatre community, such as Caryl Churchill and Naomi Wallace, whose plays were produced, and JoAnne Akalaitis, who gave a guest presentation in 1994. The subject matter of many of the productions, obvious from their titles, indicates the specifically feminist nature of material that, while nurtured within Nightwood's unique context, places the work within the international framework of the women's movement.

THE PARTICULAR CHALLENGES OF DOCUMENTING FEMINIST THEATRE

Creating a chronology for a feminist company can require an unusual amount of digging and piecing together. Lizbeth Goodman comments that "drama" is often associated with a certain degree of literary integrity, which much feminist theatre does not necessarily aim to achieve. Instead, feminist theatre often focuses on more active elements: interaction between written text and performance; extra-scenic communication between performers and audience; and the dual role of theatre as both art form and platform — a medium for social change.[22] In *Producing Marginality: Theatre and Criticism in Canada*, Robert Wallace observes, "For many who work in the fringe, theatre no longer is centred on the playwright, nor on the creation of a body of dramatic literature, indigenous or otherwise."[23] In many cases, projects initiated by Nightwood are intended to be culture building, resulting in little in the way of literary evidence, but nonetheless important within the feminist movement. *The Coloured Girls Project* is a good example. Initiated by co-artistic director Diane Roberts in 1995, it was scheduled for public performance in the spring, but instead became an in-house workshop involving Roberts and a large team of creators and facilitators. The workshop was referred to as the first part of "An Explosion Project," based on Ntozake Shange's performance poem *for colored girls who have considered suicide/when the rainbow is enuf.* While no doubt a useful exercise, it remained a private event for the actors and other participants.

Because Nightwood, like many avant-garde companies, initially worked in an improvisational manner with visual images, the work did not always result in a written script. Furthermore, like many other early women's companies, Nightwood employed a collective process, and often no one person was charged with the duties of a playwright. Of course, this lack of documentation can create gaps for the historian. When constructing a history based on material evidence, the status of the play text is significant. In some cases, the fact that a written text was never generated is irrelevant to the goals of the theatrical project, which might have had to do with the development of the performer, establishing ties with a certain community, or the exploration of an issue. In her book *Redressing the Past,* a study of an earlier era of Canadian women playwrights, Kym Bird contends that, when contemporary critics look back to the distant, or even the more recent past, they must recognize that "women's contributions to the historical record require an alternative, affective aesthetics," because the work may bring private virtues into the public, male-dominated sphere.[24]

The nature of the historical record is always problematic for a theatre historian; not least, because of the kinds of materials left behind for the researcher to use in her reconstruction. For the most part, what is preserved are the official materials demanded by government bureaucracy and funding agencies: grant proposals, fundraising letters, financial ledgers, lists of people who have donated money or corporations that have refused to do so. The paper accumulated over the years speaks volumes about how much time and effort a company must devote to raising money and the importance that holds for its survival. Furthermore, it points out a dialectic between accident and intention; when a company builds a theatrical season, its choices are dependent on the granting of funds by external bodies, and decisions are influenced in subtle or overt ways. Sometimes, projects are abandoned because no money was forthcoming. It is difficult to speculate on how an unrealized project might have altered the direction of history had it ever seen the light of day.

The funding of a feminist company might engender particularly relevant considerations. For example, has the mandate of the company, as stated on government grant application forms, been altered to reflect what the writer thinks the granting agency wants to hear? Perhaps there is an impulse to downplay the company's feminism in order to avoid the potential disapproval of a conservative agency. Or, in a more inclusive climate, perhaps it is beneficial for a company to have a socially aware mandate, since it allows the funding body an opportunity to appear supportive of minority cultures. Diane Roberts has specifically addressed this phenomenon in an interview:

> There's been a lot of pressure put on the funding bodies to incorporate a more inclusive vision of people of all nations and colours that are represented in Canada ... We, Nightwood, have an advantage in that we've been working with artists of colour for some time — it's not just the flavour of the month around here. I hope it won't be that in the funding bodies either — I hope they continue to seek out advice from the communities, which is their mandate.[25]

Her comment implies that she fears the funding bodies' commitment to inclusivity may be fickle and their professed interest in minority cultures only temporary.

Guidelines for funding tend to define the difference between mainstream and alternative, or minority, culture. This is a central issue in Canadian theatre history, given that the modern development of Canadian theatre dates from the alternative theatre movement of the late 1960s and the 1970s. As companies once considered alternative, such as Passe Muraille and the Tarragon, became increasingly well established, an even more alternative group of theatres, such as Nightwood and Buddies in Bad Times, came to occupy that minority position, shifting the definition of "minority" from criteria of nationalism and aesthetics to identity issues of gender, race, and sexuality. In his study of Canadian theatre *Producing Marginality*, Robert Wallace finds real promise of innovation only in the small fringe companies that embody marginal perspectives. Wallace calls for a restructuring of the grant process, "a reappraisal in which the social networks that have constructed the mind*set* that controls the systems of power relations that define Canadian theatre are identified and held accountable"[26] (Wallace's italics). For Wallace, there is a vital need to fund fringe companies like Nightwood because they are the only source of theatrical experimentation and critical commentary. While his claim is exaggerated, Wallace's type of passionate advocacy is necessary in order for smaller companies to get the attention they need in a competitive funding climate.[27]

HOW DOES A COMMITMENT TO DIVERSITY EXPAND THE FEMINIST MANDATE?

Besides its commitment to feminism, Nightwood's anti-racist mandate has been one of its strongest sources of creative success. According to Rita Much, when Kate Lushington began her tenure as Nightwood's artistic director (1988–1993), she "began her task by implementing Nightwood's long-standing anti-racist policy through board recruitment"[28] and through producing groundbreaking plays such as *Princess Pocahontas and the Blue Spots* (1990) by the Native actor and writer Monique Mojica. As a Jewish immigrant from England, Lushington represented a certain level of diversity herself, but Nightwood's claim to inclusivity became much more credible when Diane Roberts, a Black woman, became associate artistic director in 1992. Roberts first collaborated with Nightwood as assistant director of *The Wonder of Man,* a play that highlighted issues of race as well as gender. After Lushington left the company in 1993, Roberts was joined by Alisa Palmer as co-artistic director. As a lesbian, Palmer represented another kind of diversity in Nightwood's leadership.

Nightwood's commitment to producing work from diverse communities was in many ways a logical response to both official government policies of multiculturalism and the changing demographics of Toronto. As Diane Roberts explained, "Councils and arts organizations have been compelled to expand their vision and have been challenged to include in their vision the 'voice,' the perspective of artists of colour — the additional Canadian voices. Nightwood has been doing that for some time. So we benefit both artistically and financially."[29] Much of Nightwood's strength has come from its attempts to be open to women who have traditionally been under-represented — not only on Canadian stages, but also on feminist stages. As Roberts insists, "I want to be sure that [people] understand that this is not just racial integration for political or social reasons alone — this is primarily for theatrical innovation!"[30] Roberts's assertion has been proven correct with the success of productions like Djanet Sears's *Harlem Duet,* winner of the 1997 Governor General's Award, and Marjorie Chan's 2004 play *China Doll,* directed by Kelly Thornton and nominated for the Governor General's Award. Nightwood broke important new ground again in 2000/2001 by producing and touring Alex Bulmer's *Smudge,* a critically acclaimed show about the playwright's experience of vision loss.

DEFINING COLLECTIVE CREATION

The theory and practice of collective creation has been another major source of creative energy at Nightwood. Theatre is naturally a collaborative art form, and in some cases the notion of "collectivity" can more accurately be described as a kind of heightened and consciously implemented collaboration. The Latvian-Canadian actor, director, and playwright Baņuta Rubess, who has worked frequently with Nightwood, has done most of her directing in collectives or in situations where she has directed her own work. Rubess argues that asserting power is often painful and difficult for women, and that the collective process is conducive for women to begin thinking of themselves in positions of creative authority.[31]

Rubess outlines three different models of working collectively in which she has participated. In the first model, there is no director, but responsibility is split up in advance, with each person taking authority for some aspect of a production. In the second model, the collective has an outside director; Rubess cautions that this method can lead to conflict over who has final say, and collective members may experience a sense of aesthetic powerlessness. In the third model, the director is part of the collective and serves to translate the process, by encouraging the actors to be concerned for each other onstage and to understand the larger context of their project.

Two realizations are important for any collective to function effectively. First, the collective must acknowledge that not everyone can do everything; participants should be encouraged to do what they are best at and to discover new things they can do along the way. Second, each member must be committed to working as a collective and understand why they are doing so. Programs from Nightwood collective productions generally list certain people as being responsible for particular functions, while the show itself is credited to the group as a whole.

Because part of the feminist agenda is to build women's confidence and create bonds between them, the process by which a project is created can be as important as the finished product. A collaborative model, in which credit and responsibility are shared, as opposed to a strictly hierarchical structure, is a choice philosophically consistent with these feminist goals. Sharon Ott, the former artistic director of the Seattle Repertory Theatre, has explained:

> Women are particularly comfortable with the lateral sharing of responsibility, and not as likely to want to assume a hierarchical order with them at the top, but rather a more lateral order that, if they're the leader, has them at the center. It's a circle radiating out from something as opposed to a line going from bottom to top ... Sometimes that can be problematic, because I think that society is still based on a hierarchical behavior model or organizing principle.[32]

Collective creation offers at least the possibility for equality and a balance of power in an organization; since these are feminist goals for society at large, it seems only right that they should be put into practice in a feminist company. The benefits of a collective are practical: the individual develops more skills; increases her self-confidence by seeing herself in more powerful roles within a nurturing environment; and can add an intriguing project to her résumé. The benefits are also aesthetic and social, as the company proves that art, and the practice of theatre, can arise not just from the mind of the stereotypical lone (usually male) genius, but from sharing, equality, and cooperation — a hopeful model for all human interaction.

Collective creation has come to connote a particular kind of theatre piece: episodic in structure, presentational, and made up of a number of stories that all contribute to some overarching theme or purpose. But collective creation is more accurately defined by its process than by its outcome. Within the situation of a traditional, hierarchical production, the playwright's text is the organizing focus, but for a collective there is no such map. The end result of the process might be a play about a specific community or historical event (for example, Nightwood's 1984 production *Love and Work Enough*, which celebrated Ontario's pioneer women), and it might have an overt political motivation (such as the anti-war *Peace Banquet* in 1983). But the collective process might also result in a play like *Glazed Tempera* (1980), which was intended to explore an interdisciplinary aesthetic experience rather than to offer social commentary.

In Canada, and in some other countries — England, for example — it has become common to refer to this kind of process-oriented creation as "devised theatre." This is partly due, in Canada at least, to the connotations of the term "collective creation" — its associations with a particular historical moment and even with specific theatre companies and their methodologies (the most famous example being Theatre Passe Muraille's *The Farm Show* in 1972). But even within the relevant time period — the late 1960s until the early 1980s — it can be useful to think of devising as somewhat different from collective creation. Again, the distinction is illustrated by the difference between a play such as *Love and Work Enough* and *Glazed Tempera*. With its relatively narrative through line, named characters, and recognizable social theme, and its basis in authenticated documents and research, *Love and Work Enough* qualifies as a collective creation in the way that term has come to be understood in Canadian scholarship. *Glazed Tempera*, on the other hand, was aesthetically motivated and experiential rather than narrative, bears a stronger resemblance to performance art than to a traditional play, and might be more accurately described as devised.[33] (Nightwood, however, used the term collective creation consistently.)

Nightwood's mandate has always been to encourage diverse perspectives and to provide opportunities for women who might not find them elsewhere, and collective creation is in many ways an ideal model for this kind of empowerment. Furthermore, the work that is created through collective creation can be especially rich and powerful, benefiting from the combined efforts and gifts of a number of people, rather than being the vision of a single individual. As Maureen White commented regarding *This is For You, Anna*:

> For me the greatest reward of working collectively is seeing a vision emerge that could *never* have come from just

one person. A constant criticism of this method of working seems to be that it is a compromised vision. Yet I do
not begin working collectively on a show with *my* vision in
mind — that would certainly lead to compromise. Instead,
ideas feed off one another to develop *into* a vision.[34]

On the other hand, working collectively can be difficult and time-
consuming, particularly if all the participants are not equally
committed to or comfortable with the process. Ann-Marie Mac-
Donald acknowledged some of the hazards of the process in her
description of The Anna Project. "The collective process has
been fraught with more challenges and obstacles than any other
I have known; struggles such as fund-raising and administration
of one's own work, not to mention the constant striving for con-
sensus in a process which is also a commitment to respect each
artist's creative input,"[35] she wrote. The challenges of working
collectively will be ruefully acknowledged by any artist who has
tried to let go of traditional structures and experienced the frus-
tration of not having a leader to turn to or familiar methods to
fall back on. For people who are not used to working collectively,
the process can seem maddeningly inefficient and unproduc-
tive, even chaotic. MacDonald concludes, however, that *This is
For You, Anna* was worth "hanging in for," and a collaborative, if
not necessarily collective, method of working has continued to
be associated with Nightwood and all other Canadian feminist
companies.

There are two ways in which the collective model is significant
for feminist theatre: in how the collective working process embodies feminist principles of equality, and in how it influences the
aesthetics of the work produced. The collective projects that lead
to a mainstage production and a published script are the plays
that tend to be remembered and associated with the company's
name, and in those cases, the emphasis shifts from the collective
process to the qualities of the "finished" product. In Nightwood's
case, collective creations such as *This is For You, Anna* and *Smoke
Damage* are some of the company's most recognized works: they

have been published, anthologized, and remounted by other companies; they have been the subject of scholarly articles and are included in course curricula; they have entered the canon of Canadian theatre. On the program for the Theatre Passe Muraille run of *This is For You, Anna*, The Anna Project noted the play's adoption by mainstream culture—evidenced by its presence in university course curricula, for example—with pride.[36] The uneasy balance between a non-traditional process and a desire for mainstream acceptance has been a defining factor in Nightwood's development as a company.

COLLECTIVE CREATION AS A FEMINIST PROCESS

Susan E. Bassnett-McGuire, in her article "Towards a Theory of Women's Theatre," traces the emergence of feminist theatre collectives from the left-wing movements for social change that began in the 1960s in Europe. Bassnett-McGuire valorizes the tendency of small groups to adopt a collectively administered structure—concerning themselves as a company with both financial and artistic decision-making processes, and crediting the entire group with the final show. A production, she says, can be "described as women's theatre by what happens off rather than on-stage."[37] She also notes that feminist theatre companies often use the cabaret form because it establishes a "particular kind of performer-audience relationship that combines the distance of frame with the extreme closeness of frame breaking."[38] This form of theatre reinforces the expectations of a (feminist) audience, and works off the resulting interaction.

A good Nightwood example is the annual "Five Minute Feminist Cabaret," which serves not only as an evening of entertainment, or even exclusively as a fundraising opportunity, but also as a kind of group celebration, a reunion, a reinforcement of the spectator's ties with a particular community, and a statement of personal solidarity. In this context, an individual's attendance at an event or performance is an opportunity for her to demonstrate her support for that work in a more overt way than is typical for a theatregoer. While attendance at any event implies a certain level of support, or at least interest, an explicitly feminist event makes attendance into a political statement.

Bassnett-McGuire describes this kind of audience relationship in her discussion of Britain's Women's Theatre Group. She characterizes their performances as mere preludes to the group discussions that followed; their aim is to establish a rapport between actor and audience that transcends theatre and extends into life. The performers in the Women's Theatre Group make the audience into a "support group" and the act of theatre creation into a project for establishing group identity.[39]

Another collective feminist theatre that bears comparison with Nightwood is the American company Burning City Women. In the book *Guerilla Street Theater,* edited by Harry Lesnick, the company published an account of itself, explaining that its members were originally part of a company called Burning City Street Theater, but that, as women, they felt a great need to work with each other and to initiate a project among themselves.[40] The projects they create are not credited to any one member of the collective; their names are not even listed. They state, "The same impulse that has caused women to make theater together has been active in encouraging women to form collectives together, to put out newspapers together, write books together and make love together."[41] Clearly this is a company that sees itself as part of a women's culture. Nightwood's origins can also be traced to this "impulse," since the company's genesis was in a collective at Women's Press, which formed to edit a book entitled *The True Story of Ida Johnson.*

The seven members of Burning City Women describe their working method as collective and improvisational: "One woman would tell us an event or series of events in her life and the rest of us would act it out."[42] The result was a series of six short plays, collectively entitled *What is a Woman? A Revolutionary Soap-Box Opera,* which was performed at the "Festival of Underground Theatre" in Toronto in 1970. The plays reflect a cultural feminist perspective by aiming to identify women's common experiences and search for identity, dealing with issues such as body image, unwed motherhood, the negative impact of a sexist university education, and the mother–daughter relationship, all within a 1960s context. The plays demonstrate experimental theatre techniques, such as abstract movement and overlapping dialogue, and also show evidence of the performers' training in street theatre through their use of simple, stylized props and masks and straightforward messages.

In their early days, feminist theatre companies focused on the collective process as well as a reconsideration of the actor-audience relationship. In Susan Bennett's book *Theatre Audiences*, she locates a number of theoretical approaches that may explain the new ways in which feminist theatre practitioners communicated with their audiences. For example, Alan Sinfield is quoted as observing, "Any artistic form depends upon some readiness in the receiver to co-operate with its aims and conventions"; this seems particularly applicable to feminist theatre, which requires an audience willing to listen to its subversive perspective.[43] Bennett then cites Una Chaudhuri's formulation: "The description of how a play works on a spectator — rather than what it means — can supply the terms our criticism needs in order to erase the gap between theory and its object."[44] Again, this statement is highly relevant to the unique relationship between a feminist play and its audience, because it extends beyond the play's subject matter into a kind of shared project of celebrating cultural production; this is especially highlighted in a collective creation, where the performers may be perceived to be more personally invested in the work. In a final example, Daphna Ben Chaim considers the relative effectiveness of different levels of distance and levels of engagement between performer and audience. Ben Chaim posits: "The combination … of unreality with recognizable human characteristics seems to be the minimum requirement for identification, and both of these conditions are variable and provide the borders within which distance operates."[45] The aim of traditional realism is an intense personal relationship and a minimum awareness of fictionality, which Ben Chaim defines as "low" distance. Much feminist collective creation, conversely, aims at an intense personal relationship and a high awareness of fictionality — for example, by having one actor play multiple characters, all of them sharing a particular struggle — that produces a completely different perspective on reality for its audience.

COLLECTIVE CREATION AND THE CANADIAN CONTEXT

Nightwood's experience with the collective model, both administratively and as a method of creation, can be understood within an international feminist framework, but it must also be situated within the context of Canadian theatre. The roots of collective creation and documentary theatre go back much further than the alternative movement of the 1960s. From Erwin Piscator's theatre in Germany in the 1920s and the International Workers' Theatre Movement, collective creation can be traced to Joan Littlewood's Workshop Productions in England, and then to Littlewood's disciple George Luscombe, who brought her methods to his own Toronto Workshop Productions in 1959. Another Canadian connection was Ray Whelan, who, after apprenticing with Peter Cheeseman in England, got involved with Luscombe's TWP and then co-founded Open Circle Theatre.[46] Open Circle's method of creation was to identify local issues, create a text based on interviews with the people affected, and make the shows accessible to those people: it was "community theatre" done professionally.[47] These companies gave rise in turn to the explosion of collective creation and alternative theatre that Canada experienced in the 1960s and 1970s, and then to Nightwood.

In his introduction to *Eight Men Speak*, a collection of plays from the Canadian Workers' Theatre Movement, Robin Endres argues:

> Theatre, more than any other artistic medium, is conducive to the aims of politically conscious artists because its structure is social and public ... If the theatre is the most political of art forms, and if all theatre is in some sense political, a distinction must be made between theatre in general and theatre which is consciously political. The key to the distinction lies in the fact that consciously

political theatre, in addition to its inherent role of alter-
ing reality, attempts to convince its audience that it is desirable for *them* to alter reality through conscious activity
… it sets itself the task of literally changing the minds of
its audience in order that this audience will in turn change
the world. Given that the aims of this theatre are radically
different from other types of theatre, the aesthetic choices
it makes will also differ — indeed, attempts will be made to
change the nature of the dramatic illusion itself.[48]

Both practical aims and aesthetic choices link the political theatre of the Workers' Theatre Movement of the 1920s and '30s to
the collective creations of the 1960s and '70s, and to the birth
of feminist theatre.

In the 1930s, John E. Bonn, the chairman of the American
Workers' Theatre, specifically questioned what method of theatre-
making is most appropriate to the politically motivated. Bonn
asked, "Shall we learn from the bourgeois theater or not? Do we
need a stationary theater or an Agitprop Theater? Shall we use
scenery, costumes and make-up or not?"[49] He argued that despite
having different aims, political theatre workers could still find appropriate forms for their work by studying the bourgeois theatre:
"We cannot wait or look for a ready made style for our new theater;
we have to develop the style of the workers theater by bringing it
in conformity with its tasks and its means of expression."[50] Companies such as the Women's Theatre Group, Burning City Women,
and Nightwood all struggled with the same core issues as these
earlier activists: how to create political theatre in a manner that
was different from the theatre they were reacting against.

Workers' Theatre Movement performances were characterized
by mobility, as they needed to set up and clear out of performance
spaces very quickly; by props and costumes that were extremely
basic, but could be transformed for different uses; by a sense of
theatre as a social ritual, which heightened and formalized the
needs of the community; by the elimination of individual characters in favour of abstract representatives of class; and by the use

of mass recitation and chanting of slogans to make the working class aware of its collective strength.

The parallels between the Workers' Theatre and the collective creations of the '60s and '70s, including those produced by feminist theatres, can be attributed to common funding situations as well as to political and aesthetic goals. The minimal use of basic sets and costumes, for example, can be read as both an economic imperative and as an aesthetic and political choice — an unpretentious identification with the working class. Workers' Theatre and collective creations share the goal of reaching non-traditional audiences and take their performances to the people most affected, hence the need for mobility, simplicity, and broad, unambiguous characterizations.

A good example here is Nightwood's 1984 production *Love and Work Enough.* While hardly agitprop, it did employ a characteristically simple set, consisting of a quilt and one or two chairs, which were transformed into a bed, a carriage, and other set pieces as needed. The cast took on many different, easily identifiable characters that could be described as types, such as the eager young bride and the hard-working immigrant. Instead of mass chanting, there were songs, which served to unite the characters through their common experiences. The play was toured to senior citizens' homes, schools, parks, and other community locations where the company anticipated an interest in the subject matter. *Love and Work Enough* emphasized the great contribution of women pioneers to the history of Ontario and insisted that their stories should not be neglected. While not didactic in an agitprop sense, the play does convey its intentions to the audience in a straightforward manner. Quotations from historical documents, letters, and diaries are identified as such within the structure of the play and serve as a kind of internal authentication.[51]

Theatre Passe Muraille became the company most closely identified with the collective creation method in Canada, and Nightwood, in turn, had strong ties with Passe Muraille. Under the direction of Paul Thompson, the Passe Muraille style was a combination of dialect realism, improvisation, and presentational storytelling, guided by Thompson's belief that theatre can locate and define the motifs and images that identify a culture and point to its formative myths.[52] The actors started with recognizable characters and situations — a realistic "identifiable base" — but then employed a non-realistic, presentational technique that freed them from naturalistic portraiture and resulted in a kind of gestural storytelling.[53] Another important factor in this method of creation was the freedom of the actors to discover not only the form and structure of a play, but also its content and scope. Thompson claimed to have no preconceptions of how a play would turn out, allowing it to emerge entirely from the rehearsal process.[54] Besides legitimizing and popularizing collective creation as a genre of play-making and influencing the style of Canadian productions, Passe Muraille provided seed money, rehearsal space, and support for other artists. Paul Thompson became an early facilitator of Nightwood, arranging for the transfer of its show *The True Story of Ida Johnson* from the Annex Theatre to a longer run at Adelaide Court, as well as organizing subsequent financial assistance.

Because Nightwood came into existence at the very end of the seventies, it missed the period, ten years earlier, when the collective was at its most revolutionary — when collective creation, alternative theatre, the influence of an international avant-garde, and a passionate nationalism were all coming together in Canadian theatre. In many ways, Nightwood reflected all that had gone on a short while before, yet developed in its own unique direction. The successful experience of the 1960s and '70s gave theatre in Canada permission to be proudly nationalistic, meaning that Nightwood's mandate to produce new Canadian work fit in well with the post-colonial politics of the times. The '60s and '70s were also a time of political activism: civil rights, gay and lesbian liberation, anti-war protests, and, of course, women's rights. And finally, the prevalence of experimentation in all forms of art at the time allowed Nightwood freedom to explore new ways of working and new conceptions of what makes theatre worthwhile.

While collective creation was undeniably influential in its historical heyday, critics have disagreed about its long-term impact on Canadian theatre. In the opinion of Cynthia Zimmerman, for example, "the collective creation method is usually a way station for writers, a stop en route to greater artistic control over their own work."[55] The form has showed staying power, however; in the 1980s, Alan Filewod observed "a notable resurgence of agitprop among women's groups."[56] The Canadian Popular Theatre Alliance, for example, was formed in 1981 to promote socially active theatre (most of which was collective), and many of its member groups were women's companies. Pol Pelletier, the co-founder and artistic director of Le Théâtre Expérimental des Femmes, a Montreal separatist collective founded in 1979, presents yet another viewpoint when she claims that "collective creations are important and significant, although they are not the greatest artistic successes."[57] From her perspective, the collective is important for political and social reasons, and for the development of the individual woman, but not necessarily for the lasting value of the play.

CREATING COLLECTIVELY AT NIGHTWOOD

Throughout Nightwood's history, the kind of work the company does and how it represents itself have been largely determined by its leadership; by what the artistic director(s) are interested in doing and who else chooses to get involved. Each of the founding members of Nightwood initiated projects, directed, acted, wrote scripts, and generally found imaginative ways to create theatre projects for themselves under the company umbrella; all but Kim Renders took on the title of artistic director or coordinator at some point. Likewise, when Kate Lushington took over from the founders, in 1988, she directed, wrote, or acted in a number of key productions during her tenure. In the first newsletter published after Alisa Palmer, Diane Roberts, and Leslie Lester took over as the leadership team in 1994, they included a statement that reveals their conception of how Nightwood functioned:

> We're enthusiastic to take up the challenge of maintaining Nightwood's dual role as a leading producer of feminist art and as an important resource for women artists …

Nightwood Theatre has provided a forum for women to explore the complexity of our relationships to each other, to society and consequently to history. Its identity today is a culmination of accident, serendipity and wilful efforts to have a say in the development of women's culture. We are intrigued by the challenge of seeing the whole pattern, Nightwood's past, present and future, in order to support the contribution that each individual constituent, each artist or script or decision, can make to the whole.[58]

Alisa Palmer directed many productions, from the first one mounted after her team took over (*Wearing the Bone*, 1994, which she also wrote) to the last one before she left (*Anything That Moves* by Ann-Marie MacDonald, in 2001). Her colleague Diane Roberts initiated a workshop (*The Coloured Girls Project*, 1995) and directed *Mango Chutney* by Dilara Ally in 1996, in addition to running many "Groundswell" and "Five Minute Feminist Cabaret" productions. Indeed, the administration of "Groundswell" (and "FemCab," in the years it has been produced) has typically fallen to the artistic director, assisted by some combination of temporary staff. Kelly Thornton has directed most of the mainstage productions since she took over in 2001, and her key area of expertise, new play development, is evident through initiatives like Write From the Hip and Busting Out!

The British writer Bryony Lavery has commented that when she first began running her own women's theatre company, "I learned that just writing isn't enough. If you want to write the plays you want and have them produced and performed how you want, you also have to learn how to direct, how to raise money, deal with the Arts Council, talk people into putting your plays on in their theatre, talk to the press, talk to the actors, talk to the audience afterwards and talk talk talk talk talk talk talk."[59] The job of an artistic director is never-ending, particularly for a feminist company. In the January 1995 *Nighttalk* newsletter, Alisa Palmer worried about how her company was being perceived in the public eye with no show going on at the time, but pointed out that, since *Wearing the Bone* had closed, two months earlier, more than 200 people had circulated through Nightwood's studio and office—rehearsing, reading scripts, and meeting as an artistic advisory committee. Palmer reassured herself, "Nightwood Theatre is the foremost women's theatre in Canada. Our numbers prove our strength and the award winning quality of our art, all the art that comes from our artists, proves our commitment."[60] Both Lavery and Palmer are responding to the fact that every theatre company relies on the people who walk through its doors, but for a company that defines its mandate in social as well as aesthetic terms, participation is even more relevant.

The social mandate was not equally important to all of Nightwood's leaders; in the very beginning, aesthetic concerns were clearly more dominant. In 1979, Cynthia Grant travelled to New York on a professional theatre training grant to study with JoAnne Akalaitis of Mabou Mines, and with Spalding Gray and the Wooster Group. When she returned from New York to work on the first Nightwood production, *The True Story of Ida Johnson*, Grant described herself as:

> full of talk of imagist theatre à la Mabou Mines, courtesy of my first individual grant. My imagined career involved the creation of post-structuralist/modern style, and, like others that I met or was about to meet in forming the Theatre Centre—Richard Shoichet, Thom Sokoloski, Richard Rose, and Sky Gilbert—I wanted to "turn on" the Toronto theatre community to new work with radical artistic visions.[61]

Furthermore, Grant's co-founders Maureen White and Kim Renders had studied movement work and the theories of Jerzy Grotowski while at the University of Ottawa, and had backgrounds in the visual arts.[62] Kate Lushington has suggested that the founders' grounding in these imagistic techniques led Nightwood to do work that, while still very much collectively created, did not follow the same model as other collective creations being produced in

Toronto at the time. Lushington describes the "typical" collective creation as "a historical storytelling style, very much dependent on men," one that had "a single narrative or a chronological narrative structure."[63] In contrast, Nightwood's work borrowed more heavily from the experimental, imagistic aesthetic of its international influences.

Although each of the four founders (Cynthia Grant, Mary Vingoe, Maureen White, and Kim Renders) might take on different tasks and professional titles with each project, they shared the responsibility and credit for creating an artistic vision. At this stage, collectivity, as a philosophy and working method, was ideally about creating opportunities and encouraging theatrical freedom. Of her earliest motivations, Kim Renders recalls, "I wanted to develop my own performance vocabulary with a group of people; I thought that would be more useful than roaming the streets as a freelance actor."[64] Being part of a collective allowed Renders the opportunity not only to act, but also to write, direct, and to exercise her artistic skills through design work — a range of input normally unavailable to an actor hired by a conventional company on a show-by-show basis.

Not only does the collective creation experience provide opportunities for personal growth, it also fosters a sense of group identity. As Alan Filewod explains:

> In collective creation, the group mind must reconcile its differences to create a community statement. This can begin in one of two ways: either the cast is united by ideological consensus in the analysis of the subject ... or the circumstances of making the play become a shared experience which becomes part of the substance of the play itself.[65]

In Nightwood's case, both elements were present simultaneously. The four founders and the other members of each collective creation were united through a common ideology (usually feminist, but in the case of a project like *Peace Banquet*, an anti–nuclear weapons stance), and also a shared interest in a particular kind of experimental, multimedia aesthetic. Furthermore, financial constraints and a sense of being marginalized and avant-garde gave them a feeling of group unity and common purpose. Chris Brookes of Newfoundland's Mummers Troupe has insisted, "Any political theatre which intends to really move its audience (I am referring to activism, not emotionalism), over the long term and on a wide social level, must find a language not just of issues and ideology, but of ritual and ceremony rooted in a sense of collective belief beyond language."[66] Nightwood clearly intended something of this kind with the audience participation in *Peace Banquet*, when the actors and audience share a ceremonial dinner party with a heightened sense of social relevance.

Collective creations are more a genre of performance than of literary drama; more easily defined by their process than by the qualities of a final product. Filewod insists that traditional dramatic criticism cannot be used to evaluate these works because they reorder the fundamental relation of artist and society.[67] Authorship as a group process makes traditional dramatic criticism, with its textual orientation, difficult.[68] Many of the reviews of Nightwood's collective creations, for example, focused on the contribution or absence of a director, perhaps searching for an individual who could be identified as the "authority" in the absence of an author. This was particularly true later in the 1980s, when collective creation had fallen out of favour. For those who continue to work in alternative or popular theatre, the lack of respect for their particular art form is a common complaint. Savannah Walling claims that there is a taboo against collective creation — a fear that artistic standards will be diluted, based on an assumption of the primacy of the playwright and script. "Collective creation," she says, "circumvents the 'truth' that art comes only from the minds of bold individuals who rupture tradition and single-handedly change history."[69]

NIGHTWOOD'S COLLECTIVE ADMINISTRATION

The question of whether or not Nightwood was run collectively from the beginning is a source of controversy. Judging by the documents available — newspaper reviews, magazine articles, funding letters, and so on — it is clear that the company consistently referred to itself, and was referred to, as a collective, right until Kate Lushington took over in 1988. It is less clear at what point Cynthia Grant took on the title of artistic director and what exactly the existence of such a position might mean. In all of the documents, both the collective and traditional leadership models seem to have been employed simultaneously, in the sense that Grant is identified as the artistic director but "her" company is identified as a collective.

From the very beginning, Grant was often singled out in the press as the leader of Nightwood. For example, in a recap of the 1980 Toronto theatre season, Ray Conlogue noted that "Cynthia Grant and Nightwood Theatre ... have become the dominant force at the Theatre Centre."[70] Conlogue says, "It's nice to know that avant-garde can be fun," and issues a whimsical Squeaky Floor Award "to be shared with Grant's devoted actors." Grant was most often listed as the producer and director of Nightwood's shows and was their public spokesperson, which no doubt led the media to interpret and treat her as the artistic director as well.

In a 2004 *Canadian Theatre Review* article, "Still 'Activist' after All These Years?"[71] Cynthia Grant recounts the formation of Nightwood in a way that explicitly portrays her as the founder and artistic director. She claims, "Although [Nightwood] is often referred to as an early collective, that was not really the case,"[72] citing her membership on the Theatre Centre board and her efforts to obtain funding as evidence of her primary role. Grant also points out, "For the first seven years, I directed and produced almost every project."[73]

In refutation, Kim Renders wrote a lengthy letter to the editor, published in a later issue,[74] which disputes this interpretation of events. Calling Grant's article a "revisionist view of history," Renders insists, "We all four possessed this passion, this concept, *collectively*." She points out that she, White, and Vingoe did all kinds of other work:

Postering, making costumes and masks, organizing slide projections for our multimedia performances and putting up and taking down sets ... Plus, we all worked on scripts, acted and regularly stood outside of rehearsals to co-direct. Is Grant implying that directing and producing has more value than the less prestigious physical grunt work (read: Women's Work) required to get a show up on its feet?

Renders concedes that Grant was the first of the founding four to be in a paid position, but also claims, "We *all* agreed that she was not to be called Artistic Director, since our company was not run on the hierarchical principles that governed most other theatre companies at the time." Renders implies that by not mentioning the names of the other collective members when she was interviewed by the press, Grant had intentionally, but erroneously, fostered the impression of her sole authority.

CONCLUSION

In comparing Nightwood to other Canadian feminist companies past and present, such as Redlight, Nellie McClung, Maenad Theatre, Le Théâtre Expérimental des Femmes, Le Théâtre Parminou, Urban Curvz, and the Company of Sirens, similar struggles emerge: obtaining funding, defining a mandate, developing an organizational structure, and communicating with a desired audience.[75] The different kinds of feminist philosophy that individual theatre practitioners advocate will be reflected in the work they produce within their companies. A commitment to feminism also influences *how* a piece of theatre is created, and each company attempts to develop an appropriate, collaborative working model.

Cynthia Grant became the first of the founders to leave Nightwood. Along with a number of other activist women, she formed the Company of Sirens in 1986. In her description of the new company, Susan Bennett suggests a rift in philosophy caused Grant to leave Nightwood — ironically, that she wanted to do work that was more collective and more political. According to

Bennett, the Company of Sirens completely rejected the theatre mainstream and wanted to work directly with the audience:

> Cynthia Grant made it clear that her decision to leave her post as artistic director of the successful Nightwood Theatre in Toronto was the result of a growing dissatisfaction in working within an established institution. Her present participation in a co-operative venture, the Company of Sirens, permits a more direct and important contact between actors and audience without the constraints of the conventional theatre system.[76]

Bennett then quotes Grant as clarifying:

> Part of the move out of Nightwood had to do with making feminist theatre more accessible. Large numbers of people are put off by the idea of coming into a theatre, so we are taking theatre to them. We are very excited about playing venues as diverse as a union hall in Windsor or a cultural community centre here in Toronto.[77]

Given how relatively marginal Nightwood already was within Toronto's theatre scene, it is clear how far away from the mainstream a company like the Sirens sought to operate.[78]

In Canada's tradition of collective creation, and in feminist and popular theatre, the value of collective creation resides in both the process and the product. How this balance works itself out, however, can take different turns. Nightwood's shows were identified as collective creations and the company itself was called a collective, yet the fact that individuals took on different tasks and roles within the structure has led to some enduring conflict. At least some element of risk is appropriate to theatre-makers aiming to define themselves as alternative, but one of the biggest risks is forsaking the authority of the author or the power of a leader.

Smoke Damage
Left to Right: Mary Marzo, Kim Renders, and Maureen White in the "Lopsy Opsy" scene from *Smoke Damage*. *Photograph by Ken Martin. From the personal collection of Kim Renders.*

Three of the Founders
Left to Right: Kim Renders, Maureen White, and Cynthia Grant on a bench in front of Theatre Passe Muraille.
From the personal collection of Kim Renders.

Pope Joan
Maureen White as *Pope Joan*.
Photographer unknown. Nightwood Theatre archives.

This is for you, Anna
Back Row Left to Right: Patricia Nichols, Suzanne Odette-Khuri, Maureen White; and Front Row Left to Right: Banuta Rubess, Ann-Marie MacDonald in *This is for You, Anna*. *Photograph by Carter Brandon. Nightwood Theatre archives.*

CAUTION: WOMEN AT WORK
a weekend of performance (3 shows each night) at Partisan Gallery

FOUR-PART DISCHORD and
PSYCHO-NUCLEAR BREAKDOWN by
NIGHTWOOD THEATRE
with Mary Durkan
Cynthia Grant
Kim Renders
Maureen White

THIS IS FOR YOU, ANNA / a spectacle of revenge
Banuta Rubess / Suzanne Khuri (1982 THEATRE CO.)
Ann-Marie MacDonald / Aida Jordao / Maureen White

May 26-28 at 8:30, May 29 at 2:30
Tickets: $5.00 / $4.00 students, seniors, unemployed

Partisan Gallery
2388 Dundas West (at Bloor)
WOMEN'S PERSPECTIVE '83
RESERVATIONS 862-0659

Caution: Women at Work
Poster from 1983.
Nightwood Theatre archives.

Kim Renders for Rhubarb
Kim Renders in *Gently Down the Stream*.
This photo became the poster image for
the "Rhubarb!" Festival.
*Photograph by Robert Caspari. From the personal
collection of Kim Renders.*

Glazed Tempera
Maureen White and Kim Renders in *Glazed Tempera*.
*Photograph by Robert Caspari. From the personal collection of
Kim Renders.*

The True Story of Ida Johnson
Left to Right: Maureen White, Mary Vingoe,
and Kim Renders in *The True Story of Ida Johnson*.
From the personal collection of Kim Renders.

One
The Beginning of Nightwood Theatre, 1979–1988

An Overview: How is the Work Generated?

Nightwood's position in, and impact on, Canadian theatre can be evaluated in many different ways. There are three key elements to consider in the process by which Nightwood generates work: the company's historical context; the use of festivals and other innovative play development strategies; and the company's inclusive mandate and commitment to diversity.

Nightwood has used various methods for producing work — from the early collective creations, such as *Glazed Tempera* (1980), *Peace Banquet* (1983), and *Love and Work Enough* (1984), to plays by a single author, such as Margaret Hollingsworth's *War Babies* (1987). The company has explored many genres, from the *Soft Boiled* clown shows (performed by Kim Renders and Maureen White, as Orangeade and Cellophane, at the Theatre Centre's "Rhubarb! Festival"), to powerful political statements like *Smoke Damage*, written by Baṇuta Rubess with the cast, which deals with the persecution of women during the European witch hunts. Nightwood has produced shows ranging in scale from one-woman stand-up comedy, such as Sandra Shamas's *My Boyfriend's Back and There's Gonna Be Laundry* (1987), to shows with large casts and budgets, like Djanet Sears's *The Adventures of a Black Girl in Search of God* (2002).

To illustrate the broad spectrum of Nightwood's work, consider the two extremes represented by *The Danish Play* and Busting Out! *The Danish Play* by Sonja Mills exemplifies Nightwood's desire to promote women's plays and generate attention for the company by producing shows in high-profile contexts: in addition to its Dora Award–nominated run in Toronto in 2002, the play was taken on tour to Denmark, and presented at the "Magnetic North Festival" in Edmonton and the National Arts Centre in Ottawa. The script has been published by Playwrights Canada Press, and Nightwood remounted the show in 2007. On the other end of the spectrum are more grassroots initiatives, such as the "Groundswell" playwrights' unit, Write From the Hip, and Busting Out! — in-house development programs that do not necessarily result in a full production by Nightwood, but that encourage and develop women artists.

Write From the Hip is a development program for novice playwrights, aged eighteen to twenty-nine, who meet weekly for five months. Through workshops, seminars, and mentoring, the participants in Write From the Hip produce short works that are programmed at the end of the annual "Groundswell Festival" of new works. According to the Nightwood website, Busting Out! is

> a new theatre program for girls aged twelve to fifteen that aims to provide self esteem building and artistic expression in an open and creative, non-judgmental all-girl space. Over ten weeks, professional theatre artists work with the girls leading them through improvisation games, theatre exercises, group discussions and writing exercises. In the culmination of the program the participants create a collective project based on self-exploration and expression using the tools of theatre.[1]

Busting Out! is a free program accessible to all girls, funded through Theatre Ontario and the ministries of Culture and Education.

Nightwood also uses its "Groundswell Festival" as a means for generating new work by women. "Groundswell" has been run since 1986, making it the country's oldest women's theatre festival. As well, Nightwood hosts the annual "Five Minute Feminist Cabaret" in celebration of International Women's Day, and in 2003, Nightwood and Buddies in Bad Times Theatre inaugurated a new semi-annual festival called "Hysteria," a multidisciplinary showcase of female artists from across North America. Over ten days, the first "Hysteria" offered play readings and full productions as well as dance classes, panel discussions, and art installations. One event in particular illustrates just how diverse the festival context can be: "Tits Up: An Evening of Fearless Feminist Porn" was curated by Erika Hennebury and featured "hilarious and horny" pornographic storytelling by local performers.

While "Groundswell" was the first, there are now women's theatre festivals across the country offering variations on its model and providing a kind of network for play development.[2] For example, since 2002, the Toronto company b current has presented a festival called "rock.paper.sistahz," described as "an intimate presentation of new and original works ... focusing on themes, forms, and styles which have grown out of the black diasporic culture." At the other end of the country, Vancouver has "busTin' ouT," an annual cabaret/festival of work by women to celebrate International Women's Day, coordinated by Full Figure Theatre. The 2005 edition, in support of breast cancer research, marked the seventh year of the event. The "Her-icane Festival of Women's Art" has been sponsored by 25th Street Theatre in Saskatoon since 1999, and Sarasvati Productions presents the annual "FemFest: Plays by Women for Everyone" at Prairie Theatre Exchange in Winnipeg. The 2004 "FemFest," which took place over eight days, featured eight plays, including one in French, as well as workshops, panels, readings, and an open mic night.

REDLIGHT: AN EARLIER FEMINIST COMPANY IN TORONTO

While it can boast of other "firsts," such as "Groundswell," Nightwood was not Toronto's first feminist theatre company. That distinction belongs to Redlight, which was founded in 1974 by Diane Grant, Francine Volker, and Marcella Lustig. At the time, Marcella

Lustig and Diane Grant were working at Toronto's Open Circle Theatre and Francine Volker was working as a freelance actor at the alternative theatres, such as Passe Muraille. All three were reading a book called *Redlights on the Prairies* by James L. Gray, "about prostitution in the wild west," thinking it would make great material for a play.[3] When the women decided to apply for a government employment (Local Initiatives Project) grant, they were awarded $16,000, and they used Redlight as the name of their new company. Francine Volker insists:

> We never consciously set out to provoke or challenge by naming our new theatre "Redlight." We had read the book; we had all played prostitutes, as most female actors do. It seemed to fit. Later, when we came to realize the name's power to disturb, we made the decision to stick with it as an ironic emblem.[4]

Similarly, Nightwood had to grow into its name. Although it was a company run by women and named for a feminist novel by Djuna Barnes, Nightwood at first defined itself as a producer of imagistic, experimental work, while the explicitly feminist mandate evolved a little more slowly.[5]

Redlight Theatre spent its three seasons of existence (1974–1977) looking for an appropriate space, and used everything from nightclubs to rented theatres to a café. As Volker deadpans, "We weren't always able to match the play to the ambience."[6] Redlight is probably best known today for its play about the suffragette Nellie McClung, *What Glorious Times They Had*, which toured Canada in 1975 for International Women's Year. But the company also worked with collectives and commissioned work from important playwrights such as Carol Bolt and Margaret Hollingsworth; presented plays on serious issues like abortion (Penny Kemp's *The Angelmakers*, directed by Anne Anglin); and produced comic satires of female icons, such as *Queen of the Silver Blades*—an ironic comment on the career of figure skater Barbara Ann Scott, written by Susan Swan and Margaret Dragu.

There are numerous parallels between Redlight and Nightwood in its early days. The first is both companies' connection with Open Circle Theatre. Kim Renders explains that when she and Maureen White graduated from university and first arrived in Toronto from Ottawa, "we met Cynthia Grant and were all involved in an Open Circle Theatre piece called *The Splendour and Death of Joaquin Murieta*."[7] For Nightwood, like Redlight, books played an important role: the book that gave Nightwood its name, of course, but also the Sharon Riis novel *The True Story of Ida Johnson*, which led to the company's first production. That project began in 1976 with an editing group at Women's Press, which included Cynthia Grant. She organized a dramatized reading of Riis's novel in March of 1977 with members of the editing group, and then a workshop production in 1978 that involved White, Renders, and Mary Vingoe. The program for the subsequent full production, in 1979, listed Renders, Vingoe, and White as actors and Grant as the director; Renders also worked on the design. These four women, who came to be considered the founders of Nightwood, and six others who helped with the production, were listed in the program as the "Theatre Collective and Associate Members." In terms of its formal qualities, the production was described as "a highly innovative and fascinating social document" by the *Toronto Star*.[8] According to Grant, "The work didn't abandon but rethought plot and character. The style wove a fabric of sense impressions through music, dance, mime, mask and visual images."[9] Kate Lushington writes, "Using slides and nonlinear text to illuminate the relationship between two women and their worlds, a new style of feminist theatre was born."[10] The plot was simple but disturbingly ambiguous: Ida Johnson, a waitress in small-town Alberta, relates her life story to Luke, a Native man, who at the end turns out to be Lucy, Ida's childhood friend. Ida's story is both tragic — she has killed her husband and children — and untrustworthy, creating the ideal framework for an allusive and imagistic production.

There is one further connection to conclude the comparison between Redlight and Nightwood: in 1989, Redlight founder

Francine Volker engaged with what she called "the second wave of feminist theatre" when she worked with Nightwood to produce her own one-woman show about the Russian-Canadian artist Paraskeva Clark, a play entitled *The Paraskeva Principle.*

1979: ALTERNATIVE THEATRE AND THE THEATRE CENTRE

In the January 1995 issue of Nightwood's *Nighttalk* newsletter, Kim Renders reflects on both her original and more recent involvement with the company:

> In those days we really didn't see ourselves as a women's theatre group. We were four artists with ideas and we got together to make theatre. But as Nightwood grew, we realized the terrific need for feminist expression in our culture. We realized that Nightwood could and should be a vehicle for many women's voices and passions, not only that of we four ... Now, after almost seven years, I am very happy to be back on the Nightwood "squeaky floor" boards. I am thrilled to see that the ship ... she still sails![11]

Renders has commented that, as an actor newly arrived in Toronto in 1978, she did not want to wait passively for someone to cast her in a show; instead, she and the other founders of Nightwood chose to create their own opportunities.[12]

Nightwood can be considered to have emerged at the tail end of what theatre historian Denis Johnston refers to as the golden age of Canadian theatre: a time in the late 1960s and early '70s when a new and exciting wave of alternative theatres sprang up across Canada, especially in Toronto.[13] These small, experimental companies, such as Theatre Passe Muraille, were reacting against the domination of the established regional theatre system by foreign productions. While these new companies were initially inspired by the international avant-garde — companies like the Living Theatre in New York, for example — their motivation quickly came to include a passionate nationalism. Johnston argues that the failure of a "second wave" of young Canadian companies was their inability to define a permanent mandate, to offer something different from the original alternative theatres like Passe Muraille.[14] Nightwood is part of what Johnston calls the "third wave" of small theatres in Toronto, those established in the late 1970s and early 1980s, which proved more durable than their immediate predecessors because they did succeed in offering fresh perspectives.[15] Certainly, Nightwood's longevity can be attributed in part to its unique and evolving mandate, which has always dealt with the production of women's art, but has adapted the means and manner by which this is done.

The definition of what qualifies as "alternative" theatre can be endlessly problematized. In an article published a few years after his book on documentary drama,[16] Alan Filewod concludes that there are actually two models of alternative theatre: the first, a political theatre that speaks for a defined constituency, which may include a variety of institutional structures and aesthetic approaches; the second, a theatre that defines "alternative" in relation to the institutional structures of Canadian culture.[17] When these two models overlap, as they did in Toronto in the 1970s, confusion results because a single term is used to describe both. Filewod also points out that the existence today of "fringe" and "popular theatre" companies and festivals constitutes yet another level of "alternative." Nightwood bridges the two models of political theatre Filewod identifies. During its early years as a member of the collective Theatre Centre, Nightwood was defined as an alternative to the institutional structures of Canadian culture, marginal even in comparison to the alternate theatres such as Passe Muraille. In interviews and articles, the member companies of the Theatre Centre defined themselves in terms of their physical space, their artistic vision, and their marginal status — on the furthest outer edge of the mainstream–alternative opposition. Nightwood was further specialized in being run by and producing works by women, thereby fitting into Filewod's first category as well, as a political theatre that speaks for a defined constituency, and that may include a variety of institutional structures and aesthetic approaches. In Nightwood's case, this meant identifying itself as both an experimental and a women's theatre company.

Nightwood's ongoing concerns were already clearly established in its first few productions: in 1979, *The True Story of Ida Johnson* introduced an enduring interest in literary adaptation; the 1980 production *Glazed Tempera* was a non-narrative, imagistic look at a famous public figure; and in 1981, *Flashbacks of Tomorrow* cemented the importance of multicultural and anti-racist work in Nightwood's mandate. This early work, which involved both the collective process and collaboration with outside companies and projects, would continue to define Nightwood's production history. While some Nightwood productions dealt with non-feminist themes (the male painter Alex Colville was the inspiration for *Glazed Tempera*, for example), the very first show dealt with issues of gender, sexuality, and race, was created collectively, and used experimental staging techniques—all attributes that situated Nightwood within the concerns of feminist theatre.

Nightwood was founded at the same time, and in conjunction with, the Theatre Centre, an artist-run facility established in 1979 to provide rental space and services to its members and other independent companies. It was legally incorporated on 10 February 1981 with the registered name B.A.A.N.N. Theatre Centre, reflecting the names of the five member companies: Buddies in Bad Times, AKA Performance Interfaces, Autumn Leaf, Necessary Angel, and Nightwood. During the period that Nightwood was associated with it, the Theatre Centre occupied three different addresses: 95 Danforth Avenue (1979–1981); 666 King Street West (1981–1984); and 296 Brunswick Avenue, known as the Poor Alex Theatre (1984–1986). Nightwood was very much affiliated with the Theatre Centre in its early years, and this status as a collective within a collective helped to define its place in the theatre community. However, after 1986, Nightwood no longer identified itself as part of the Theatre Centre and remained in the Poor Alex space even after the Centre had departed. After many interim years of occupying space in industrial, multi-use buildings, Nightwood moved in 2003 to its current location in the

Distillery District, a cluster of renovated warehouses now home to theatres, galleries, shops, and restaurants. The move marked a significant return to a specifically cultural environment and, for the first time, a noticeably upscale one.

Nightwood, Buddies in Bad Times, and the other resident Theatre Centre companies were characterized in the media as a "fringe of the fringe" — an even more alternative form of theatre than the alternates like Theatre Passe Muraille. Within the context of the Theatre Centre, the fact that Nightwood was run by women was not highlighted and the focus was squarely on the alternative and experimental nature of its work. For example, when Nightwood teamed up with Buddies to present the "Rhubarb!" annual festival of new performance for three of its years (1980–82), Nightwood's program note read, "Nightwood Theatre operates as a collective to produce original or adapted material in a style which emphasizes the visual, musical and literary elements of the presentation." Many of the artists involved with the earliest "Rhubarb!" festivals went on to work with Nightwood over the following years.

"Rhubarb!" was initially described as "a Festival of New Canadian Plays." The program boasted, "Rhubarb! is a workshop production presented to give artists a chance to explore new works. Plays will be presented at various levels of performance from staged reading to fully mounted production."[18] The festival was sponsored as a Theatre Passe Muraille "Seed Show." Two of Nightwood's first contributions were a study in contrasts, demonstrating the founders' wide range of interests. *Psycho-Nuclear Breakdown* by Cynthia Grant was a sombre piece that involved Grant, wearing a bathrobe and seated in a rocking chair, performing a monologue and reading from *Nuclear Madness* by Helen Caldicott. Her live reading was juxtaposed with a tape-recorded voice reading from another book, called *The Denial of Death*, and with a video, produced by Chris Clifford and VideoCabaret, showing Grant on the verge of a nervous breakdown. At the other extreme was the first of Renders and White's charmingly comic *Soft Boiled* clown shows.

Sky Gilbert, the founding artistic director of Buddies in Bad Times, recalls, "When Nightwood joined us in the spring of 1980, the Rhubarb! pieces moved from scripts to directorial and conceptual pieces." The emphasis was on allowing artists from one discipline to experiment in another, while avoiding financial pressures or the need to be aesthetically "slick." Gilbert admits, "The cross-fertilization among the disciplines and the audience results in a happy though hectic experience."[19]

1983: "WOMEN'S PERSPECTIVES"

Besides "Rhubarb!" Nightwood was involved with more explicitly feminist events, like the legendary "Women's Perspectives '83," a month-long art exhibit sponsored by Partisan Gallery that included a weekend of performances from Nightwood entitled "Caution: Women at Work." Two of the shows presented (*Four-Part Discord* and *Psycho-Nuclear Breakdown*) had previously been done at "Rhubarb!" but the third was the groundbreaking collective creation *This is For You, Anna/ a spectacle of revenge*, written and performed by Suzanne Khuri, Ann-Marie MacDonald, Baṇuta Rubess, Aida Jordão, and Maureen White. While The Anna Project collective had an arm's-length relationship to Nightwood, the connections were always evident: Maureen White was one of Nightwood's four founders, and Ann-Marie MacDonald and Baṇuta Rubess have been on its board of directors as well as directing and writing some of its best-known productions.[20]

That 1983 performance event was part of an amazing spring in Toronto, as Women's Cultural Building (a collective of women hoping to establish a building in Toronto as a central place for women's groups and women's cultural activities) presented a wide-ranging "Festival of Women Building Culture" at various venues. On 8 March, the first "FemCab" was held at the Horseshoe Tavern. Kate Lushington recalls, "There were line-ups around the block...it was just tremendous. And some things were started there that have gone on for the rest of peoples' lives."[21] Jan Kudelka's play *American Demon* was produced in March, and Pol Pelletier performed *Night Cows* by Jovette Marchessault and *My Mother's*

Luck by Helen Weinzweig in April, both at Theatre Passe Muraille. *American Demon*, directed by Kate Lushington, went on to "Brave New Works" at the Factory Theatre and then a fully produced run at Passe Muraille, while Kudelka went on to be involved with the "Groundswell Festival" in later years. Nightwood's contribution to Women's Cultural Building had further consequences. First, the two groups began to produce "FemCab" together every year (until 1990, when it became solely Nightwood's annual fund-raising celebration). Second, many of the women involved with Women's Cultural Building continued to work for Nightwood, including Tori Smith, the stage manager for *This is For You, Anna*, and Kate Lushington, who became Nightwood's artistic coordinator in 1988.

NIGHTWOOD IS DESCRIBED AS AN EXCITING NEW THEATRE — BUT NOT A FEMINIST ONE

In a 1983 article in *Canadian Theatre Review*, Patricia Keeney Smith discusses "the many expressions of Nightwood": its adaptations from literary sources, such as *The True Story of Ida Johnson* or *The Yellow Wallpaper*; its use of visual art in *Glazed Tempera*; and its collaborations with the Latin American and Greek communities on *Flashbacks of Tomorrow*. Keeney Smith writes, "One of their latest shows, *Mass/Age* has been called McLuhanesque but, as [Cynthia] Grant readily acknowledges, it owes more to Mabou Mines, a New York company with which she apprenticed ... The biggest problem with Nightwood Theatre is honing a piece; there are always too many ideas and never enough time for the experiments to gestate properly."[22] Nightwood's imagistic style is conveyed through Keeney Smith's detailed description of *Glazed Tempera*, a collective creation the company considered an unqualified success:

> The piece used both taped commentary and original material worked up by the company. Slides of Colville's paintings were juxtaposed with still figures behind scrims to produce a flat light effect uncannily similar to the artist's.

They had some fun too; in one scene, actress Maureen White shoots her silhouette across a slide of Colville's "Stop for Cows!" while Kim Renders looks fixedly out at the audience through binoculars; and in the famous "Horse and Train" painting, a little toy train comes chuffing along; the Canadian coin series evoked animal noises. There was magic in these colour-washed atmospheres that dabbled in fantasy, tinkered detachedly with perception and constantly surprised.[23]

Keeney Smith's article was published the same year that Nightwood produced *Smoke Damage*, a project with an explicitly feminist message. Yet the focus in her article is on artists, rather than women artists. For example, Cynthia Grant is quoted as complaining that artists are not sufficiently recognized in Toronto: "She points out that we still lack both foresight and hindsight, a strong enough reason for doing, for seeing the potential of what we're lucky enough to have happening here."[24] There is discussion of the lack of a practical division between commercial and experimental theatre in terms of government funding, but no mention of the specific problems or potential of a company run by women.

THE EARLY AESTHETIC

After *The True Story of Ida Johnson* and *Glazed Tempera*, Nightwood's next big production was *Flashbacks of Tomorrow/Memorias del Mañana*, a collective presentation by Nightwood and the Open Experience Hispanic-Canadian Theatre, along with a musical group called Compañeros. *Flashbacks of Tomorrow* was presented as part of the Toronto Theatre Festival's Open Stage in May of 1981, at the Toronto Free Theatre downstairs space (26 Berkeley Street), and was supported by the Ontario Arts Council and Theatre Passe Muraille. The program described it as

an original theatre production, presented in a mosaic of dance, ritual, personal experience and music, based on legends, documents and the art of Latin America. The musical adaptation has been written by and will be performed live by Compañeros ... a political group formed in Toronto in 1978. They have participated in many political, cultural and creative gatherings in order to sing their message of their culture and their peoples' struggle.

Compañeros and the bilingual company composed original music and based the text on their research about, and/or personal experiences of, Latin American culture. The form of the piece reflected the collective approach: "*Flashbacks* ... celebrates a festival on the Day of the Dead, when the past may be told by the people who lived it. ALL are here...and their collective memory spans more than one hundred years."[25] Nightwood took on the role of facilitator, providing a creative centre around which a large group of people could build their story.

The next summer, Nightwood mounted another large-scale collective piece. *Mass/Age*, subtitled "A McLuhanesque Look at our Lives," a multimedia spectacle of life in the nuclear age, was produced 25 to 29 August 1982, in a tent at Harbourfront Centre. In the program, Nightwood is described as a B.A.A.N.N. Theatre Centre satellite; the "collaborative production" was performed by Jay Bowen, Kim Renders, Daniel Brooks, Allan Risdill, Gordon Masten, and Maureen White. The director was Cynthia Grant, choreographers included Johanna Householder (of the lip-synch trio The Clichettes), and the visual artist John Scott worked on the design. Also listed "for Nightwood Theatre" are administrator Anna Barron-Schon and publicity director Anne H. Kear. Nightwood is described as a professional company that operates within the jurisdiction of Equity—so at this early point, Nightwood was already employing short-term administrative personnel for its shows and operating as a professional company.

In the press release ("Nightwood Theatre presents *Mass/Age*, High-Tech Theatre in a tent"), Nightwood is described as "one of Toronto's most innovative experimental theatre companies." The press release also boasts, "Nightwood's artistic director Cynthia

Grant has established a reputation as the challenging director of such productions as *The True Story of Ida Johnson* ... and *Glazed Tempera*," and mentions Kim Renders's Dora Mavor Moore Award nomination for her work in *Staller's Farm* at Theatre Passe Muraille. These statements suggest that Nightwood wanted to be taken seriously as part of the Toronto theatre community: identifying Grant as artistic director signals a cohesive structure, and labelling her "challenging" suggests an avant-garde vision, while Renders's Dora nomination communicates a recognized standard of quality. The credentials of the other collaborators were also celebrated, placing Nightwood within a creative community of equals.

Reviews of *Mass/Age* discuss it not only in terms of avant-garde theatre, but also in the context of an established Nightwood style. In his review, Ray Conlogue depicts the set as a runway with high platforms at each end.[26] He mentions projections of da Vinci paintings, John Scott's ghost figures (faces painted on dangling Styrofoam), and slogans and poetry blown up gigantically over the actors' heads. A soundtrack of familiar popular music was used and action faded in and out as the audience's attention was focused on different spaces in the huge playing area. Furthermore, Conlogue refers to Renders and White as "Nightwood's customary actors." Evidently, Nightwood was already identifiable in terms of its style and performers, building on the striking visual design and the attention garnered by its first shows.

Further documentation from this period reinforces Nightwood's status as an experimental collective operating within the small theatre community of Toronto. Cynthia Grant, interviewed in *NOW* magazine, is said to be creating a theatre of images, broadening the theatregoing experience by bringing in other art forms. Jon Kaplan notes:

> The opening of *Mass/Age* has a filmic quality typical of Grant's work. A voiceover description of humanity's coming into the cosmos glides into a personal monologue about coping with today's world. Then the focus of the

play zooms out again to look at experiments on the brain, including memory distortion.

Grant wants to present the negative, alienating implications and contradictions of the individual in today's high-tech society: "The work will try to evoke certain responses in the audience so that people can see themselves in perspective." Kaplan comments that the work sounds reminiscent of Mabou Mines.[27]

After discussing Nightwood's aesthetic style, Kaplan and Grant turn to the company's placement within the Toronto theatre context. Grant sees disappointingly small progress in Toronto theatre but believes "that the sort of collective, ongoing process of a group like Nightwood is important to the growth of theatre." She is cynical about change because of the absence of funding and lack of support from the media: "Our area of theatre is research/development. Because those organizations that fund don't distinguish between our area and that of commercial theatre, the pressure is on us to become more commercial." Again, the shape of Nightwood is coming into focus in the public eye — that of an experimental theatre company with a strong visual sense and a collective way of working, but with Cynthia Grant assuming the role of leader and spokesperson.

The next large-scale production after *Mass/Age* was *Peace Banquet* ("Ancient Greece Meets the Atomic Age"), collectively written and presented in November of 1983 as an adaptation of Aristophanes' play *Peace*; it was produced and directed by Grant. Reviewer Carole Corbeil describes the structure of the play: in the first half of the show, actor Dean Gilmour visits heaven in search of Miss Peace and meets actor Sky Gilbert as the God of War, attended by Kim Renders and Maureen White as Corruption and Chaos. Gilmour is told that Peace is actually Force "in drag." The second half of the play takes the form of a banquet in which the audience participates.[28] Again, critics attempted to place the work on a continuum of Nightwood productions. In his review, Henry Mietkiewicz praises the coherence of the piece and the appropriateness of its broad tone, "unlike earlier Nightwood efforts which have too often tended towards incoherence (*Mass/Age*) or verbosity (*Hooligans*) [a "Rhubarb!" show]."[29] Except for the four Nightwood founders, there was no overlap between the other collective participants who created *Peace Banquet* and *Mass/Age*, and yet there is an attempt to find an identifiable Nightwood style in both.

The earliest Nightwood shows do demonstrate a consistent aesthetic vision: reviews of *The True Story of Ida Johnson*, *Glazed Tempera, Flashbacks of Tomorrow*, and *Mass/Age* speak of the innovative use of multimedia techniques and the fragmented, nonlinear structure. But by 1984, when Baņuta Rubess and other women had become a strong presence at Nightwood, reviewers perceived a corresponding diffusion of the "Nightwood show." In fact, one reviewer of Rubess's *Pope Joan* (1984) comments that the plot is unusually linear for a Nightwood production, indicating that there had been a certain loosening of the established model for the company's work.[30] The obvious though unacknowledged difference, of course, is that *Pope Joan* was not a collective creation.

1983 TO 1986: THE IMAGIST AESTHETIC MEETS FEMINISM IN *THIS IS FOR YOU, ANNA*

The twenty-minute version of *This is For You, Anna* was so well received at its Partisan Gallery premiere that the five performers were encouraged to expand it into a full-length play. Further workshops were held at the Factory Theatre Lab in Toronto and Playwright's Workshop in Montreal; collective member Aida Jordão left to work as an actor in Portugal, and was replaced by Patricia Nichols. In 1984, funded by a variety of government grants, the collective added Tori Smith and Barb Taylor as stage manager and administrator and began touring to community centres, women's shelters, law schools, and a prison. In 1985, Patricia Nichols left the collective and the play was rewritten for four performers. *This is For You, Anna* also toured in England, had runs at Theatre Passe Muraille and at the Great Canadian Theatre Company in Ottawa, and was invited to the 1986 "duMaurier Theatre Festival" in Toronto. It was published in *Canadian Theatre Review* in

1985, credited to the pared-down collective of four perform-ers — Baṇuta Rubess, Ann-Marie MacDonald, Suzanne Odette Khuri, and Maureen White — as well as to Tori Smith and Barb Taylor. It was published again in *The CTR Anthology* in 1993.[31]

The process behind *This is For You, Anna* illustrates some im-portant features of feminist theatre in general and of Nightwood's work in the 1980s. The piece was created collectively, initially performed at a women's event, and based on a real-life incident that provided the basis for further invented material and research into related issues. Beginning with a newspaper item about a Ger-man woman who took revenge against the man who killed her child, the collective members expanded their material through research on violence against women and consultations with po-lice officers and rape crisis workers.[32] This process was in keeping with the tradition of collective creation, but in a feminist context it also served as a kind of consciousness-raising around feminist issues; furthermore, it reflected a materialist feminist concern with analyzing the specifics of oppression.

Another important element in the collective method is the sharing of credit, demonstrated here by the inclusion of Tori Smith and Barb Taylor (stage manager and administrator) as col-lective members in the published version of the script. As Smith explains, the script was written by the performers, but "the the-atrical experience was the work of the whole collective."[33] This demonstrates an awareness that a theatrical performance is made up of many elements and situates the script as just one factor. Awareness is further demonstrated by the collective's decision to perform outside of traditional venues and to take their piece to an audience most directly affected by its subject matter.

In her essay "The Politics of the Script," Ann Wilson agrees that the text should be viewed as only one element of a produc-tion and not its centre. She argues that feminist theatre should reflect a sense of flux and multiplicity; that it should reject the constraints of linearity and finality in order to convey the open-endedness of women's discourse.[34] Wilson also applauds The Anna Project's emphasis on collective process: in order to be truly feminist, a production must not only deal with women's concerns and subvert the conventions of linearity and closure; it must also be born out of a politically conscious theatre practice. As Maureen White insists, "I think it is not coincidence that a lot of feminists are choosing to work collectively: in exploring new material and breaking down old structures, a new process also should be explored."[35] The Anna Project also included its audience in the play development process by holding a question-and-answer session after each performance and by remaining open enough to rewrite the script when collective members departed. The collective did not regard its play as a finished product but as an ongoing process, even when a version of the script was published in *Canadian Theatre Review*—a quality of openness that Wilson identifies as particularly feminist.

Many of the decisions regarding process and content in *This is For You, Anna* reflect a basis in materialist feminism. The materialist position concentrates on the specific nature of women's oppression within their historical circumstances, and *This is For You, Anna* is specifically concerned with issues of class and sexuality. As Ann Wilson observes, the story of Marianne Bachmeier and her daughter, Anna, is used as a framework in which to explore women's anger at the violence committed against them.[36] The women onstage tell the stories of other women because the experience of violence is held in common, yet it is always placed in a social context. The anger of the women in the different interwoven stories—Marianne, legendary victims Agate and Lucretia, and the battered Canadian women Eena, Maria, and Jenny—is situated in relation to the economic and political organization of the societies in which they live.

In addition to socio-economic factors, materialist feminists also emphasize the necessity for change in male/female relationships. *This is For You, Anna* places Marianne within her particular social class, family history, occupation, and nationality, and explores her troubled relationships with men. Because we hear Marianne's story in her "own" voice (and in some cases, her own words, taken from newspaper accounts of the trial), she acts as the subject of her own experience in the play. While fragmented, the perspective is always from her point of view.

The combined talents of the collective resulted in a play that is unusually layered and aggressively nonlinear. The play's subtitle, "a spectacle of revenge," signals a heightened sense of theatricality and a certain detachment of tone. A number of stories are told, often in the third person; the actors do not assume the same roles throughout; and a single character is played by many different actors, either serially or simultaneously. The effect in performance is one of fragmentation, as the audience is prevented from identifying with one particular actor and instead focuses on the gradual buildup of detail and imagery. The audience is reminded of the separation between performer and role and is required to actively participate in bringing meaning and connection to the stories.

The deconstructionist tools of parody and satire draw attention to the distance between expectation and reality, particularly evident in the use of fairy tales to frame individual stories and to define Marianne's relationship with her daughter. Throughout the play, Marianne communicates with Anna through stories—sometimes playful and reassuring, at other times more ambivalent. For example, in one scene she says:

> **Marianne 3**: Alright, Anna. You want a story? I'll tell you a story. Once upon a time there was a little girl and she was born and her mother was miserable.[37]

As collective member Suzanne Odette Khuri points out, fairy tales have traditionally been used to tell violent or extraordinary stories about women.[38] In one way, the fairy-tale format suggests a commonality between the women onstage, a shared cultural vocabulary, but on the other hand, the characters are all too aware of the irony of their usage, the gap between their own material realities and the happily-ever-after promise of the fairy tale.

The deconstructive project is most clearly demonstrated in the treatment of motherhood. The set is a multi-levelled white playing area that includes a refrigerator, a laundry line, a hamper, and four red chairs, minimally representing the homebound environment of a traditional mother. Trapped within this space, Marianne Bachmeier serves as a challenge to the one-dimensional ideal of motherhood: she is not only the devoted mother, but also a complex woman who can be selfish and neglectful. Her act of revenge against her child's killer exemplifies an extreme, even grotesque, image of protective motherhood. The play suggests that society (and perhaps the audience) is of two minds about the act of revenge: the court punished it as a crime, but the general public applauded it as the right action of a good mother. Later, when details of Marianne's troubled past and relationships with men came out in the press, public opinion turned against her. Her sexuality was somehow incompatible with her previous idealization as a mother.

In the process of creating the play, The Anna Project collective became increasingly aware of the power of the motherhood myth and the seductiveness of revenge. Baņuta Rubess remarks, "Whereas in 1983, we were angry and volatile, by 1984 we were very concerned not to endorse violence, to make clear that we do not idolize Marianne."[39] In the published text, a provision in the copyright information forbids any "graphic depiction of violence, weapons, or blood in any production of this script."[40]

The collective was very conscious of the signifiers they employed and rather than using concrete items (like a gun, for example), they selected objects that could have multiple resonance for the spectator. In the first scene, entitled "The Story of Marianne Bachmeier," the circumstances of Marianne's life are related in a series of short sentences delivered by the Narrator. With each sentence, she places a nail on a piece of black cloth on the floor, forming a circle. Marianne's life story culminates in Anna's death:

A man called Grabowski strangles Anna when she visits him in his room. Marianne is away, driving around town. He tells the court that Anna flirted with him. Anna was seven years old. Marianne walks into the courtroom and shoots him seven times. (*Narrator drops seven nails*)... A thousand tragedies, a thousand sins. (*with empty hands*).[41]

The Narrator picks up the black cloth full of nails and carries it offstage, cradling it like a baby and counting under her breath. Nails have a variety of connotations — crucifixion, construction, "hitting the nail on the head," "a nail in her coffin," "hard as nails" — but their specific meaning in the context of the scene and the play is left up to the spectator. There is a grim irony in the image of the infant represented not by a doll or even a soft bundle of cloth, but by nails, each of which signifies an event in the troubled life of the mother. The child, or the image of the child, is yet another cruelty in this woman's cruel life.

Another powerful image in the play is the pouring of milk. At the beginning of the play, Marianne pours a glass of milk from the refrigerator and offers it: "This is for you, Anna." At the end of the play, Marianne stands at the refrigerator pouring milk into a glass until it overflows and runs onto the floor. She simply states: "I did it for you, Anna." As Khuri explains, the image is one of terrible absence: Anna does not take the proffered glass of milk because she is not there anymore.[42] As with the baby bundle, a conventionally positive image is given a much darker undertone. Milk is an image or metaphor easily found in cultural feminist work, where it might represent the nurturing female body of the mother,[43] but in this instance it resonates with grief, violence, and loss. The fragmented nature of the storytelling and the use of all the actors to portray Marianne preclude audience identification with a particular character throughout the play; instead, the emotional power of the performance comes from the repetition of visual imagery.

1986: CRITICAL BACKLASH

While *This is For You, Anna* was groundbreaking for Nightwood, it also provoked a response from one prominent male theatre reviewer that illustrates why the company might be reluctant to engage with the feminist label. The fear that one's work will be misinterpreted is very real for theatre practitioners in general, when the future of their theatre company relies on the box-office returns and favourable reviews that translate into grant money. In an article in the national *Globe and Mail* newspaper entitled "Cathy Jones Steals World Stage Festival Show," the well-known theatre critic Ray Conlogue compares two productions by women at the 1986 "duMaurier World Stage Festival."[44] Conlogue starts by praising comedian Cathy Jones's show, but then warns that it is a "ready contrast" to the "victim fetishism" of *This is For You, Anna*. "Much has been written about this show," he begins, "an incontrovertibly powerful piece of theatre created by a feminist collective in Toronto and revived for the festival." Conlogue makes a number of factual errors in recounting the plotline of the show, and spends most of the review discussing not the play itself or its performance values, but his personal opinions on gender relations.[45] He philosophizes at length:

> It is true that some men are physically violent to women, and that most women cannot respond in kind. But this does not mean women are helpless to fight back. They do so by other means, responding … with psychological sexual humiliation. Often they do so not toward the men who have abused them, but toward other men they meet at some subsequent time. Our society is engulfed in gender tension right now, and women are responsible for a good deal of it … Sexual violence in our society is a syndrome in which men and women alike are caught, and to which both contribute. Plays in which women are seen as incapable of any wrong action (or any action at all, a convenient by product of "victimization") misrepresent women as well as men.

Conlogue concludes by stating that *This is For You, Anna* "is a negative image of shattered, crippled women and its implied message to any male viewer is one of blame." Conlogue is entitled to his opinion as a theatre critic, but much of his argument has nothing to do with the play at hand, nor with its performance. Instead, he uses his column to air his vitriolic take on a social issue, and as a forum to express his anger at feminism (and perhaps at women in general). The force of his condemnation and his high profile as a critic for a national newspaper could not help but negatively affect Nightwood's potential audiences.

Given this experience of a hostile reaction from an influential reviewer, it becomes understandable that the women involved with Nightwood sound at times as if they are trying to avert criticism before it arises. A few months after Conlogue's review, Mary Vingoe assured readers that, although Nightwood was a feminist collective, "We do not ask writers to toe any particular political line ... We want theatre that has integrity and its roots in real experience, rather than just being doctrinaire."[46] In another article, Baņuta Rubess elaborates:

> Nightwood ... never consciously set out to make a grand, feminist statement, let alone an angry diatribe ... The point here is not to proselytize. Since we happen to be feminists, we ask certain questions, but this show isn't meant as agit-prop. What we want to avoid is being ghettoized to the point where people say, "If it's Nightwood, it must be feminist, so I probably wouldn't like it."[47]

The author of the article in which this quote appears goes on to assure readers that Nightwood's emphasis on "solid theatrical values rather than dogmatic statements" has resulted in Dora Mavor Moore Award nominations for best new play (*War Babies*, 1987) and featured male performance (Sky Gilbert in *The Edge of the Earth is Too Near, Violette Leduc*, 1987). The message being pushed is that Nightwood produces high quality shows that have been given a seal of approval by arts organizations, and that the prospective audience member need not fear an experience like Conlogue's. Ironically, Nightwood's 1987 production of Margaret Hollingsworth's play *War Babies* provoked at least one review that continues to illustrate the way critics write from biases that have less to do with the production at hand than with preconceptions of what a feminist show must be like. The critic comments, "After seeing a play of the quality of *War Babies* produced well by Nightwood, I am reluctant to see them do more of their traditional collective creation. It's encouraging to see that Nightwood's vision of feminism isn't as dogmatically rigid as much of their previous output suggests."[48] Here, the reviewer implies that he was able to enjoy this particular production in spite of the expectations he had developed from seeing previous Nightwood shows (how many and which ones he does not specify). The reader of the review is led to assume, therefore, that Nightwood generally produces "dogmatically rigid" work (like *This is For You, Anna*, perhaps?) and may approach the next Nightwood creation with whatever prejudice this phrase brings to mind.

ANOTHER 1983 COLLECTIVE CREATION: SMOKE DAMAGE

Following *This is For You, Anna*, Nightwood's next project, in the fall of 1983, was *Smoke Damage*, a play about the European witch hunts, written by Baṇuta Rubess with a collective cast that included Ann-Marie MacDonald. Susan G. Cole has described Rubess and MacDonald as part of the first wave of women who got involved with Nightwood and widened the sphere of the original four founders by creating *This is For You, Anna*, *Smoke Damage*, and Rubess's *Pope Joan*. Cole writes, "These early '80s productions used Nightwood as a collective laboratory, and emphasized the need for a feminist company on the theatre scene, for no other troupes were confronting such issues as church violence and hypocrisy from women's perspectives."[49] These projects in particular helped to formulate Nightwood's growing identification in the public eye as a feminist company. As we have seen, Nightwood was not without external detractors; unfortunately, it was also not free from internal challenges.

Nightwood's early commitment to the collective process and its rejection of a strictly hierarchical structure can be seen to reflect cultural feminist values, as do a number of its productions, such as *Smoke Damage*. Cultural feminism is often associated with groups that operate as women-only collectives, such as At the

Foot of the Mountain or Le Théâtre Expérimental des Femmes, for example, and much feminist performance art expresses the female body in profound ways, which can be considered cultural feminism.[50] The story of a group of women travellers who encounter the history of the European witch hunts, *Smoke Damage* draws explicit connections between the common oppression of women in previous and contemporary ages. The play links historical misogyny with the repression of a separate women's culture and its traditional, oral transmission of women's knowledge — the skills of the midwife, for example. *Smoke Damage* emphasizes that women were oppressed in the past and continue to be oppressed today precisely because they are women. At the end of the play, two of the characters plan to hijack an airplane in order to force the Catholic pope to stand trial at Nuremburg, accused of "the annihilation of three centuries of women."[51]

Smoke Damage employs an actual historical text about punishing witches, the *Malleus Malificarum*, and even represents that text's authors, Kramer and Sprenger, onstage as chilling examples of misogyny. Interestingly, the same book was used by the British playwright Caryl Churchill when researching *Vinegar Tom*, her 1976 play about witches. Churchill developed her play while working with Monstrous Regiment, a company that initiated new work through a period of time in which the writer and actors "discuss central themes, read historical material, travel, talk to experts, and explore character possibilities."[52] This would be followed by a period of writing, then rehearsals and productions, as the work was shaped in a complex exchange between writer and actors. Churchill has expressed enthusiasm for this working method, which does seem particularly suited to the witch-hunt material. Like the women in the *Smoke Damage* collective, Churchill found that her research on the witch hunts led her to a cultural feminist conclusion: "I discovered for the first time the extent of Christian teaching against women and saw the connections between medieval attitudes to witches and continuing attitudes to women in general."[53]

The origins of *Smoke Damage* can be traced to the summer of 1983, when a collective called The Midnight Hags was initiated in

Toronto by Mary Ann Lambooy, a director from Ottawa. The collective created a play called *Burning Times*, which was performed at the Theatre Centre (then located at 666 King Street West) from 17 to 28 August, and produced with the assistance of the Canada Council Explorations Program and the Ontario Arts Council. The program for the production gives a good indication of how carefully feminist collectives try to assign credit for their work: the play is said to be written by Baņuta Rubess in collaboration with Peggy Christopherson, Mary Ann Lambooy, Ann-Marie Mac-Donald, Mary Marzo, Kim Renders, and Maureen White. The play was directed by Lambooy in collaboration with the same names, including Rubess. The cast collaborated with both the writer (Rubess) and the director (Lambooy), and they also collaborated with each other. Furthermore, the project is stated to have been "conceived by" and produced by Lambooy, while the set and costume design is credited to "the company." Midnight Hags was considered a professional company operating within the jurisdiction of Canadian Actors' Equity Association.[54] The connections between Midnight Hags and Nightwood are evident from the involvement of Renders, White, MacDonald, and Rubess.

The play's source material is explained in a program note — an example of how collective creations often aim for internal authentication. The program note begins, "*Burning Times* is based on fact and fiction, poetry and personal anecdote." It goes on to stress the authenticity of the quotations from the *Malleus Maleficarum* by Kramer and Sprenger (1486), mentions a 1927 edition of the book published by Montague Summers, which is also quoted, and cites other books of a similar nature. The program note concludes, "All the various individual case histories presented in this piece are based on documents." The aim of this note is clearly to assure the audience that the examples of persecution and misogynist writing used in the performance are not inventions of the collective, and the tone implies that the audience should find the reality of these examples as appalling as the collective does.

In an interview in the collection Fair Play, Rubess explains that Lambooy invited her to work on a collective creation called *Burning Times*, which we were going to workshop. We did two weeks of improvisations in a search for characters for these five women in the company, gestural texts, story lines, etc. After these two weeks I took the loads and loads of notes that had accumulated and went off for about three weeks to write a first draft. We then got together and workshopped the script.[55]

According to Kim Renders, during the process of creating *Burning Times* there was some conflict between Mary Ann Lambooy and the rest of the company about how the collective should be run — a disagreement serious enough that it had to be resolved through an appeal to Equity.[56]

Shortly after the production of *Burning Times*, Cynthia Grant and Nightwood Theatre began arrangements to rework and remount the show with Rubess and the original collective, minus Lambooy, who had gone back to Ottawa. There was an immediate difference of opinion about the appropriateness of this action. In a letter from Lambooy to Grant dated 20 September 1983, Lambooy states that, in regards to their previous discussion about Nightwood's interest in reworking and reproducing *Burning Times*, she has come to the conclusion that she does not want this done so shortly after its premiere. "Under the Copyright Act," Lambooy writes, "I am the first owner of the copyright for *Burning Times* and am registered as such with the Copyright Office. Should Nightwood oppose my decision and reproduce any part of *Burning Times*, other than the sections open to public domain e.g. *Malleus Maleficarum*, such action would constitute an infringement of copyright. I do not wish to have to be put to the initiative of enforcing my rights but if I have to I certainly will." Lambooy concludes by saying she regrets the severe tone of her letter, but feels she must avert a serious situation.

Grant's response, dated 30 September 1983, is that all contractual arrangements for the new play, which was being called *Smoke Damage,* had been made with Baņuta Rubess, "whom we understand to be the principal playwright." If, Grant writes, after seeing the play, Lambooy still had a question about ownership, Nightwood would be willing to discuss it. The implication of Grant's letter is that if Lambooy had a conflict, it was with Rubess and not Nightwood, which did not recognize the situation as problematic. Rubess has stated, "*Smoke Damage* marked the first time I began to think of myself as a real writer,"[57] and certainly she was treated as such by Nightwood.

Smoke Damage was produced by Nightwood at St. Paul's Square, 30 September to 23 October 1983. The program states that it was written by Rubess in collaboration with the cast: Peggy Christopherson, Ann-Marie MacDonald, Mary Marzo, Kim Renders, and Maureen White. The "direction consultants" were Rubess and Grant. The program uses the same "note of interest" regarding the source material as was used for *Burning Times*, and both the program and the press release acknowledge that the current play was developed from *Burning Times* (which was referred to as a "workshop") and mention Lambooy's involvement with that project. The program also stresses that the play was developed through a collective process. In 1985, when *Smoke Damage* was published by Playwrights Union of Canada, the same credits and information were used again, with a note that reads, "*Smoke Damage* develops several themes from the successful workshop of *Burning Times*, written by Baņuta Rubess and presented by Midnight Hags at the Theatre Centre, Toronto, in August 1983. *Burning Times* was initiated and produced by Mary Ann Lambooy. *Smoke Damage* was developed through a collective process. Although the main writer, Baņuta Rubess, gave the play its final shape, the five actors contributed largely to its content."

Smoke Damage demonstrates many of the same qualities as *This is For You, Anna*, which Rubess, MacDonald, and White all worked on as well. There are repetitive actions, such as sweeping, washing, and the opening and closing of doors, and the play makes use of emblematic props such as a green cloth, a bouquet of flowers, and dripping water. There are symbolic costumes, such as men's suit jackets as metonyms for Kramer and Sprenger, the figures of male authority. There are wild changes in tone, from comedy to horror, and changes in style, from realism to absurdism to musical theatre. Different time periods — Medieval, Renaissance, contemporary — are interwoven, as are dream sequences. Scenes are layered with images, an accompanying soundtrack, and simultaneous actions, all building to a cumulative effect. Finally, there are scenes that relate the persecution of Medieval witches to the persecution of contemporary women — as in, for example the character of Madeleine, an abused wife.

Although *Smoke Damage* did not do particularly well at the box office, it received good reviews and was eventually published. In response to Ray Conlogue's favourable 5 October review in the *Globe and Mail*, a letter to the editor was published on 26 October. The letter, signed by Roger Ware "and six others," is headed "Reassessment of credit." The letter writers were disturbed that Mary Ann Lambooy had not been mentioned in the review. They write that she had "conceived of the theme of the play, assembled the cast, hired the writer and directed the development of the play largely into its current form," and that the review had incorrectly attributed these functions to Cynthia Grant. Grant responded in another letter to the editor, saying that Conlogue's review was "positive and well-considered" and that if there was any reassessment to be done, "it would be in acknowledging the collective input of the company toward the creation of the script as well as the staging of *Smoke Damage*." Grant acknowledges that the same writer and cast worked on both shows and that both were collective creations, so "it is natural that a stylistic and textual progression consistent with the intentions of the original workshop production would be apparent in the further development of *Burning Times* into *Smoke Damage*." Grant also points out that the *Smoke Damage* program credited Lambooy for her work on *Burning Times* but that, since it was a collective work, it would be inaccurate to say she "largely directed the show into its current form," or to attribute a final product to any one guiding hand.

At this point, the dispute became a legal matter, as both sides engaged legal counsel and sought some agreement over matters of royalty and further production. Nightwood's documentation included its contract with Rubess and her copyright for *Burning Times*, which was issued prior to Lambooy's. The company's correspondence to Lambooy (8 November 1983) summarizes Nightwood's handling of the matter: it had credited *Burning Times* in the press release, and the program had credited *Burning Times* and Lambooy's role as "initiator and producer" of that show. Grant also reiterates that Nightwood's contract for *Smoke Damage* was with Rubess, the principal author, and that it was her responsibility if there was any copyright infringement. Copyright for *Burning Times* "was issued to Rubess on September 6, 1983, and *Smoke Damage* is in the process of being issued a separate copyright." The tone of this letter is conciliatory, and a copy was sent to the Ontario Arts Council.

The response from Lambooy came on 11 November. In this letter, she refers to a conversation she had with Grant on 9 November, in which Grant made a verbal offer of $400 "as royalties for Nightwood Theatre's production of *Smoke Damage*." This was followed by a formal offer in which terms were set:

> 1. Nightwood agreed to pay Lambooy $400 "in settlement of any claim which she may have at this time or in the future for breach of copyright or for any other reason";
> 2. Lambooy waived claims against Nightwood concerning its production of *Smoke Damage*;
> 3. Nightwood would continue to acknowledge Lambooy as "initiator and producer" of *Burning Times*;
> 4. Both parties acknowledged Rubess as the principal author of both *Burning Times* and *Smoke Damage*, in collaboration with the companies in each case.

The letter concluded by asking Lambooy to sign a copy and return it, upon which she would be issued a cheque.

Lambooy responded on 2 December 1983 by saying that she refused to sign the letter and accept the conditions. She states that she would not give up copyright for *Burning Times* in regards to future productions,[58] and she would not acknowledge a principal author of *Burning Times*. Lambooy wanted the Nightwood letter to be amended so that the payment of $400 represented a royalty fee and settlement for the recent production of *Smoke Damage*.

The last piece of correspondence on this matter, from December of 1983, came for the first time from the *Smoke Damage* collective — Peggy Christopherson, Ann-Marie MacDonald, Mary Marzo, Kim Renders, Baņuta Rubess, and Maureen White — and was addressed to Lambooy as a kind of position statement and final offer. They again offer a settlement of $400 for her to waive all present and future actions against them for the September/October 1983 production of *Smoke Damage*. For future productions, they had worked out a distribution of royalty payments ("We presume that you know that there were losses on the Nightwood production and no royalty payments," they write). The agreement was that Rubess would receive all revenue up to $500 as playwright's royalties; any amount above that would be split as follows: 51 percent to Rubess, 45 percent to the *Smoke Damage* collective, and 4 percent to Lambooy.

On the second page of the letter, there is an interesting paragraph that questions Lambooy's status as the producer of the original production, even though she was credited as such in the program. The collective thought that the producer was the society "Midnight Hags," for which Ann-Marie MacDonald had served as official secretary, and of which they were all members. They were under the impression that it had been this society (that is, their collective group) that had received the funding grant and held the bank account, and now they wonder if it was in fact some other legal entity of which they were not aware. In any case, the collective concludes, they are willing to credit either Lambooy or Midnight Hags as the producer — whichever she would prefer. The implication is that they are questioning Lambooy's claim to having been the producer, or having had as much importance to the original production as she claimed.

This disappointing incident illustrates that collectives sometimes work better in theory than in practice. Part of the problem may be inherent in the process of collective creation itself, in that "job descriptions" may be largely self-defined and therefore easily subject to dispute. Individuals who put a lot of time and effort into a project are not always able to give up a sense of personal "ownership" of that work for the greater good of the company, and there are many who argue that they should not have to. But the issues can be further complicated when the collective members are assumed to share the same feminist principles. Unspoken assumptions can be made that everyone is more in agreement than they really are, and individuals can be afraid of voicing dissenting views for fear of looking "not feminist enough."

On the other hand, the majority of the women in this collective do seem to have worked well within the model. Reviews of *Smoke Damage* speak about the obvious energy and commitment to the material that the actors displayed, and the end result was one of the most successful plays of Nightwood's early period. Apparently, collective creation may involve a discrepancy between process and product. In some cases, a beneficial feminist process does not necessarily result in a concrete product, while in the case of *Smoke Damage*, an extremely troubled feminist process still resulted in a valuable feminist play.

1984: New Feminist Developments

By March of 1984, in an application to the Laidlaw Foundation requesting funding for an upcoming production called *Penelope*, Nightwood's status as a women-led company was given prominence. The application was written by Mary Vingoe, who notes that, over the previous five years, Nightwood had produced "original and innovative work for the stage" including plays that dealt with contemporary issues such as "the concerns of the women's community," the role of technology in our lives, and the "peace problem." She mentions *Glazed Tempera* and *Flashbacks of Tomorrow*, but also the overtly feminist *Smoke Damage*. Vingoe even makes use of Rina Fraticelli's report on the status of women in Canadian theatre, by attaching an article about it from *FUSE* magazine. She states that Nightwood had designed its 1984/85 season to specifically address the gender imbalance documented by Fraticelli. "We wish to fully educate the public on the status of the 'invisible majority' in the theatre while providing opportunity for many women artists," she writes. Vingoe explains that the upcoming season would include *The Euguélionne*, adapted from the novel by Louky Bersianik, "which electrified Quebec women when it was first published," as well as a play developed through The Women's Immigrant Centre in Toronto. The fate of this particular application provides a good example of how decisions by funding agencies shape the direction of a company, and how projects that are proposed in one form may turn into something quite different. The immigrant women's play did not receive funding, so it never happened at all; and Cynthia Grant did not direct *The Euguélionne* until considerably later, and then only as part of the November 1987 "Groundswell," not as a main-stage production.

The main focus of Vingoe's application, however, is the proposed production of *Penelope*. Nightwood planned to commission ten women writers to interpret female characters from *The Odyssey*, with some of their prospective participants to include Sharon Riis, Ann Cameron, Jan Kudelka, Jane Rule, Susan Musgrave, and Rita MacNeil. They then planned to challenge any of Toronto's male-run companies to do the same, creating the "male version," and to run the two works on alternate nights as *Penelope/Ulysse* (sic). Nightwood would sponsor the production costs, but salaries were to be paid by the "male company" within strict limits. An external judge would interpret the "rules," and neither company would be allowed to see the other's rehearsals. Vingoe concludes that the project would provide "a unique forum and a good humoured context by which to explode some of the dark myths which exist about men and women in the theatre." As with *The Euguélionne*, the proposed project did take place, but on a considerably reduced scale: *Penelope* was eventually staged 3 to 6 October 1985, as a workshop production at the Theatre Centre, with poetry by Margaret Atwood adapted by Cynthia Grant, Peggy Sample, and Susan Seagrove. Later, it was developed further and performed in 1992/93 by the Company of Sirens, and published in *Canadian Theatre Review*.[59]

Vingoe makes some significant statements in the application: "Our wider purpose is to stimulate a better awareness of the female aesthetic in the theatre, a field which even today is dominated (90%) by men," and, "The theatre has always had the power to shock public consciousness into an awareness of our true social values." The nature of the *Penelope* project and the use of the term "female aesthetic" clearly point to a theatre company coming to terms with its status as woman-centred, and feminism runs as an unspoken subtext throughout the application. As the journalist Meredith Levine has commented, "The artistic community's diminishing resistance to feminism has enabled Nightwood to 'come out' as a feminist theatre."[60]

A similar willingness to push its role as a resource for women is evident in Nightwood's promotional brochure for the 1984/85 season, which states that Nightwood chooses "programming that reflects the voices of women in Canadian culture. Over the past five years we have produced 20 new or adapted plays ... We focus on a broad spectrum of modern concerns. Using comedy, we provide our audiences with entertaining and thought-provoking evenings." The 1984 summer tour of the collective creation *Love and Work Enough* and the fall 1984 production of *Pope Joan* by Baṇuta Rubess, which played an extended run at the Poor Alex Theatre (at that point, the home of the Theatre Centre), are highlighted. The brochure lists upcoming productions in Nightwood's season, including *The Woman Who Slept With Men to Take the War Out of Them* by Deena Metzger; a piece about the artist Kathe Köllwitz; *Penelope*; and *Before and Beyond Testubes* by Amanda Hale, which dealt with reproductive issues. Obviously, the work was by that point consistently dealing with women-oriented themes and characters. This piece of publicity sums up what appears to have become Nightwood's official strategy at this stage in its development: the Nightwood women never used the word "feminist," but they did market themselves as being unique and they did start talking about things like a "female perspective," a "female aesthetic," and their role as an employer of women theatre artists.

In its application to the Toronto Arts Council for 1983/84, Nightwood applied for $4,000 for the period May 1983 to May 1984 (it had received $1,700 the previous year) and the company is described as "operating as a collective." The application also provides some interesting statistics about the number of Nightwood performances: over the previous year the company had done 32 performances for an audience of 2,900; in the upcoming season it projected 40 performances for an audience of 3,500. The average audience per performance was 91 and the special audiences it addressed included women's groups, the literary and visual arts community, and the Spanish-speaking community.[61] In fact, the application form asked all companies to list which "special" audiences they might be addressing, so Nightwood was encouraged to include outreach in its mandate and to identify itself as a women's theatre company because of the advantage of having a unique and identifiable niche in the eyes of potential funders.

1985: REACHING OUT TO FEMINIST THEATRE INTERNATIONALLY

In May of 1985, Nightwood hosted two American theatre companies as a fundraising event. Both companies — Ladies Against Women and Time and Space Limited — gave performances, and TSL also conducted a workshop. These American connections exemplify not only Nightwood's interest in establishing an international feminist context, but also how broadly motivated women-led companies can be. Ladies Against Women was a satirical performance troupe based in San Francisco, active throughout the 1980s and eventually disbanded in 1990. In addition to actual shows (*Plutonium Players in: Bad Mothers...The New Adventures of Ladies Against Women*), they staged various public demonstrations and protests, using outrageous costumes and slogans. Their favourite targets were the Reagans and other right-wing political figures. A still-active website archives the activities of Ladies Against Women, including their visit to Canada.

Time and Space Limited was established in New York City in 1973 to create and present adaptations and original works, which were performed in theatres and alternative spaces in the U.S., Canada, and Europe. TSL moved to Hudson, New York, in 1991, and is still active. The company's founders, Linda Mussman and Claudia Bruce, converted an old bakery in Hudson into a multi-use building where two productions (by Mussman and Bruce) are presented per year, along with weekly film screenings and a lecture series. TSL's mandate is to enhance the artistic quality of life in Hudson by creating opportunities for artistic expression, and to support the evolution of a community that embraces diversity.

Hosting these two American companies, Ladies Against Women and Time and Space Limited, remains a unique event in Nightwood's history. It was both an innovative fundraising venture and a significant opportunity to position the company alongside and within an international feminist cohort.

THE MID-1980s: NIGHTWOOD'S EVOLVING ADMINISTRATIVE STRUCTURE

As multiple projects developed and more people besides the founders became involved, as grants were applied for and received, a concrete organizational structure was being set in place for Nightwood. By 1982, a small board of directors had been created; in 1985, it was restructured as a volunteer board made up of approximately ten women, including a president, vice president, treasurer, and members, who met every month to discuss policy issues. Paid staff ran the organization on a day-to-day basis.

Like most theatre companies, Nightwood is associated with its artistic director, or with whoever is perceived to be fulfilling that leadership role. For the first decade, that person was one of the founding four, who rotated titles and responsibilities among themselves. By about 1982, Cynthia Grant was consistently referred to as the artistic director. In 1985, Mary Vingoe became the artistic coordinator and Linda Brown was hired in the important job of office administrator. Brown eventually became the general manager and was a valued contributor for many years. In 1987, Maureen White took her turn as artistic coordinator. Of the founding four, only Kim Renders did not hold this position.

In its application to the Ontario Arts Council for 1985/86, Nightwood's administrative structure was laid out explicitly: Rosemary Sullivan was the president of the board; Cynthia Grant was the artistic director; Christopher Bye was the administrator; Maureen White, Mary Vingoe, and Kim Renders were listed as collective members; and Brenda Darling was the fundraiser. The purpose of Nightwood is "to provide programming that speaks to the women's community and to provide job opportunities for women." This application represents the culmination of influences at work in Nightwood for some time — both the need to set up a more stable administrative structure, and the need to acknowledge the company's significance within the feminist theatre community.

1986: RESTRUCTURING THE COMPANY

In many ways, Nightwood was moving more toward the mainstream by the late 1980s, in what could be seen as a transitional phase of its development. In 1986, Cynthia Grant left Nightwood to form the Company of Sirens, a feminist collective that works at a much more grassroots level than Nightwood, most often outside the framework of traditional theatre. In a retrospective article in *FUSE* magazine from 1990, Susan G. Cole suggests that the creation of the collectively based Sirens freed Nightwood to concentrate less on collective work and more on developing individual writing talents.

In Nightwood's 13 February 1986 funding application to the Municipality of Metro Toronto, Mary Vingoe introduces herself as Nightwood's new artistic "coordinator," and Linda Brown as the first full-time office person. Their application emphasizes events that traditionally define success: the fundraising productions by Ladies Against Women and Time and Space Limited made $8,000 in one week; *Love and Work Enough* won a Dora

Mavor Moore Award; the tour of *This is For You, Anna* sold out in England, was voted one of the top fifteen shows in London, and was also invited to the "duMaurier World Theatre Festival." Upcoming projects included the English-language premiere of *The Edge of the Earth is too Near, Violette Leduc* by Jovette Marchessault and a 1987 production of *War Babies* by Margaret Hollingsworth — two very literary scripts by individual authors with little previous contact with Nightwood.[62]

In her application, Vingoe mentions that the company began to reach out in 1985/86 to new audiences and artists through touring abroad and co-productions, and planned to continue working with Passe Muraille, Factory, and Toronto Free Theatre. In addition to a new artistic focus, the company had expanded its board of directors to include nine working artists. Furthermore, the creation of the two new positions — artistic coordinator and general manager, both part-time — "marks a significant change in the structure and organization of the company ... Nightwood has gone through a major transition this year."[63]

The adjustment of the title from "artistic director" to "coordinator," adopted throughout Mary Vingoe and Maureen White's terms of leadership, signalled Nightwood's desire to retain its image as a collective. The position of coordinator was supposed to change hands every two years, further avoiding the perceived dangers of a traditional hierarchy.

In a letter to the Canada Council dated 17 March 1986, Vingoe explains the reasons for the new title:

> For this season at least, we have created the position of artistic coordinator, as an alternative to artistic director, in order that the day to day artistic concerns of the company can be efficiently handled, while allowing more "collective" input on major decisions such as company programming.

Vingoe also describes Nightwood's decision to hire a staff person through the creation of a permanent, part-time administrative position as an important step for the company:

For the first time there is a sense of stability and consistency in the office. Organizational systems are beginning to be put into place to allow others easier access to information. The day-to-day concerns of the company are being handled more efficiently and the workload is being shared, thus relieving the burden on just one person. The long-term plan is to secure enough financial support to make this a full-time position.[64]

The subtext of Vingoe's comments hints at a growing unease with the collective structure. Collectivity works when there is a committed core group, but Nightwood was becoming not one group but several, each working on different projects with different combinations of people. The collective ideal was no longer fashionable, and was gradually becoming a burden. Throughout the changes in leadership and board structure, Nightwood still continued to identify itself as a collective, although it might be more accurate to say that it had become a producing company that supported the creation of collective projects.

1986: "GROUNDSWELL"

Besides emphasizing Nightwood's continuing commitment to collective creation, Vingoe also highlights the company's attention to "innovation in theatrical form," as evidenced by the workshop production of *Penelope*. Research and development is also mentioned as an important component of Nightwood's work, which led to "two landmarks in the 1985/86 season": the "Transformations" reading series, in the fall of 1985, and the newly created "Groundswell Festival," to be presented in the spring of 1986.

The "Transformations" reading series consisted of public readings of four international feminist plays and received letters of praise from Susan Feldman, executive director of the Performing Arts Development Fund of Ontario; *Canadian Theatre Review* editor Robert Wallace; and Margaret Hollingsworth. While the reading series was very successful and resulted in a further production for one of the plays (*War Babies*), it was conceived as a one-time event. "Groundswell," however, marked a crucial development in Nightwood's history because it became annual.

A festival in which new works in progress by women are given staged readings or workshop productions, "Groundswell" has become the most consistent means by which Nightwood develops new material for its mainstage productions and reaches out to the wider community. This is a conscious choice to privilege an in-house play development strategy rather than relying solely on pre-existing, higher-profile scripts. The first "Groundswell" was supported financially by the Jackman and Laidlaw Foundations and involved an outside company, Montreal's highly respected Le Théâtre Expérimental des Femmes. Nightwood's strategy was to reach a wider audience by combining known and unknown names and co-producing with other companies. In some ways, this model is paradigmatic of the Nightwood method: finding corporate sponsorship and mainstream audiences for works that would not be produced otherwise. By 1989, only three years later, more than fifty authors had already had work presented at "Groundswell."

Nightwood quickly realized how important and popular the "Groundswell Festival" could be and applied for funding to make it an annual event. In a letter to the Laidlaw Foundation, dated 10 October 1986, Vingoe explains how an in-house series over the summer had given the company a head start on the festival for the next year. It was already receiving submissions after putting out a call in several publications, and actively soliciting material from theatre artists it wanted to encourage. The letter also mentions that Nightwood wanted to invite outside writers and directors into the company to work with the many experienced people on its board and in its "extended circle":

Rina Fraticelli, Baņuta Rubess, Maureen White, Mary Durkan, Peggy Thompson, Johanna Householder and Kim Renders have all furthered their own development through

Nightwood and through Groundswell they will provide support for other theatre artists in kind. This involvement insures that the collective sensibility that we have built into our structure is carried through to the grass roots level. By sharing programming decisions among a group of artists Nightwood reaches a wider cross section of the community than could any one individual. By having within our number alternate approaches to new work we are able to offer not just one, but a number of perspectives.[65]

This statement sums up how Nightwood hoped to continue its collective tradition through "Groundswell," while still producing mainstage shows. In a 22 October 1986 application to the Ministry of Citizenship and Culture, Internship Training Program, Vingoe explains, "Major decisions such as programming are made in conjunction with a programme committee from the Board. The new structure has allowed Nightwood to retain a functioning collective sensibility while evolving an efficient management structure."[66]

The critic Rita Much has heralded "Groundswell" as "a rare opportunity for women writers and directors and performers to present their work at an early stage in a celebratory and supportive atmosphere."[67] In only its second year, "Groundswell" provided a venue for important work such as Djanet Sears's first play, the autobiographical *Afrika Solo.* Another example, *A Particular Class of Women* by Janet Feindel, was performed in excerpts at various locations, including the Theatre Centre (where Nightwood was still one of the managing companies), before the entire piece was featured in the January 1987 "Groundswell," directed and dramaturged by Mary Durkan.

A Particular Class of Women consists of a series of monologues by women who work as strippers, and attempts to portray the diversity of the individual women and their attitudes toward their work. Feindel portrayed all of the characters, which she based on women she knew, employing slight costume changes and music for each monologue. The intent was to convey a politicized message about the derogatory stereotypes that strippers face; the audience finds itself implicated in the perpetuation of these stereotypes, since as theatregoers they are asked to assume the position of voyeuristic strip club customers.[68] This dynamic would undergo substantial shifts depending on the venue in which it was performed and the configuration of the audience: Feindel presented the play at fringe festivals, feminist conferences, and at an actual Toronto strip club. In a performance context, Feindel's body is displayed onstage, but for the purpose of celebrating other women in a positive way. Because the characters portrayed are engaged in the business of being sexually provocative, the ability of the actor herself to evoke that response is more than usually pertinent. It would be intriguing for a feminist theorist discussing the play in performance to consider Feindel as both skilful actor and sexualized female presence, and to speculate on the implications for her varying audience members. Were they expecting to be titillated or to disapprove? Was the play's message what they thought it was going to be? And how did their experience reflect their own assumptions about what they might see at a feminist theatre festival like "Groundswell"?[69]

In many ways, the cross-fertilization that occurs in "Groundswell" is as important as any mainstage or full production Nightwood mounts. "Groundswell" commands a third of the company's budget, and over the years has served a number of important purposes, including being an incubator for new work that finds its way into the season.[70] The festival has been programmed during some periods by a specially designated committee; at other times by the Artistic Advisory or the Play Group; and at still others by a festival director. "Groundswell" has been the place for very new writers to see their work "on its feet," often with experienced actors, directors, and designers, but without the pressure of being critically reviewed. It has been an opportunity for mentorship and a door through which many women have entered the company and stayed on. It has also been the place where celebrated playwrights such as Judith Thompson and Linda Griffiths have been able to connect with Nightwood, lending their support and credibility to the company by having their new work done while still in progress, and offering their own considerable wealth of experience to emerging artists. The festival has been a venue for work from across the country, as well as for occasional entries from the United States, and a place where a greater range of genres, such as performance art and physical theatre, can be incorporated. In many ways Nightwood's commitment to diversity, in all the ways that diversity can be interpreted, is most vibrantly embodied in "Groundswell."

1987: MOVING AWAY FROM COLLECTIVE CREATION

With a growing interest in reaching a wider audience, Nightwood became increasingly concerned with marketing itself to potential sources of funding. Nightwood launched an aggressive fundraising campaign at the beginning of 1987. A package was developed to send out to potential sponsors with an introductory letter signed by Carlyn Moulton, a member of the board of directors. Nightwood is defined as "a successful and growing Toronto theatre company; a critical success in many of its 30 productions in past seasons; a strong commitment to developing new work and new talent; a charitable organization; a theatre company without a deficit! Maturing fiscal management, developing talent, critical acclaim and popular success — the combination feels terrific." In describing Nightwood's mandate, the letter reads, "In addition to creating and adapting our own plays, we are committed to encouraging the development of contemporary material from a women's point of view. *New York Times Magazine* critic Mel Gussow refers to the recent emergence of women playwrights as 'The most encouraging and auspicious aspect of the current theatre.'"

The letter emphasizes the range of topics dealt with in Nightwood productions, and argues that Nightwood is uniquely important because it was founded by, and usually produces plays by, women, and because its artistic, technical, and administrative staff was seventy-five percent female. "We are committed to the collaborative process," the letter states, and "committed to working with women whose individual vision challenges the way we see society through their politics and their dramaturgy. Nightwood is a feminist collective with an active board of directors who advise on matters of policy and programming." In this instance, Nightwood's commitment to collectivity is centred in its administration, while the creative focus is on individual women playwrights. The quote from the *New York Times Magazine* and references to fiscal management indicate a company attempting to appear legitimate to potential funders.

The founding members were well aware that the introduction of single-author texts was a new direction for the company. In an article published in 1987, Kim Renders acknowledges that the production of scripted works was a new development for Nightwood: "The promotion of female talent is still one of the company's strongest features. But in the past two and a half years, Nightwood has been putting on fewer collectives and become more script-oriented. This is a broadening of the group's method, since previously it had been adamantly opposed to scripted material."[71] And in a later article, Maureen White and Mary Vingoe comment on their working relationship as director and playwright for the 1989 production of Vingoe's play *The Herring Gull's Egg*:

> "This is the first time we've worked together in this configuration," says White. "In our earlier days at Nightwood, collective creations were more common. It's exciting to see Nightwood now, at a time when more input is coming from outside people, those who weren't founders. It's good," she smiles, "that the company can exist without its mothers."[72]

We can see the accident and intention dialectic at work here: when company members and related groups were interested in creating collectively, collective creation was defined as part of Nightwood's mandate. But as the founders became more interested in writing and directing conventionally scripted plays, the mandate changed to emphasize the production of Canadian work and the creation of opportunities for women, while shifting the collective ideal to aspects of the company's administration.

1987: A FINAL COLLECTIVE CREATION — THE LAST WILL AND TESTAMENT OF LOLITA

In her letter to the Canada Council of March 1986, Mary Vingoe makes it clear that Nightwood was not quite ready to give up its collective status entirely:

> While we have begun seriously to work with writers and scripts, we have not abandoned our commitment to the more innovative, collaborative way of play-making which has been our strength in the past. Both *This is For You, Anna* and *Love and Work Enough* were created through painstaking collective work, refined over a number of workshops and productions.

Vingoe explains that this commitment would be demonstrated through "a collective, comic collaboration on the theme of female eroticism, inspired by photography by Marcia Resnick." The creative team working on this project included Baṇuta Rubess, Maureen White, Louise Garfield (a member of The Clichettes), and the playwright Peggy Thompson. Collectively they were called The Humbert Humbert Project. Although some of the presentations at subsequent "Groundswells" were by collectives,[73] *The Last Will and Testament of Lolita* was Nightwood's last mainstage collective creation.

The show started out with great promise, receiving ad hoc funding from the Canada Council as one of only seven applications out of sixty to receive grants, and winning special funds from the Ontario Arts Council multidisciplinary jury and $5,000 from the Woodlawn Foundation for development of its visual component. The piece was inspired by a book of photographs entitled *Re-Visions* by the New York artist Marcia Resnick, published by Coach House Press in 1978 and dedicated to Humbert Humbert, the central character in Vladimir Nabokov's famous novel *Lolita*.

Images and text in the book depict "the life of a bad girl from 10 to 19." The play takes her further, to the age of thirty-one.

The project application describes a collective effort: "From the very start the project has been an exchange of skills — [Louise] Garfield's studies in movement have offset White and Rubess's improvisation games and [Peggy] Thompson's insights in writing techniques and semiotics. Since the scenario is developed collectively, the initial process constituted a learning process in and of itself." In an interview published in the book *Fair Play*, Rubess recounts an incident in the creation of the piece that illustrates their collaborative method:

> The very funny and erotic bread image in *Lolita* ... evolved in a curious way. It was inspired first by a picture in Marcia Resnick's *Re-Visions* ... of a girl crushing a loaf of white bread between her thighs with a caption reading something like, "She learned the facts of life from a friend during a trip to a bread factory." The choreographer, Louise Garfield, asked Maureen White to do a movement study with the bread and without her pants, and she did, bless her. The movement study was very abstract, though, so we decided we would not use it. We also didn't like the nudity. Yet, the picture stayed with me and when we were trying to resolve a different section of the work, I took the bread and said, "Look at this," and I began playing with it in a way that was inspired by watching Maureen ... it was a most successful image.[74]

As part of the development process, a twenty-minute, multimedia version of the project was presented at "Groundswell" in March of 1986. In Nightwood's subsequent application for funding, this version is described in detail. Four slide projectors allowed images, text, and action to integrate. For example, as a male voice crooned, "You're leaving me baby," a slide of a hand holding a candy cigarette swooped and slid across the entire space of the theatre, and selections of text were projected on a sleeping figure and a closing door. The slides were not intended to function merely as an addition to the theatrical scenery, but as active agents of the performance.

In the final version of the play, the multimedia component was represented by a five-minute film, created by director Peter Mettler. Lolita appeared on film to address the characters onstage, representing the past interacting with the present. The onstage characters—stereotypical "bad girls"—were former students in an acting class once taught by Lolita, reunited at her death to explore her legacy. *The Last Will and Testament of Lolita* ran from 2 to 21 June 1987 in association with Theatre Passe Muraille. Subtitled "A vile pink comedy," the play was advertised with the lines: "Four bad girls steal, revise and reconstruct the Lolita Myth," and "created and performed by the strange and wild feminist theatre collective of Louise Garfield, Baṇuta Rubess, Peggy Thompson, and Maureen White," with Jim Warren as the Sandman and Jackie Burroughs on film as Miss Lolita.

Despite its promising beginnings, *Lolita* was not well received, and even its creators came to regard it as a failure. Rubess comments:

> The only collective creation that I've worked on that really didn't achieve its potential was *The Last Will and Testament of Lolita*, a work I frequently forget is a part of my career. The circumstances surrounding it weren't the most favourable. I think we were collectively under an emotional dark cloud. When I watch the videotape of the production, I feel quite regretful, because it's so clear where the piece is strong and where it suddenly comes apart. We were trying to wed madcap humour with strong image work, and thereby alienated some part of the audience most of the time. Either they just wanted to laugh, or they just wanted to be mesmerized. I do want to say that there was a substantial part of the audience which accepted and appreciated the thing as a whole. But we knew we could have done better. It was a heartache.[75]

In the interview, Rubess uses *The Last Will and Testament of Lolita* as an example of what she considers to be a gender bias among theatre reviewers. "What I resent about much male criticism of writing by women is the grudging tone," she says. "For example, *Lolita* got 'terrible with flashes of brilliance,' which makes no sense to me. It should have read 'Brilliant with some major flaws.' In general, our critics are terrible. Most aren't at all versed in theatre language and they look for failure. Their focus is on why things fail and not why they succeed." She is most likely referring to the review by Christopher Hume, in which he writes, "Despite occasional flashes of brilliance, the play doesn't hold together."[76] Reviewers in general seemed to have difficulty critiquing a play with no one writer or director; they frequently comment that a director was needed to "whip *Lolita* into shape" and to give the play focus and cohesion.

Despite professions of interest in its funding applications, Nightwood's commitment to collective work had clearly diminished. Combined with resistance to collective work by reviewers, and the members' own "emotional dark cloud," *Lolita* had a lot working against it. The combined efforts and enthusiasms (or lack thereof) spark the creative process in a collective. Individual moments of genius may not add up to an overall production, but the effort and its multifaceted result may convey something about the process and the feminism of its participants. Rubess admits that it was at about this time when she lost interest in writing about women's issues,[77] and her comments to the media about *Lolita* reflect a fear of being "ghettoized." One of the motivating factors behind the decision to work collectively is the desire to communicate with the audience in a new way; however, as in the example of *Burning Times*, the process is fraught with pitfalls. Rubess's comments suggest that The Humbert Humbert Project was unable to fully connect with its audiences — possibly because they, too, had lost faith in the collective process.

1987: CHANGING PERSPECTIVES, ENTERING THE MAINSTREAM

In the spring of 1987, in *Theatrum: A Theatre Journal,* an article by Meredith Levine appeared entitled "Feminist Theatre — Toronto '87." In an attempt to explain the more conservative programming choices at Nightwood for the 1986/87 season, Levine hypothesizes that Nightwood had always been relatively conservative and that its recent choices were consistent with the company's latent tendencies. Levine allows that a feminist sensibility was always evident in Nightwood's choice of politically controversial plays and nonlinear, imagistic forms, but argues, "The cautious rhetoric of the early years, and the long-standing desire for mainstream recognition reveal recent changes at Nightwood to be more consistent than it may first appear."[78]

Levine observes that, by 1987, Nightwood had an eleven-woman management board and operational funding, and that Cynthia Grant had been replaced by Mary Vingoe as artistic coordinator. She concludes, "Nightwood is pursuing the middle-class, main-stream audience which involves using larger, more expensive venues. These are not fundamental changes, but a reflection of recent structural and financial abilities to realize their original goals." Levine quotes Vingoe as saying that Nightwood felt pressure from the government to achieve greater box office revenue, "but the pressure towards the mainstream is coming from the inside too, the artists want to reach a broader audience."[79]

In the article, Vingoe is unapologetic about the company's desire to appeal to a larger audience. "We don't say mainstream is bad," she says. "We want to have an influence in the mainstream. We don't want to be ghettoized .... Still it remains very important in the work that I do that I challenge the status quo."[80] She contends that to survive in the centre while presenting work with political content is an act of subversion: "I guess what we are trying to do this year is create sophisticated pieces of work that are attractive to mainstream audiences. And imbuing them with a feminism the audience didn't expect. We are still looking for different ways of redefining the images we see around us. We are just using a different means of snaring people." Levine sums up by questioning the type of feminism Nightwood will reflect. She notes that the board "represents a range of feminist perspectives" and wonders how much commitment to the most political aims of feminism will remain intact.

Levine contrasts Nightwood with the Company of Sirens, conceding that while most feminists would applaud the presentation of positive female images in highly visible places, not all share Nightwood's view on how this is to be done. She writes, "Perhaps one of the more notable dissenting voices is its former Artistic Director Cynthia Grant, who left Nightwood last June [1986] to form the Company of Sirens with Lina Chartrand, Shawna Dempsey, Peggy Sample and Lib Spry." Part of the impetus for forming this new theatre group was a difference of opinion about the definition of theatre and its audience. The mainstream is not such a bad place to be, but Grant and the Sirens were unwilling to have it become a major focus of energy, preferring to concentrate on non-traditional audiences and performance venues.[81]

Levine structures her comparison of the companies around the kind of audiences they attract, writing, "One must ask: which post-isolation audience is the group trying to reach and what venues are being used to reach them? The choice both of public and of public space indicates a particular concept of feminism and therefore feminist theatre." She concludes, "Ultimately, it is not the particular public space and audience that tests the validity of each group's work, but rather their ability to be heard beyond their own parlours."[82] Levine sets up an opposition between the "mainstream" Nightwood and the "grassroots" Company of Sirens that was perhaps not as sharply divided as she makes out.[83] Both Diane Roberts and Alisa Palmer, future artistic directors of Nightwood, worked with the Sirens early in their careers. But Levine does point to the differing routes companies calling themselves feminist may take. Her article suggests that there was a spectrum of possibilities ahead, even in the limited context of Toronto theatre in the late 1980s.

In an article by Malene Arpe entitled "Feminist Theatre," which appeared in *Bark* magazine, Cynthia Grant is quoted regarding her work with the Company of Sirens: "We see ourselves as part of a larger feminist movement, which I think is very important in terms of feminist artists — that they work within the larger feminist movement. I think sometimes artists end up sort of 'out there on their own.'"[84] In the same article, writer and performer Diane Flacks responds to the criticism that feminist theatre only "preaches to the converted" — that is, attracts an audience that already agrees with a feminist philosophy. Flacks contends that such "preaching" is in fact valuable because it reinforces those ideals and gives the audience more things to think and talk about. She states, "I think the media has done a really good job of turning feminism into a dirty word. But the theatre community is wonderful, because the theatre community is conscious and not interested in buying into that." The same article contains a quotation from Kate Lushington:

> There are a lot of lines drawn. Maybe it's Canada, maybe it's art, maybe it's theatre. It's either political or it's purely aesthetic. It's either popular or it's non-professional. It's either academic or it's practical. And it seems to me that there is a lot that feminism can offer in joining together all these either/ors. With them we fall into too many traps of exclusivity.

All three of the women quoted illustrate how feminist theatre practitioners understand themselves to be part of the larger feminist social movement, and how this understanding is important not only as a source of strength, but also as an impetus for ideas and creative inquiry.

ANOTHER OVERVIEW: ISSUES AT AN EARLY STAGE

Feminist theatre practitioners in Toronto, like their international counterparts in the 1970s and '80s, were coming to terms with the possibilities and the limitations of their careers. Despite

Nightwood's growing appeal to a wider audience, the fact remains that women are not as welcome in the theatre world as their male counterparts, their careers not as encouraged; unfortunately, the situation has not changed much today. Concerns with being pigeonholed as a particular kind of writer, different communication styles as a director or within a collective, fear of hostile reviewers, and the common pressures of personal relationships and childcare all compound the perception. Perhaps no other American woman director has enjoyed as much acclaim as Julie Taymor, the Tony Award–winning creator of *The Lion King*, and yet Taymor can remark:

> There is an excitement about the 20-year-old male director, and women directors have not really been part of that club. A woman who's that young and doing that much is "risky," rather than the next bandwagon everyone wants to hop on. When it was JoAnne Akalaitis or Anne Bogart or whoever, they never got that kind of attention. Neither did I until I got *Lion King*. And yet look at what I've done.[85]

In 1970, JoAnne Akalaitis and Ruth Maleczech of the experimental company Mabou Mines included child care expenses as part of the production expenses for their shows, insisted that children be welcome on their tours, and ensured that tours would be limited to three weeks "so as to be minimally disruptive to family life."[86] More than thirty years later, such provisions still seem radical and remain the exception.

The dilemma of the talented woman balancing a successful career with the demands of a family is a frequent theme in 1970s and '80s British, American, and Canadian feminist writing. In her discussion of contemporary women's plays, Michelene Wandor concludes that political activism and a personal life cannot go together, or at least cannot be represented together on the stage.[87] The British director Pam Brighton came to the same conclusion while working in Canada in the late 1970s. She spent time at the Stratford Festival, but also worked in Toronto, where she directed *Dusa Fish Stas and Vi* by the British playwright Pam Gems. Brighton reminisces:

> Women's theatre up until that point in Canada had had a very low profile and this was the play that could (and in fact did) open up that area of work ... The women of Toronto practically stormed the theatre; we played to 103 percent capacity, and the show had to be transferred.[88]

The play is based on the suicide of Buzz Goodbody, a feminist director whom Brighton had known well. In Brighton's assessment, Gems's play is about the central contradiction in contemporary women's lives: the apparent impossibility of being both independent, with a successful career, and also maintaining an equal relationship with a man.

In the American context, Wendy Wasserstein won a Tony Award and the Pulitzer Prize in 1989 for *The Heidi Chronicles*, a play that deals with the same dilemma. Wasserstein was acclaimed for her comedy and was compared to Neil Simon for her farcical situations and snappy dialogue, but she herself believed the work to be political, revealing deeper truths about the crises of an intelligent, independent woman. The problem is addressed again in the hugely successful play *The Search for Signs of Intelligent Life in the Universe* by Jane Wagner, which premiered 26 September 1985 at the Plymouth Theater in New York City, starring Lily Tomlin. Among the many characters that Wagner writes and Tomlin portrays, one of the most developed is Lyn, who struggles with wanting to pursue a career while also keeping her husband and family content. Lyn utters the memorable line, "If I'd known this is what it would be like to have it all, I might have been willing to settle for less."[89]

The play from Nightwood's repertoire that best addresses this theme of professional versus private lives is *War Babies* by Margaret Hollingsworth. In association with Toronto Free Theatre, Nightwood presented *War Babies* 26 February to 29 March 1987, directed by Mary Vingoe. The production of *War Babies* was nominated for a Dora Award for best new play, while the playtext itself was nominated for a 1985 Governor General's Award for Drama. The press release for the production reads:

> *War Babies* centres around a couple in their early forties, she a playwright, he a war correspondent, as they await the birth of their first child. Slowly they are overshadowed by their fictional doubles, characters from a play Esme is writing. As Esme creates her play within a play, the distinctions dissolve between past and present, real and imagined, private and public.

In *War Babies*, as in no other play produced by Nightwood until *Mathilde* in 2006, the dynamics of a marriage are dissected and interrogated. The main character, Esme, is a playwright who worries that the horrors her husband has witnessed as a war correspondent will distance him from her and will poison their ability to be good parents. Her world is private and imaginative, while his world is public and descriptive. The contrast between the two gendered realities infects the couple's ability to communicate and ultimately undermines Esme's mental stability.

Twenty years later, in Véronique Olmi's play *Mathilde*, the title character reacts to a stultifying "career" as the perfect doctor's wife by having an affair with a teenage boy. The play begins with her release from a correctional facility, and her return home to confront her husband. Here, to an even greater degree than in *War Babies*, the playwright offers a psychological portrait of a very strained private relationship at the point when the public façade has been breached. In this French play, translated by the Canadian playwright Morwyn Brebner, staged by Nightwood and performed by two of Canada's most respected actors, Tom McCamus and Martha Burns, we find the perfect example of international congruence — a dialogue among women of different nations that has been going on for as long as feminist theatre. From its inception, Nightwood has been part of the dialogue, reflecting — in its organizational structure, its working methods, and its struggle to define its feminism — the preoccupations of women working to create a new theatre.

Goodnight Desdemona
Tanja Jacobs as Constance Ledbelly in *Goodnight Desdemona (Good Morning Juliet)*. Photograph by Cylla Von Tiedemann. *Nightwood Theatre archives.*

Charming and Rose: True Love
Djanet Sears and Kristina Nicoll as the Fairy Godmother and Rose in *Charming and Rose: True Love*. Photograph by Greg Tjepkema. *Nightwood Theatre archives.*

Princess Pocahontas
Left to Right: Alejandra Nunez and Monique Mojica in *Princess Pocahontas and the Blue Spots*. *Nightwood Theatre publicity.*

A Fertile Imagination
Kate Lynch and Robin Craig as Del and Rita in *A Fertile Imagination*. Photograph by Liz Kain. *Nightwood Theatre archives.*

Random Acts
Diane Flacks in her one-woman show, *Random Acts.*
Photograph by Greg Tjepkema. Nightwood Theatre archives.

Leaders
Left to Right: Leslie Lester, Alisa Palmer,
and Diane Roberts for the "Groundswell"
Festival 1996.
Nightwood Theatre archives.

Leaders
Left to Right: Diane Roberts, Leslie Lester, and Alisa Palmer at a VideoCabaret event.
Photograph by VideoCabaret. From the personal collection of Leslie Lester.

Two
Breaking Away and Moving On, 1989–1993

RESISTING AND EMBRACING THE FEMINIST LABEL

Artists, particularly those working in the avant-garde, seldom like having their work defined for them, and they are reluctant to be pigeonholed in the media. This is not just a Canadian perception: the British playwright Bryony Lavery remembers how her initial reluctance to define herself as a feminist gave way once she actually began working with and appreciating feminist theatre companies (in her case, Monstrous Regiment and the Women's Theatre Group). Her experience of working in a feminist theatre environment led her to embrace the feminist label with pride.[1]

In the Canadian context, the magazine *Broadside* (vol. 4 no. 5) ran an article in November of 1983 entitled "No Mean Feet," by Amanda Hale (who would later have a play produced by Nightwood and go on to work at the Company of Sirens with Cynthia Grant). Hale's article begins by describing an abbreviated version of Rina Fraticelli's report on the status of women in Canadian theatre that had been published in the September 1982 issue of *FUSE* magazine. Hale announces that in response to the report, a group of about forty-five women had recently formed a Women in Theatre group in Toronto and were meeting on a monthly basis. Two of these women, Susan Padveen and Kate Lushington, had taken a further step by forming a company called Mean Feet, the aims of which were: to give visibility to the problems women encounter as a result of gender stereotyping; to create opportunities for female directors and playwrights; and to develop the skills required to capitalize on those opportunities. Lushington is said to have felt isolated as a female director, and Mean Feet was an attempt to create a community of women.[2]

Because *Broadside* is a feminist publication, Hale is careful to specify the kind of feminism that Mean Feet represents: "Both Lushington and Padveen are feminists of the liberal, broad spectrum variety rather than the separatist perspective, and they intend to reflect this in their work by giving visibility to the feminist perspective." Both felt that male artistic directors were not willing to take a chance on women directors, and that an individual woman's success or failure unfairly reflected on all other women directors. But at the same time, they were concerned that they would contribute to their own "ghettoization" if they dealt only with women's issues or were seen to be producing "agitprop." Hale explains, "Lushington and Padveen feel they must compete on the open market rather than retreating into 'women only' theatre justified by the all-too-true excuse of discrimination." This is an interesting statement, considering that Kate Lushington took over as Nightwood's artistic director in 1988 and, if anything, moved the "women-only" company in a more explicitly feminist direction. During Lushington's tenure at Nightwood (1988–1993), its mandate statements, publicity materials, and choices of shows tended to emphasize politics as much as, or even more than, artistic concerns.

Lushington's comments in the 1983 article express an ambivalence with the feminist label and the threat of ghettoization that are echoed in Cynthia Grant's comments about the founding of Nightwood: "Personally, I wished to have a career as a director, not as a woman director. Although I was already clearly defined as a feminist, I knew the derogatory, second-class implications of such terms."[3] Although theatre practitioners like Grant and Lushington readily defined themselves and their politics as feminist, they went through an initial period when they resisted having their work labelled as such.

The times were changing in the early 1980s, though, and with the release of Fraticelli's report and the growing strength of feminism, women began to understand their marginalized position in the theatre as part of a much larger problem, and came to embrace the movement that was identifying and critiquing that condition. In an interview in 1996, Lushington acknowledges the gap that had existed earlier between her personal feminist politics and her discomfort with being labelled as a "woman director." The disjuncture was so extreme that she even refused to be interviewed by Fraticelli for her report. When the report came out, however, Lushington remembers "being totally bowled over by her conclusions and being able to relate to every single one of them." Lushington came to embrace the idea of Nightwood as a kind of "sheltered workshop" where women could hone their skills, talk, and pursue common interests; "where you wouldn't have to explain yourself every second word for somebody who didn't know what you were talking about … Nightwood is trying to be a safe place for people to write about things that are dangerous as well as scary."[4]

While still conscious that their careers have been categorized in a way that a man's might not have been, women like Grant and Lushington accepted the label and attempted to make feminism fit their own individual work, as opposed to making the work fit feminism. Both, for example, have done solo performance art pieces that tackle social issues that are not exclusively feminist, yet this work is clearly situated within their own personal understandings of political and aesthetic practice. As feminism has evolved, it has expanded to include more women, who have, in turn, shaped feminism by expanding what are considered "feminist" issues. For example, like Grant, Lushington was involved with Women's Cultural Building, and it was there that she met Johanna Householder, a member of The Clichettes. In 1987, Lushington wrote a "Groundswell" show about housing issues for the performance-art trio; *Up Against The Wallpaper* was then picked up for a full production by Nightwood at the Factory Theatre in January of 1988, directed by Maureen White. Later that spring, Lushington was hired as Nightwood's new artistic coordinator.

1988: A NEW ERA — KATE LUSHINGTON

In a 1988 application for a Grant in Aid of the Arts to the Municipality of Metropolitan Toronto Cultural Affairs Division, Nightwood defined itself as "a feminist collectively-run professional theatre company, dedicated to the development of new Canadian work and to supporting the work of women writers and directors." But a real break with the past would come that year, when Kate Lushington was hired as artistic coordinator, replacing Maureen White, and none of the founding members were involved any longer at the organizational level. It was an inevitable progression, as each of the founding four was involved in outside endeavours, but it was also a tricky thing to negotiate: would a new artistic leader maintain the founders' original vision, or choose to distance herself and start fresh? For her first season, Lushington inherited what Maureen White had already programmed, and was charged with organizing a national tour of *Goodnight Desdemona (Good Morning Juliet)*, a surprise hit from the year before. But when she began her own programming, Lushington ushered in a new and more politicized era at Nightwood by working with Diane Roberts, as her artistic associate, to enlarge the company's mandate to include anti-racism work and to become more inclusive of women of colour.

When Lushington was hired in 1988, she was initially called "artistic coordinator," but in 1990 the title was changed to "artistic director," and it has remained so ever since. The title and its adjustment reflected an ongoing struggle to balance different agendas that were not well served by collectivity: the desire to be taken seriously within the theatre community, which demands artistic leadership; the desire to retain the support of the feminist community, which prefers alternative approaches to organization but also wants strong work; and the desire for a clear relationship between the board and the staff. Lushington was hired as artistic coordinator with the idea that, as with Vingoe's and White's terms, the position would rotate again within two years, but instead she felt encouraged to stay on and follow through with the changes she had begun.[5]

Shelley Scott • Nightwood Theatre

Nightwood's board of directors also changed its structure and purpose that year. At first it had been an artist-run board, emulating the Theatre Centre model; under Lushington there was more of an emphasis on attracting women with certain skills, such as legal expertise and fundraising experience, and the board was referred to as "community-based."[6] The artistic decisions were taken over by the Play Group, a collective of artists working in conjunction with the board and staff. At a meeting of an ad hoc Structure Committee in November of 1988, it was decided that the board should encompass a balance of community and artist members. The artistic coordinator and general manager were to be informed of all meetings and could attend with "a voice but no vote." The Play Group was to include the artistic coordinator and one or two board members, plus four to six artists appointed by the board.

In a July 1989 application to the Ministry of Culture and Communications for money to hold a board retreat, Lushington clarifies:

> Since I joined Nightwood last September as the first Artistic Coordinator from outside the group of founding members, the Board has been under-going a year of structural transition, from an open ended collective approach to a more traditional structure, with the establishment of standing committees to handle tasks, intensive Board recruitment, and the setting up of terms for Board Members.

Nightwood's mission statement had also been rewritten as follows: "To provide opportunities for all women to create and explore new visions of the world, stretching the concept of what is theatrical, and to hone their skills as artists, so that more of us may see our reality reflected on this country's stages, thus offering theatre goers the full diversity of the Canadian experience."[7] The term "collectively run" is noticeably absent, and instead, the word "diversity" takes on a new prominence.

Nightwood was consciously abandoning the collective administrative structure for a more traditional model. The whole concept of collectivity is about sharing responsibility and power, but among feminist artists, there was a growing dissatisfaction with collectivity as a philosophy. When Kate Lushington eventually left the position of artistic director in the fall of 1993, the enormous search committee was made up of Baŋuta Rubess, Sally Han, Jennifer Ross, Ann-Marie MacDonald, Kate Tucker, Monique Mojica, ahdri zhina mandiela, Amanda Mills, Astrid Janson, and Diane Roberts, as well as the rest of the board. A revealing note from the minutes of their 30 August meeting mentions that Rubess had turned down the position of artistic coordinator back in 1988, when Lushington was hired, because she felt her need for personal artistic expression would not be encouraged or desirable in a collective structure. Apparently, this concern had been echoed in similar terms by several other potential candidates: they feared their own need for personal artistic growth would be incompatible with a collective administration.[8] Lushington alleviated the problem by actively distancing the company from its collective past.

By the fall of 1989, in the first issue of a brand-new Nightwood newsletter called *Nightwords*, Lushington explicitly charted what she saw as the company's new identity in a column entitled "A Word, or two, from the Artistic Coordinator." The 1989/90 season was celebrated as Nightwood's tenth anniversary, and in her column Lushington recounts Nightwood's origins with *The True Story of Ida Johnson* and expresses the opinion that Nightwood had grown beyond the wildest dreams of its founders: "No longer a collective, the collaborative spirit lives on in the artistic heart of the company, The Play Group, consisting of Martha Burns, Jennie Dean, Pat Idlette, Astrid Janson, Kate Lushington and Djanet Sears." With this statement, Lushington redefined the way Nightwood would present itself. There would be a stronger focus on administration, on having adequate office staff and large enough budgets to mount higher-profile shows. The board was increasingly made up of professional women, including lawyers, accountants, and executives, and there were more fundraising events. The "collaborative spirit" shifted to the collective Play Group, who formed the selection committee for "Groundswell" and planned each season. Instead of sponsoring co-productions with collectives, such as The Anna Project or The Humbert Humbert Project, Nightwood supported its own playwright-in-residence; for the 1989/90 season, Sally Clark worked on her play *Life Without Instruction*.[9]

While in 1982, Lushington had been quoted by Amanda Hale as saying she was uncomfortable with "women-only" theatre, once she took over Nightwood, she started seeing the value of, and advocating for, that unique environment. As early as 1985, in her article "Fear of Feminism," Lushington makes the analogy that both Canadian theatre and feminist theatre need the same encouragement and protection. Why, she asks, are people so terrified when women claim their true voice and equal participation in culture as women? Lushington challenges, "Feminism is not just a matter of doing non-sexist plays or replacing the boys at the top by girls. Feminism, rather, is a search, a constant questioning of accepted beliefs and hidden assumptions. It's not a state, not an imperative, but a process, a dynamic."[10] As valuable as it may be to have more plays written and directed by women within mainstream theatre structures, the ongoing project of feminism and feminist theatre is far more wide-ranging and complex, and part of this larger project can only be carried out within the space of a women's theatre company such as Nightwood.

Going further in her 1989 article "The Changing Body of Women's Work," Lushington provocatively claims, "All women theatre practitioners are by their very nature marginalized, disenfranchised, from prestigious 1988 Toronto Arts Award Winner Judith Thompson, to the community theatre workers from coast to coast who labour to give voice to the silenced."[11] Lushington cites statistics released by the Playwrights Union of Canada in 1988 showing that, of all new plays produced in the 1987/88 season, only seventeen percent were by women; even fewer were directed by women, and there were also few roles for women actors. (These statistics were collected as a follow-up, six years later, to Rina Fraticelli's original survey). Yet in the same article, Lushington quotes Janet Amos, who, during her 1985 term as artistic director of Theatre New Brunswick, fretted, "The danger (in labelling women's work feminist) is that the work will either be rejected as propaganda, or worse, it will become more important that the work be done by women, than whether or not it is any good."[12] Lushington criticizes Amos for her timidity, using the Playwrights Union numbers to note sarcastically, "Don't worry, Ms Amos, we are in no imminent danger of affirmative action."

Many of the problematic issues around feminist theatre are illustrated by Lushington's article and her examples. While activists like Lushington are incensed by the statistical under-representation of women in theatre employment, which is at least partly a sociological and economic issue of employment equity, an artistic director like Amos is concerned with more ambiguous issues, like audience reception and "artistic quality." While Lushington might advocate the tactical use of the word "feminist" to highlight the marginalized status of women's work in a male-dominated field, Amos fears the word will evoke connotations and assumptions that will overshadow the work itself. The two women share certain concerns, both economic and aesthetic, but the word "feminist" inhabits diametrically opposed degrees of importance and has very different implications for their respective understandings of theatre.

1990: LOOKING BACK ON A DECADE; REPOSITIONING

The ideal of Nightwood as an independent, woman-centred company was presented to the media as a better alternative than trying to fit women's work into male-dominated theatres. In a 1990 article in the *Toronto Star* newspaper, Kate Lushington asserts, "Finally, we don't have to change something because somebody else tells us to. We want power — not huge power — but just enough power to be able to put on a play the way we want to. That's what Nightwood is all about."[13] While Lushington's comment is not meant to be separatist, the clear implication is that women must have the space and the means to create from an independent vision. Sometimes this has been fulfilled through the very existence of Nightwood as a women's theatre company, and sometimes it has been explicitly expressed in the creation and content of a particular play, such as *Smoke Damage.*

In the spring of 1990, *FUSE* magazine published the article "10 Years and 5 Minutes: Nightwood Celebrates a Decade of Feminist Theatre," by Susan G. Cole, a member of the Nightwood board. In direct contrast to the 1987 article by Meredith Levine, Cole starts off by saying that Nightwood has been substantially transformed from its original concept and is grappling with fundamental questions: How does a theatre company remain true to its alternative roots while fulfilling a political mandate of reaching out to a large audience? How does it function within a theatre community unfamiliar with, and sometimes hostile to, feminist principles? How does any theatre survive in the 1990s? Like Levine, Cole believes that Cynthia Grant's resignation represented a shift in Nightwood's direction, but rather than seeing Nightwood's move toward the mainstream as a natural emergence of latent tendencies, Cole problematizes the move and characterizes it as part of an ongoing struggle for definition. New audiences and the involvement of an increasing number of artists demanded a re-evaluation of the company's ability to fulfill all the requirements of a feminist mandate and remain accountable to the community: "The structure, which worked well for a small group, couldn't be expected to function for Nightwood's slowly changing political priorities. In 1985, Nightwood established a board of directors, employed a general manager as its first paid staff and hired Mary Vingoe as its first artistic coordinator."

While Cole is correct in depicting a growing move toward structure within Nightwood, her dates are in dispute: by 1982, Nightwood had a first board in place and Cynthia Grant was consistently referred to as artistic director, at least in the press; in fact, Levine goes so far as to refer to Grant as "Nightwood's founding Artistic Director."[14] Cole writes that the founders agonized over every move, making sure that there were artists on the board and naming an artistic coordinator instead of a director in order to "institutionalize the collective values they thought might be leached out of the company under the aegis of a board." But this concern for artist representation on the board and the coordinator title really came about during the terms of Mary Vingoe and Maureen White, between 1986 and 1988, after Grant had left. Cole believes that if these women had been labelled artistic directors (as Grant was) they might have been considered more legitimate by their counterparts at other theatres and by government funding bodies. This is difficult to judge, but it is noteworthy that Kate Lushington made a conscious switch to the title artistic director.

The most interesting aspect of Cole's article is her discussion of the "Five Minute Feminist Cabaret." Cole declares, "In many ways, FemCab has become emblematic of Nightwood's internal philosophical tensions. Originated by Women's Cultural Building in 1983, it started out as a quintessentially grassroots event, with an open call to anyone female with a feminist bent to submit ideas." For the first two years there were no auditions and bars were the venues, but when Nightwood took over as producer of the event, it was mounted in legitimate theatre settings. According to Cole, "FemCab supporters, proud of the roots of the event, challenged this turn of events. They believed that it would work against Nightwood's philosophy of encouraging new theatre artists." While Cole leaves her discussion at that, she is correct in identifying "FemCab" as a source of potential philosophical conflict over the issue of inclusion versus professionalism. In fact, when a new leadership team took over from Kate Lushington, they suspended the annual event for two years before resurrecting it in 1996 — at least in part to create a period of distance between themselves and the past.

Cole concludes her article with the telling statement, "Many theatre artists call it a support group, but they couldn't really tell you all the women that are in it. But in spite of the elasticity of its definition and the fact that the company has never had a permanent theatre space, many women playwrights, directors and actors call Nightwood home." Nightwood is loosely defined in this regard; very much a theatre of people, and yet an influence and force for many who may barely be acquainted, despite the mutual benefit of their community bond.

1988–1990: GOODNIGHT DESDEMONA (GOOD MORNING JULIET)

Ann-Marie MacDonald's *Goodnight Desdemona (Good Morning Juliet)* is one of the most successful plays in English-Canadian theatre history, and it is no exaggeration to say that its surprise breakthrough changed the course of Nightwood's history. First produced by Nightwood in 1988, directed by Baņuta Rubess, it was remounted in 1990 and won the Governor General's Literary Award and a Chalmers Canadian Play Award for Best Production. It continues to be produced frequently in Canada, the U.S., and England, often at colleges and universities, where it is also part of many academic curricula.[15] Kathleen Gallagher has written about *Goodnight Desdemona (Good Morning Juliet)* as a text to use when working with female students, and cites the play's treatment of sexual identity and gender construction as factors that make it useful in sociological terms. Considering the frequency with which this play is produced in school environments, it is significant that a good part of its popularity comes from its particular brand of feminism. Despite the fact that the play dates from the late 1980s, its feminism can be recognized as fitting into the Third Wave model in its irreverence and insistence on pleasure.[16]

Ann-Marie MacDonald's play breaches all boundaries — between texts, historical periods, nations, genders and sexualities, and certainly theatrical conventions such as language and spectacle. The critical assessment of the play has focused on its postcolonial content (Wilson 1992), its treatment of Shakespeare's female characters (Porter 1995), its sociological uses in teaching (Gallagher 2002), and its use of a recognizably feminist mode of comedy (Hengen 1995). The play has also been criticized (by, for example, Ric Knowles and Marianne Novy) as an affirmation of the privileged cultural position and "high culture" theatrical tradition of Shakespeare.[17] This very affirmation is what situates the play as Third Wave and post-modern: the breaching of boundaries between "high" and "low" culture, and the simultaneous embrace and critique of its source material.

The main character, Constance Ledbelly, is an exploited junior academic who is working on the thesis that Shakespeare used a source by some unknown author to create the plays *Romeo and Juliet* and *Othello*, but suppressed the comic Fool character in order to turn them into tragedies. Shakespeare then gave his source book to his friend Gustav the Alchemist to preserve in an undecipherable code. Constance is trying to decode the Gustav manuscript in order to determine the original author. After a first act in which we come to understand both Constance's quest and her dreary life circumstances, she is magically transported into the worlds of *Othello* and *Romeo and Juliet* and succeeds in turning them back into comedies through her intervention in the fate of the characters.

Although Constance is a university professor, her low status and poor self-esteem mean that she inhabits a "youthful" subject position that students can relate to more easily. As Laurin Porter points out, "For all practical purposes, as the play begins Constance is a child, an innocent."[18] Her desk is covered with remnants from her childhood, and during the course of the play she recounts incidents from her experiences in grade five (when she was tormented by bullying girls) and grade eight (an erotic encounter with her classmate Ginnie Radclyffe). The play can be seen to chart Constance's journey through her own unconscious mind, the process by which she explores the different sides of her personality and sexuality and finally emerges a whole, adult woman.[19] This is a journey especially relevant to young feminists and to students in general. As Shannon Hengen observes, it is of central importance to the play's comedy and its revolutionary potential that the audience empathizes with a marginalized protagonist.[20]

The aspect that most clearly signals a Third Wave attitude in the play is the treatment of gender and sexuality. In her study of contemporary young women's sexual behaviour, Paula Kamen claims that, "using their own taste as their barometer, they have a broad menu of choices at their fingertips"[21] and that "the greatest sexual revolution has taken place inside women's heads."[22] In Act Three, when Constance arrives in the Verona of *Romeo and Juliet*, she has lost her tweed skirt and appears only in a jacket, long underwear, and boots. Thus clad as a man, she is understood to be male by all who meet her. Both Romeo and Juliet desire Constance as a boy. Romeo believes the boy, "Constantine," to be heterosexual, so dresses as a girl to win "him." Sexuality is cued entirely by clothing, something one can easily put on and take off. All Constance has to do to "be" male is to lose her skirt, and all Romeo has to do to "be" a female love interest is to gain a skirt. Juliet believes the boy, "Constantine," to be homosexual, and so dresses as another boy to win "him." When, in her bedchamber, Juliet discovers that Constance is, in fact, biologically a woman, and a much older woman at that, her desire is again swiftly accommodated:

> **Constance**: I'll have to trust you with the truth. /My name is Constance. I'm a woman.
> **Juliet**: Oh
> **Constance**: That's right. So that's that.
> **Juliet**: And art thou of Cyprus?
> **Constance**: Not originally.
> **Juliet**: Then art thou of Lesbos?!
> **Constance**: What?! I've never been there in my life.
> **Juliet**: O most forbidden love of all!
> **Constance**: Oh no.
> **Juliet**: Unsanctified desire, more tragic far/than any star-crossed love 'twixt boy and girl!
> **Constance**: Now wait.
> **Juliet**: Once more I am a virgin maid. /O take me to thine island's curv'ed shore, and lay me on the bosom of the sand.[23]

The characters do acknowledge societal strictures and gender expectations: at least partly, Constance is thinking of personal safety when she goes along with the mistaken perception that she is male, and part of Juliet's desire for Constance as a woman lies in the "forbidden" nature of that love. But as Laurin Porter observes, "While these scenes are played tongue-in-cheek, MacDonald uses Juliet in a more serious fashion to awaken Constance to her own sexuality."[24] Romeo, too, desires indiscriminately, male and female, with sweet abandon: first he pursues Juliet and Constantine, then Desdemona when she also arrives in Verona, and at the end he is carried offstage by Tybalt.

In MacDonald's play, fluidity of sexual practice is not matched by an insistence on essential identity. As Sophia Phoca explains, "Queer politics challenges the essentialist assumption that 'the queer' emerges from a uniquely gay sexuality. Queer sexuality expresses a desire for polymorphous sexual configurations and fantasies which do not stem from a need to regulate, control and organize the sexual subject according to compulsory identification."[25] All the characters are free to sexually pursue each other, but no one is required to claim a label, and no one is punished for what they want. The fluidity of sexual choice, the celebration of desire of many kinds, and most importantly, the lack of angst around the subject, all mark the play as Third Wave. Theorists such as Laurin Porter point out that the cross-dressing "allows MacDonald to reveal the extent to which not only our social exchanges but our very identities are shaped by gender constructs."[26] The real subversion lies in the flagrant and gleeful manner in which these constructs are flouted and disregarded. As Ann Wilson has argued, "The text is a sort of Arden ... where, free from the demands of the actual world, we can live imaginatively,"[27] placing us in the role-playing, polymorphous playroom of the Third Wave. To once again quote Phoca (a theorist who uses the term post-feminism as interchangeable with Third Wave), this movement is about "retaining a desire for empowerment without telling women how to experience their sexuality. By celebrating difference, post-feminism invites women to explore the complexities inscribed in the construction of the sexual subject."[28]

As Ann Brooks observes, "the truly resistant female body is not the body that wages war against feminine sexualisation and objectification, but the body ... that uses simulation strategically in ways that challenge the stable notion of gender as the edifice of sexual difference."[29] The Third Wave embrace of pluralism can be highlighted by challenging assumptions and clichés about race, as well, especially through casting choices. In a 2001 production of *Goodnight Desdemona* in Toronto, for example, Desdemona was played by a Black actor, Alison Sealy-Smith — challenging traditional Shakespearean production conventions, opening up further layers of possibility for political identification and new resonance in the text, and playing with the supposed transgressiveness of interracial eroticism. Such casting choices further align the play with Third Wave feminism through live production.

This liberating effect is truly obvious only in performance. Martha Tuck Rozett, for example, misses the subversiveness of the action set in Verona when she writes that, after the wedding banquet scene early in Act Three, "The play degenerates into silliness and confusion ... and though it would be tempting to see this as MacDonald's comment on the improbable complications and mistaken identities of *Othello* and *Romeo and Juliet*, parody for its own sake threatens to overwhelm the play's feminist agenda."[30] Rozett claims that MacDonald only "regains control of the action at the very end," in a "long scolding oration to both Juliet and Desdemona" in which she teaches them to eschew their predispositions toward violence and suicide. Later in her critique, Rozett wonders how Juliet and Desdemona can possibly return to their respective husbands after what they have experienced, and notes that Romeo and Othello do not appear in this final interaction with Constance, which she takes to be the moment when the two female characters learn their lessons.[31] But Rozett disregards the fact that the actor who plays Othello in Act Two also plays Juliet's Nurse in Act Three, and that Romeo has been wearing a dress since the wedding banquet. The visual effect of these two characters in drag is thoroughly redemptive, at least for the spectator at the live performance. If Juliet and Desdemona have changed, so have their mates. Furthermore, we do see the two men again: after the scene in which Constance "scolds" the two women, the play concludes with an epilogue in which the entire company enters dancing, clearly suggesting unity and acceptance as in any traditional comic structure.

Production choices can sway audience perceptions, and it would be possible for a director to downplay some of the play's subversive effect. Ric Knowles, for example, describes the play's "representation of polymorphous sexuality and lesbian eroticism" as "muted."[32] But this depends on choices of casting, costuming, and direction. And for many mainstream heterosexual spectators, especially those outside of urban centres, who may not see much theatre, the very fact that they have found themselves empathizing with and enjoying characters who display homosexual behaviour is in itself a significant response.

Not all audience members will respond in the same way, of course, or necessarily in a positive way. As Natalie Fenton explains, audiences "use and interpret ... according to their own social, cultural and individual circumstances—the audience is involved in making sense of the images they see—the message does not have the total monopoly on the meaning."[33] The play's popular success, however, does suggest that it has widespread appeal. Of particular interest is its appeal for young women. The oft-repeated criticism of Third Wave feminism—that it is largely media-obsessed—discounts the critical importance of representation to self-definition and identity for young women and men. Heywood and Drake paint a picture of today's academics "facing classrooms of young women and men who are trained by the media caricature of 'feminazis,' who see feminism as an enemy or say 'feminist' things prefaced by 'I'm not a feminist, but'..."[34] Kaschak also identifies the phenomenon of negative media portrayal as a significant obstacle to young women claiming a feminist identity: "Specifically they face the dilemma of reconciling two different cultural discourses, that of the classroom which tends to credit feminism for many cultural strides and that of the popular media, which portrays feminists negatively."[35] As a result, Kaschak advises that educators may have to take into account initial negative responses to feminism in younger women.[36] Much of the appeal of *Goodnight Desdemona (Good Morning Juliet)* as a teaching tool, then, is its ability to frame feminism in a way that students can appreciate.

The very silliness and confusion that Rozett condemns produces a carnivalesque fantasy of permission. The play demonstrates, rather than lectures about, an agency free from gender assignment for all its characters. Citing Kathleen Rowe and Mary Russo, Fiona Carson has argued that the ribald excess of the unruly woman in comedy can be used affirmatively to destabilize and provoke social transformation. Perhaps critics like Rozett are overlooking this crucial aspect of theatre, which can make feminist meaning in performance as much as through written lines. Indeed, Rozett seems relieved when Constance finally has a speech with a concrete, recognizable message, although the message (to live by questions and confusion rather than answers and certainty), is redundant at that point. In fact, the Third Wave feminist spectator might not be convinced that Desdemona's violence is such a negative quality, if by "violent" one reads physically strong and capable of action: consider the many female heroines in popular culture who exist in similar realms of fantasy and display just these attributes. And the audience has already seen demonstrated the childishness of committing suicide over lost love, as Juliet readily recovers from heartbreak to find one new love after another. In comedy, perhaps in any theatrical performance, the audience does not necessarily have to be told a character's behaviour is folly, or liberating, because we can see it for ourselves. Again, the fact that *Goodnight Desdemona* models a forgiving world means that its "silliness and confusion" are part and parcel of its Third Wave feminism.

The second aspect that makes the play Third Wave is its postmodernism; specifically, its simultaneous embrace and critique of both high and low culture. *Goodnight Desdemona* employs two texts in which traditional power relations result in death for the tragic heroines, Desdemona and Juliet, and shows how the internal contradictions of those texts produce an undermining protest in the viewer (we feel, for example, how preventable and unfair Desdemona's and Juliet's deaths are). As a reading of canonical literature, *Goodnight Desdemona* foregrounds the act of feminist resistant reading—its plotline is explicitly based on a female academic choosing to re-investigate the authority of its source texts—and as Ric Knowles points out, the audience finds its interpretive role inscribed as a resisting one.[37] Djanet Sears would later use a similar strategy in her play *Harlem Duet*, even using one of the same Shakespearean plays, *Othello*, to simultaneously appeal to and undercut the audience's investment in the canon. As theatre, *Goodnight Desdemona* uses theatrical tradition and conventions to produce its comic effect and make its feminist meaning, through the familiar devices of cross-dressing, mistaken identity, and even vaudevillian humour. And as Canadian theatre, it parodies its colonial relationship with its source material. MacDonald's play alternates between different time frames and different fictional worlds, and uses ambiguity and indeterminacy to develop not only the play's comedy, but also its clever subversion of audience expectation.

Goodnight Desdemona uses plays by Shakespeare as inspiration and source material for its plot and language (primarily *Othello* and *Romeo and Juliet*, but with references to others, most notably *Hamlet*). The play cleverly works with the concept of authority by having Constance, an exploited female Canadian academic with no personal "authority," searching for the source material of the most highly respected male literary authority (Shakespeare) and discovering that she herself is that Author. This draws attention, of course, to the play as a work created by an author, Ann-Marie MacDonald. Familiar characters and lines from Shakespeare are appropriated into a new text, which makes for a highly satisfying experience for the audience, as they can recognize the source material and take pleasure in its witty reinterpretation—they are able to admire both authors simultaneously. While the plotlines of Shakespeare's plays and the fates of his female characters are critiqued, the audience is never actually required to give up their affection and respect for Shakespeare — a complicity with dramatic tradition that is very post-modern, and an attitude toward problematic cultural artefacts that is very Third Wave.

Goodnight Desdemona takes the traditional versions of Desdemona's and Juliet's stories and reverses them. This is done for comic effect, but it also serves to point out, and effectively dismiss, the ideology underlying their traditional portrayal as passive victims. When MacDonald reconstructs them as powerful women capable of efficacious action, she not only creates delightful characters, but also empowering ones. In response to the question, "Is parody almost an inevitable part of the portrayal of women on the stage today?" MacDonald has responded:

> It's like opening up a trunk that used to be full of instruments of torture and now everything has turned into toys. When you reclaim and transform ideas and methods that have been used against you as a woman, you become empowered. Subversion of this kind is healthy.[38]

The audience member (especially the contemporary feminist) is not satisfied with Desdemona's and Juliet's preventable deaths and objects to their function as sacrifices within male narratives, a dissatisfaction that MacDonald consciously remedies. By embracing a vision of female wholeness that encompasses an intriguing variety of desiring and desired characters, *Goodnight Desdemona (Good Morning Juliet)* is uniquely in tune with the kind of representation young feminists respond to. MacDonald's technique clearly moves in the direction of embracing her cultural sources, yet uses them to empower her female characters, particularly sexually and particularly in the realm of "the revolution within," to use the phrase coined by Gloria Steinem. MacDonald's choices make the play appealing to viewers who are more comfortable with Third Wave feminism's embrace of contradictions. The critics Linda Burnett, Ellen McKay, and Marianne Novy have all suggested that it is not

Shakespeare's work that is patriarchal and imperialist, but the subsequent critical interpretations (whether literary criticism or productions) that have allowed only one possible reading. They argue that a parody like MacDonald's actually restores a sense of what is already there, or at least what might be possible.[39]

Juliet's seduction of Constance is set up in a way that makes it "acceptable to spectators often uncomfortable with same-sex wooing"[40] and the play as a whole makes a good text for teaching students because "many will enjoy it while few if any complain about its subversive laughter."[41] MacDonald herself has stated that it is her "crusade" to bring the spectator to identify with a character she had previously thought of as "alien or deviant."[42] Certainly, in terms of Nightwood's profile and mainstream success, *Goodnight Desdemona (Good Morning Juliet)* was a huge breakthrough.

1990: Nightwood's evolving mandate

Throughout her tenure, Kate Lushington addressed the definition of feminist theatre and Nightwood's mandate in a number of articles. The topic is introduced in the Winter 1990 issue of the retitled newsletter, *Night Talk,* when Lushington discusses her experiences on tour with *Goodnight Desdemona (Good Morning Juliet).* Because the presenter in Edmonton, Gyllian Raby, emphasized Nightwood's position as a feminist theatre more than the other host companies had, Lushington spent her three days in Edmonton at talks, interviews, and meetings, trying to define Nightwood's position. The experience resulted in a list of her conclusions: that feminist theatre challenges fixed ideas; it is woman-centred; it offers access to the means of production to women theatre artists; it is collaborative and non-hierarchical in process "yet unafraid to seize and wield power"; and it combats isolation, reaching out to other under-represented groups to promote alternative visions of the world. Lushington agrees that there are many other women and companies across Canada with different kinds and styles of feminist theatre, but with similar ideals and desires: "Nightwood does not represent all feminist theatre, and looks forward to trying on many different shoes in the future."

Shelley Scott • Nightwood Theatre

In an article in the *Toronto Star* later that same year, Lushington elaborates further on the subject:

> We don't do issue-oriented theatre … It almost seems that
> if you're talking about real issues then you can't be theat-
> rical and if you're being theatrical then you're talking in
> a kind of abstract way about art and can't deal with real
> issues. We like to put the two together … Some people
> are saying Nightwood is going soft: "They used to do plays
> about violence against women (*This is For You, Anna*) and
> now they're doing a play about a university lecturer who
> finds herself visiting the worlds of Shakespeare." Those
> people want to plug us into their stereotype of what a femi-
> nist theatre company should do. But Nightwood is about
> exploding stereotypes. And that involves knocking conven-
> tional ways of thinking sideways a bit — our own as well as
> other peoples'.[43]

Lushington's conception of feminism as being a matter of perception, rather than a series of specific political demands, is addressed in a 1991 article in *NOW*, in which she states:

> It's easy to mistake us for a social action theatre company
> because we have such a strong political bent, but we're
> not just interested in social action … Everyone at Night-
> wood agrees that they want to affect change in society, but
> the nature of that change is an opening of the mind, a
> shifting of perception, a looking at things from different
> angles … Nightwood is given to exploding stereotypes,
> but one of those stereotypes is what a feminist theatre
> company is.[44]

In a way, these kinds of statements can be read as a response to
Nightwood's sudden, high-profile success. With the tremendous
response to *Goodnight Desdemona (Good Morning Juliet)*, Nightwood
was no longer quite as marginal and alternative as it used to be.

Perhaps paradoxically, with greater mainstream acceptance, the company had to reinforce its feminist principles. Nightwood did just that, by next taking on plays that addressed new communities and broke new ground — such as *A Fertile Imagination*, which Lushington directed in 1991.

1991: SEMIOTICS AND SEXUALITY — A FERTILE IMAGINATION

A Fertile Imagination is a great example of how Nightwood has nurtured new work within its network of programs, events, and opportunities for involvement. Susan G. Cole, an editor at the alternative weekly *NOW*, served on Nightwood's board from 1986 to 1988. During that tenure, she performed an autobiographical monologue at "FemCab." Her piece was further workshopped at the 1989 "Groundswell," and Cole went on to develop it into a full-length play in collaboration with Kate Lushington and the cast. It opened in February 1991 at the Poor Alex Theatre, directed by Lushington and featuring Kate Lynch, Robin Craig, and Patricia Idlette, who was also a board member. A year later it was remounted at Theatre Passe Muraille, directed by Layne Coleman, with Yanna McIntosh replacing Idlette. Cole comments that when she first did the piece as a monologue, "It seemed to cross a lot of different sensibilities and communities. That's what I remember most. It wasn't one particular group of people who were touched by it."[45] Nightwood is defined by this kind of example — by people who become involved in one capacity and move on to doing more. Kate Lynch had been in the cast of previous Nightwood productions, *The Herring Gull's Egg* and *Goodnight Desdemona (Good Morning Juliet)*, and would return to participate in several "Groundswells" and to act in *Smudge* in 2000. Robin Craig would later appear in the 1993 "Groundswell" reading of *Charming and Rose: True Love*, also directed by Kate Lushington. *A Fertile Imagination* also illustrates Nightwood's commitment to diversity and willingness to address lesbian issues, as it deals with two women having a baby together through artificial insemination. In the advance publicity for the show, Lushington revealed,

"Along the way, those involved in the production have been challenged in their heterosexist assumptions — something they hope will also happen with the audience."[46] In 2005, Nightwood embraced the topic of lesbian motherhood again with Diane Flacks's autobiographical play *Bear With Me*, produced in association with Buddies in Bad Times, and directed by Kelly Thornton. To celebrate the premiere, Nightwood presented a panel discussion called "Ms.Conceptions: Queer Mothers and Children Tackle the Politics of Family," moderated by the popular lesbian comedian Elvira Kurt.

A Fertile Imagination is a largely autobiographical account by Cole, a well-known Toronto journalist, chronicling a lesbian couple's attempts to have a baby. The main characters, Del and Rita, are looking for a sperm donor so that Rita can be artificially inseminated, or, as they prefer to call it, "alternatively fertilized." Between scene transitions, a recording of the fictional couple's answering machine messages is played. The following example, from the transition between Act One, Scenes Two and Three, suggests the play's humorous tone and its placement in a specific social milieu:

> — Hi gals, this is Audra. I'm getting on with the legal paperwork. Your guy's lawyer wants to come Tuesday at 5:30 pm. Make sure you're home.
> — Del, this is your editor. I have a question about your sexual harassment piece. You say that a male professor's comment on a female student's clothing might constitute harassment. Don't you think it should read that it could constitute sexual harassment?
> — Rita, dear. It's mum. I wish you wouldn't put on that machine. I'm taping the Donahue show for you. He's interviewing some women who are, you know, in your situation.
> — Hey Del. Dykes on Donahue. Turn it on.[47]

The play is written in a situation comedy format, taking material that, for many in the audience, might be unfamiliar and possibly threatening, and making it seem friendly and familiar. Lushington, as director, chose not to use blackouts between scenes, instead showing the characters continuing to live within their home environment in an attempt to really involve the audience in the onstage world. A series of short, fast-paced scenes introduce likeable, easily identifiable characters who find themselves in an unusual situation and deal with it in a light, comic manner. Helpful information about reproductive technologies is offered within a highly normalized portrait of lesbian life. (Interestingly, this is the same strategy employed by *Ellen*, an actual television sitcom of the same time period that dealt with lesbian life).

According to Lizbeth Goodman, the British writer Libby Mason's play *Double Vision*, produced by Women's Theatre Group in 1982, was described in the press as being "like a Woody Allen script for lesbians."[48] This is similar to the way *A Fertile Imagination* was marketed in Toronto, and also brings to mind some of the critical response to Wendy Wasserstein's plays in America, where her serious intent was sometimes overlooked in favour of the work's lighter, comic elements. Nightwood chose not to produce the play at Buddies in Bad Times, Toronto's gay and lesbian theatre space, and advertised it as a "courageous comedy" in anticipation of some resistance to its content. The production was designed, at least in part, to attract a non-homosexual audience, and Cole's choice to use the non-threatening sitcom format fit in with this agenda. In fact, Kate Lushington has commented that fathers often responded to the play in an unexpectedly positive manner, since they found they could relate to Del's role and feelings as the non-pregnant parent.[49]

However, Cole also had a socially transformative agenda for her play. In both the script and the program for the second production, there are a number of cues that the playwright is making every effort to place her play within a contemporary social and political, and specifically feminist, context. For example, the script calls for the third actor (who plays a variety of other characters) to be Black, in an attempt to reflect Toronto's multicultural makeup. A sarcastic reference is made to the "politically fantastic element" of having a "radical feminist" like Del write a regular column for a daily newspaper. Reference is made to the Morgentaler Clinic, Toronto's free-standing abortion facility (predating the destruction of the clinic by arson in the following year, 1992), and program notes dedicate the play to the pro-choice movement and thank the Gay and Lesbian Community Appeal for seed money.

The match between form and content was an uneasy fit. The superficiality of the form tended to undermine the attempt to get audiences to do any real questioning of the multitude of issues being raised. Reviewers either concentrated on the comedy and ignored the politics, or argued that the form undermined the politics. On one end of the spectrum are reviews in which well-known American television sitcoms are cited as a way to sum up the play: Del is called "a gay Rhoda for the 90s," and Del and Rita are described as being such warm characters that "even Archie Bunker might want to know them."[50] The critic Vit Wagner complained that the play "is such an odd mix of radical politics and sitcom convention that one is tempted to call [Cole] a lesbian Neil Simon. This is *Barefoot in the Park* for the same-sex crowd."[51] Wagner identifies the "odd couple" pairing of Del and Rita, and the "familiar, comfortable way the comedy works" through one-liners, as further evidence of its sitcom format.

At the other end of the spectrum, Sandra Haar, writing for a gay and lesbian newspaper and describing the play as having a "linear plotline" with "skit-like segments," faults the comedic form for undermining the play's politics. Haar comments that while "lesbians everywhere" were no doubt encouraged to see a "mainstream" company like Nightwood mounting this play, Cole was too obviously trying to appeal to a broad audience. As evidence, Haar points out that some jokes and references were "extended to permit a small explanation ... Because lesbians live a different reality than non-lesbians, the extending [of jokes] served to pander to the needs of a mainstream audience."[52] The review makes it apparent that the sitcom formula was not necessarily an effective match for a more politicized spectator — one attracted to, rather than wary of, the play's content.

Haar also comments that she did not find the actors' portrayal of lesbians convincing, and as a result, she, as a lesbian audience member, could not relate to them or enjoy the play. Haar complains that the actors were too stiff with each other and that humour "consistently threatened the intensity of the most sexual of scenes. From the very beginning I was unable to identify with the characters' sensibilities or connect with their presence."[53] At this point she reveals that neither of the actors is lesbian and that "the actors' inability to reflect the particularity of the situation they were representing was masked by the steady flow of jokes." One might interpret this as an instance where the actors took on a "disguise," knowing that some of their audience would see through it because of prior or "specialized" knowledge, and hoped that their attempt would be artful enough to convince the viewers-in-the-know to suspend their disbelief. But Haar found fault with the production specifically because the two actors playing the couple were known to be heterosexual. She writes, "Of course, reality is not what theatre is about, but authenticity is. The relational, emotional framework that Cole has claimed to want to contextualize lesbian sexuality cannot support the sex and sensuality in *A Fertile Imagination* and little heat is generated."[54] This is interesting semiotically, as the actors, as signs, relate to the stage world of meaning, and are in turn intended to be read by spectators in relation to the real world. But for this reviewer, and perhaps for other audience members, the process broke down from the beginning, disrupting the relay of signification throughout. While gender and race are generally evident to the audience, perhaps sexual orientation requires another kind of perception. Jill Dolan, in *Breaking the Code: Musings on Lesbian Sexuality and the Performer,* argues that all production choices are inherently political because a person's gender and race have cultural meanings that bear ideological weight: "A lesbian required to pass as heterosexual on the street or stage is placed in a Brechtian position of commenting on her role, editorializing on the trappings of her impersonation *for those who can see*"[55] (Dolan's italics).

Shelley Scott • Nightwood Theatre

For this reviewer, authenticity has to do with recognition, with the perceived comfort level of the actors, and with their "real-life" sexuality. In the politicized arena of gay theatre, the emphasis is not on a traditional approach to inhabiting a role, but on reading the performers *as* performers and as members of a particular community. The artist's physical presence, her body, becomes the signifier of authenticity and the site of lived experience, and is just as important as the veracity of the playwright's script. Particularly in work that positions itself as autobiographical, or that seeks to represent the experience of any marginalized community, the visible reality of the physical body is of enormous importance, much as it would be with the issue of race. While a non-lesbian actor cannot be excluded from playing a lesbian character, she must be prepared to withstand a different kind of scrutiny, both within the public discourse around the production and in the confines of the theatre space.

Concern with an authenticity that can be read on the body is directly related to the ongoing anxiety throughout the play with "natural" behaviour. For example, in one sequence, Del resents the fact that she and Rita have to involve a midwife to teach them the insemination procedure:

> **Rita**: You know we can't do this alone.
> **Del**: But a fourth party? It's bad enough we have to go sperm-hunting a third.
> **Rita**: Del, we've been through this before. Why are you making it so complicated?
> **Del**: Midwives don't have to help other people get pregnant.
> **Rita**: Since when do you care what other couples do?
> **Del**: Well, the whole thing makes me feel...unnatural. I hate that feeling. I hate feeling marginalized.
> **Rita**: So, we could use the support.

In addition to being something "other than" their "unnatural" situation, nature is a mystery to be figured out, and Rita superstitiously worries that they might somehow tamper with this force.

She insists on throwing away all of the tampons in the house while she is trying to become pregnant, claiming they are "bad luck," and she chastises Del for reading about miscarriages on the grounds that "just thinking about it" can somehow bring it about. When Rita does in fact miscarry, she sees nature as an angry god:

> **Rita**: We got what we deserved. Messing with nature.
> **Del**: You don't think what we do is natural.
> **Rita**: We made a baby with a plastic syringe.
> **Del**: We made a baby with love.
> **Rita**: We're being punished.

By the end of the play, however, Rita has become pregnant again and they have devoted themselves to constructing a new family model that will work for them. Del, who has resolutely refused to discuss their experience in her newspaper column, finally writes a personal, first-person account and identifies her situation: "I'm not Daddy Del…I'm a woman who loves a woman and we're going to have a baby. I'm going to be a mother."

Despite the characters' determination to do things in a new way, and, by implication, to develop a more consciously chosen and constructed, individual sense of what is natural, the normalizing tone of the play lingers. The penultimate scene makes clear the playwright's belief that, in a fundamental way, Del and Rita are more like, than unlike, other parents. In discussing the pitfalls of raising a child, Del predicts ruefully, "He'll hate us because we're lesbians," and Rita ironically reassures her, "No, no she won't. That's too simple. She'll hate us for some reason we can't even dream of." Onstage, the picture is iconic: Del's hand is on Rita's belly and she reacts with joy as she feels movement. Different productions of this play, especially various casting choices, might well have different degrees of success in subverting the TV sitcom format; and despite (or perhaps because of) her choice of this form to appeal to a heterosexual audience, Cole's content does strongly suggest that she hopes to have a transformative effect on them. Interestingly, however, the power of this form is so containing that it manages to undermine the potentially subversive sight of two women onstage embodying lesbian desire and a radically new form of reproduction.

In her introduction to *Performing Feminisms*, Sue-Ellen Case identifies characteristics of feminist theatre theory that, she argues, define both the content and the nature of the field. One of the points that Case makes is that the "double" of feminist theatre is the historical moment in which it takes place, the real material conditions that are addressed by feminist political action and that move within the gestures of the stage. As plays that deal with lesbian motherhood, Cole's *A Fertile Imagination* and Flacks's *Bear With Me* are good examples. The performance of either of these plays within their fictional worlds onstage will be constantly echoed by the status of the social issues in the external world which is its "double." When *A Fertile Imagination* premiered in 1991, Cole and her female partner did not have the legal right to marry in Canada, but by the time of the premiere of *Bear With Me* in 2005, that right had been won. A consideration of the play by a feminist critic, therefore, would likely address how the play and its performance evoke these kinds of "real-life" circumstances and issues for the spectator.

1989 AND INTO THE '90S: THE ANTI-RACISM MANDATE

Nightwood has embodied the materialist feminist position most obviously in its commitment to producing work by, and opening up its organizational structure to, women of colour. Feminism became increasingly concerned with issues of race in the late 1980s, as women of colour charged feminism with being run by and for middle-class white women.[56] Nightwood responded by launching SisterReach, an anti-racism campaign aimed at opening the company up to a wider community. The first mention of the new anti-racist agenda was in Nightwood's inaugural newsletter *Nightwords* (vol. 1 no. 1, Fall 1989). Plays such as *Princess Pocahontas and the Blue Spots* (1990) by Monique Mojica and *The Wonder of Man* (1992) by Diana Braithwaite came to represent the new face of Nightwood. These plays attempt to construct new identities for their subjects that take into account the conditions of race, class, nationality, sexuality, and other culturally specific factors, in addition to and inseparable from the construction of gender.

Because the women who worked on these productions — as theatre practitioners and members of various communities — were active in the creation and transmission of new cultural values, they affected the audiences who came to see them, inspiring them to initiate projects of their own. In a 1993 interview with the African-Canadian playwright Djanet Sears, reporter Jill Lawless describes Sears as a longtime arts organizer and a powerful force at Nightwood, a woman responsible for its "admirable diversity." Sears explains:

> I've been to board meetings and argued policy, helped out with shows, directed shows, chosen shows. But mostly my contribution was just placing certain people in the same orbit. There are a lot of people who are part of my world, so when I joined Nightwood the circle of Nightwood opened. That's the interesting thing about any predominantly white organization wanting to invite in people of other cultures. You can't do it just because you think that's what you should do. And you can't expect other people just to fit in. You must not only have people of colour in the hierarchy of your organization — you must expand your ideas about your organization. You have to rethink everything, your whole structure. Structures fit some people, but not all people. And with Kate [Lushington] I sensed that openness ... I don't find Nightwood limited to a single dialectic, which is a very difficult thing to find.[57]

At that stage, Nightwood's commitment to a materialist approach to feminism had largely come to define the company, particularly since the anti-racism mandate was implemented. Rather than taking a cultural feminist approach to inclusion by assuming all women have the same issues, Nightwood had adopted a materialist project of targeting specific women — those previously marginalized within feminism and theatre — and letting their voices be heard.

As Sears suggests, this idea finds its most direct expression in the relationship between company and audience. This is particularly evident at the annual "Groundswell Festival" of new work, where the atmosphere is informal, with audience feedback encouraged in a variety of ways. In 1989, for example, the audience was invited to write comments on the paper-covered tables where they sat, cabaret-style, at the Annex Theatre, while in 1994, a form asking specific dramaturgical questions was enclosed with the program. Kate Lushington emphasized Nightwood's desire to reach out to a different audience with "Groundswell." As early as 1988, "Groundswell" had a selection committee made up of women from outside Nightwood who were mandated to take into consideration a wider representation of the theatre community. Participating playwrights were also invited to "Groundtalk," an informal discussion group led by Susan Feldman (executive director of the Performing Arts Development Fund of Ontario), and were offered feedback from established playwrights including Carol Bolt, Sally Clark, Ann-Marie MacDonald, and Judith Thompson. In an article in *NOW*, Lushington comments on the cross-fertilization that occurs between participants and audience members at "Groundswell": "We hope people will come to see the whole Festival, not just one or two readings ... We want audiences to see the whole fabric of a developmental process. Maybe some viewers will be inspired to go home and write something themselves. We're always looking for new material."[58]

Audience involvement continued to be crucial to Nightwood, as evidenced by the Spring 1996 newsletter, retitled *Nighttalk* (sometimes called *Night Talk*). In reference to the annual "Fem-Cab" fundraiser, associate director Soraya Peerbaye writes, "An idea I've had of Nightwood for a long time suddenly crystallized, an image of Nightwood being not the handful of women who are the staff, nor the cluster that forms the Board and Advisory, nor even the multitude of artists who illuminate Nightwood's productions; it was an idea of Nightwood defined not by its artists, but by its audience."

In an 1990 article in *Performing Arts Magazine*,[59] Kate Lushington explains that Nightwood's anti-racist mandate was to be implemented in four ways: there would be increased representation of women of colour on the board; priority would be given to women of colour when development money was available; various artists connected to Nightwood would be involved in a project called *The Colour Collective*, based on individual experiences with and attitudes towards racism, and co-written by Lushington and Djanet Sears; and Nightwood would hold a forum targeted at progressive arts organizations. These last two initiatives developed into, respectively, *Untitled*, created and performed by Lushington, Sears, and Monique Mojica in 1993; and *Do the Thing Right*, an anti-racist forum that was planned but never materialized. According to Lushington, the forum was abandoned partly because of limited resources and partly because the board felt it had work to do within the company on issues of racism before it attempted to advise outside organizations.

In the 1991 newsletter, in a note about a recent board retreat, the anti-racist mandate is specifically reiterated: "In a key historical moment, the board committed to form an anti-racist policy." This commitment had already been described in the program for *Princess Pocahontas and the Blue Spots*, produced in 1990. The program note again recounts Nightwood's origins as a four-woman collective and its growth into a collaborative, non-profit, artist-run company with a mandate unique in English Canada: to promote and produce the work of Canadian women playwrights and directors exploring alternative visions of the world. The production of *Princess Pocahontas and the Blue Spots* is celebrated as an example of the commitment to anti-racism that would be reflected throughout the next decade. The terms "collaborative" and "artist-run" are significant, in that Nightwood clearly wished to retain its image as an alternative company. The implication is that the collective structure has been outgrown, but the original spirit—of being alternative and unique in pro-moting women—has remained. Even the commitment to anti-racism can be read as something newly highlighted, as opposed to a radical change. According to Lushington, one measure that could be considered more radical was a resolution that "we would not do another play until we rethought it—not forever, until we rethought it—with an all white cast."[60] Nightwood adhered to this resolution throughout the 1990s, opening the door to more performers of colour, such as Djanet Sears and Monique Mojica.

1990: PRINCESS POCAHONTAS AND THE BLUE SPOTS

Monique Mojica's play *Princess Pocahontas and the Blue Spots* was produced by Nightwood in 1990 and published by the Women's Press in 1991.[61] Mojica had come to Toronto from New York to be a founding member of Native Earth Performing Arts and had taken on a number of significant acting roles: she played Adele Starblanket in Tomson Highway's *The Rez Sisters*, and the title character in the February 1986 Theatre Passe Muraille produc-tion of *Jessica*, directed by Linda Griffiths and Clarke Rogers.

Mojica's involvement with Nightwood has been extensive, be-ginning with the 1987 "Groundswell," when she and Makka Kleist presented *Swindler's Rhapsody* and Mojica performed in that year's "FemCab." In 1991, she was part of Nightworks, an in-house work-shop series with Diana Braithwaite and ahdri zhina mandiela, as part of the larger SisterReach anti-racism campaign. By the end of 1991, Mojica was Nightwood's playwright-in-residence, working on *A Savage Equilibrium*, which was presented at "Groundswell" in 1992, performed by Mojica, Fernando Hernandez Perez, and Jani Lauzon, and directed by Floyd Favel. Mojica was also a member of the planning committee for "Groundswell" that year.

In May of 1993 at the Nightwood Studio, Mojica performed a piece called only *Untitled: A Work in Progress*, a workshop explora-tion about issues of race and friendship, with Kate Lushington and Djanet Sears.[62] According to the Nightwood newsletter, *Un-titled: A Work in Progress:*

investigates the contradictions of race, culture and friendship ... Formerly titled The Colour Collective, the group has since dreamed up many titles: Storm Warning in Effect, Cooking Up a Storm, Seven Onion Soup, Bloodlines and Lifelines, Treacherous Remedies for Amnesia, and This Ain't the June Callwood Show. Fragments were performed at FemCab, and now the creators are joined by animators Michele George, Diane Roberts and Banuta Rubess, and designer Teresa Przybylski. Cheryl Francis is production stage manager.[63]

Mojica's friendship and close working relationship with Sears and Lushington was the subject of their collective piece, in which they explore their common bonds as women (a cultural feminist trait), but also the material condition of their racial differences, all while cooking and serving food to the audience. In 1996, Mojica went on to play a major role in Dilara Ally's play *Mango Chutney*, and in 2002 she was a member of the chorus in Sears's *The Adventures of a Black Girl in Search of God*, both Nightwood productions. She continued to be associated with Nightwood as part of an ongoing collaboration called The Turtle Gals.[64]

Princess Pocahonatas and the Blue Spots was workshopped by Mojica and Alejandra Nunez, with direction and dramaturgy by Djanet Sears, in the spring of 1988. It was workshopped by Nightwood and Native Earth Performing Arts in May 1989, directed by Muriel Miguel (one of the founders of Spiderwoman, "a radical feminist theatre group,"[65] and also Mojica's aunt), and dramaturged by Sears and Lushington. The play was then read at the "Weesageechak Festival of New Work by Native Playwrights" at the Theatre Passe Muraille Backspace in June 1989, and presented at "Groundswell" in November 1989, directed by Sears. It was given a full production at the Passe Muraille Backspace in co-production with Nightwood from 9 February to 4 March 1990, directed by Miguel. The family relationship between Miguel and Mojica is significant in that it relates to the cultural feminist idea of matrilineal tradition and Mojica's concern with heritage in the play.

The play has a complex structure, and the two actors onstage play a large number of characters.[66] The published version explains the play's structure, which consists of thirteen "transformations." These can be sudden or lingering, but are divided into four sections: "they are the transfigurations of three women who are one."[67] The playtext stresses that these transfigurations came out of the characters and were not imposed, illustrating the cultural feminist tendency to respect experience and organic process, and to see women as "one," a unified field of subjecthood. In performance, the distinctions between each character or entity were not as evident as they are when reading the text. As Mojica moved from one transformation to the next in performance, it was as if she were illustrating different aspects of a single subject, the Native Woman.

The tendency to collectivize women is part of what feminist theory objects to in traditional, patriarchal theatre, yet here the technique is clearly intended to establish solidarity rather than to erase individuality. It may help to remember that the main difference lies in who the play is "for": the traditional male spectator, for whose gaze the Woman is presented, versus the author herself and an audience to whom she wishes to communicate her respect for what she sees as her lineage — her female and indigenous cultural inheritance — by presenting powerful, almost archetypal, images. Ric Knowles and Jen Harvie have described the play as "an antihegemonic revisioning of dominant myths of Native women, written and performed by Mojica out of a strong and resisting subject position, from which its various characters, historical and contemporary, seem to emerge — it can be seen as a kind of spiritual/historical autobiography."[68]

The cultural feminist concern with nature is reflected in the richly detailed mise en scène for *Princess Pocahontas and the Blue Spots*. The set, as described in the text and as it appeared in the 1990 Theatre Passe Muraille production, is a pyramid with steps. There is a tree with a platform: a basin, cup, water, red paint, sand, and popcorn; a pole pegged for climbing; faces and clothing of Métis women; a picture frame, cloth, a circle on the floor, and the foliage of trees. Each prop is transformed into many things over the course of the performance.

The play begins with a scene called "500 years of the Miss North American Indian Beauty Pageant." Princess Buttered-on-Both-Sides enters, distributing corn, as the Host introduces her. The Princess performs a parodic "Hollywood Injun Dance." The use of stereotype and satire is employed repeatedly throughout the play and might suggest a more materialist approach to the subject, given the association of parody and satire with materialist textual strategies. This suspicion is reinforced by the next scene, in which the two actors, as Contemporary Women #1 and #2, talk about being a "real Indian" and about how one's authenticity was traditionally established by the appearance of a blue spot at the base of the spine. There appears to be an awareness of how "realness" is complicated by other factors besides biology, and of how the presence of a physical characteristic (in this case of race, but one could extrapolate to sex) does not guarantee identity.

There is also an investment in truth, however, which the play comes to emphasize through a series of scenes that attempt to tell familiar stories from the perspective of the voiceless female. Pocahontas's story, for example, is told in both its "storybook" and its "real" versions, suggesting that there is an essential truth to her experience, which can be recaptured by looking at her life from a new perspective. This is very much in keeping with the cultural feminist aim to recreate women's culture and to reclaim forgotten or neglected women of the past.

The cultural feminist perspective is also evident in an important scene in which Mojica is transformed into the child Matoaka. The musician becomes an entity called Ceremony, beating a rhythm as Matoaka chants a song, entitled "Nubile Child," about the traditional initiation ceremony for becoming a woman. Mojica paints the outside of her arms and the tops of her feet with red paint, and declares that she is invoking "woman's time."[69]

The cultural feminist agenda is complicated here by the

inclusion of a scene about male/female relationships, called "Grandfathers/Stand up." Contemporary Woman #1 talks about what she finds attractive and familiar about her male partner and discovers his resemblance to her grandfather and his connection with their male traditions. Woman #2 becomes a man and the couple perform a semi-comic routine, with the woman trying to get the man to stand tall on his own feet, to not be drunk or dependent, or pursue white women, but to rebuild their nation. But when she succeeds in making him strong, he leaves her. The scene is not entirely materialist either, however, focusing as it does on an archetypal, non-individualized situation related from the woman's perspective.

The play continues to explore increasingly grim material, focusing on the abuse of Métis women by their white husbands, the torture of a young woman in Chile, and the murder of the American Indian Movement activist Anna Mae Aquash. In the final scene, entitled "Una Nación," Contemporary Woman #1 talks about the difficulty of fitting into "feminist shoes," which do not represent all Aboriginal women. The two actors wash and purify each other. They offer a range of quotations from various writers, culminating in the image of a Rainforest woman confronting a riot squad in Brazil. There is a final dance and a last quote: "A nation is not conquered until the hearts of its women are on the ground."[70]

Princess Pocahontas and the Blue Spots attempts to link the experiences of the Aboriginal peoples of North and South America through a few scenes of parallel storytelling, especially near the end, but mostly through mixing different kinds of music. Mojica is accompanied in performance by a musician, Alejandra Nunez, who is Chilean-Canadian, and who contributed material about the *mestiza*, the offspring of the Spanish and Native Americans. Mojica, as the child of a Kuna-Rappahannock mother and a Jewish father, is herself concerned with issues of hybridity. As Knowles and Harvie point out, "The myths of Native identity that it attacks or constructs are indiscriminately drawn from all of North, Central and South America; and the hybrid nature of

Native and other ethnicities is asserted at every turn and embodied in the author-performer."[71]

Mojica's play is similar to Djanet Sears's *Afrika Solo* in that it is one woman's story, but other people on stage also play parts (in both cases, the others are also musicians). In both plays, the woman is responding to her image or absence in popular culture in an attempt to establish an identity, and eventually finds a sense of herself by reclaiming her ethnic heritage. As with Mojica's mixed parenthood, Sears also has a less than straightforward task: her mother was born in Jamaica and her father in Guyana, and Sears was raised in England and Canada. The experiences of both playwrights/performers are representative of the multi-cultural, mobile society we live in and the sense of confusion and increased opportunity that can result.

Another example of this phenomenon is the 1993 play *Dryland* by Pauline Peters, a "story cycle" that was performed at "Ground-swell" in 1992 and 1993, and then at the Nightwood Studio, which celebrated a Black cultural aesthetic in both language and visual design. Monique Mojica contributed to the show as one of a large collaborative team of designers and facilitators. In an interview in *Night Talk*, Peters expresses her interest in finding a hybrid identity, one rooted in her parents' heritage as well as her place within Canadian society. Peters explains that, as a second generation West Indian, she feels adrift because her parents have not passed on their stories, preferring to forget the past as part of the process of improving their present lot: "Some of us are desperately seeking black culture and others completely subsumed into white culture. So it's important to create our own, because stories are what anchor you, give you a sense of belonging in history. It's a discovery really."[72]

The task of these plays is multiple: part of their value is therapeutic, enabling the author to give voice to her own experiences and concerns through the process of writing and performing. Furthermore, they attempt to communicate that process to an audience, by way of explanation and education, perhaps, for those of a different background, and as a means of empowering others with similar circumstances (Sears's play, for example, toured to high schools in Ontario and was clearly seen as having a valuable message to convey). These goals are consistent with the cultural feminist desire for community, and as a result, the plays exhibit a cultural feminist aesthetic that is affirmative and inspiring for performer and audience alike: they impart a sense of group identification that is tied to geography, artistic expression, common experience, and cultural pride.

Mojica's more recent work continues to be a boundary-defying mix. As a member of Turtle Gals Performance Ensemble, with Michelle St. John, Sandra Laronde, and Jani Lauzon, Mojica created *The Scrubbing Project*, which was developed at the 1999 and 2000 "Groundswell Festivals," while the women were in residence for the 1999/2000 season.[73] In 2007, as a trio (minus Laronde),[74] Turtle Gals produced a show called *The Only Good Indian...* which explores the history of Native performers "from the 1880s in Buffalo Bill's Wild West shows through P.T. Barnum's side shows, the 1904 St. Louis World's Fair (and other expositions), the silent film era, vaudeville, burlesque, and Hollywood."[75] Like *Princess Pocahontas and the Blue Spots*, the work may not be autobiographical in the traditional sense, but it seeks to place the artist within her very particular lineage. In an article entitled *Stories from the Body: Blood Memory and Organic Texts*, Mojica writes, "First, what you need to know is that I come from a family of show Indians." She talks about her grandfather making up ceremonial skits and dances to accompany the sale of "snake oil," and her mother and aunts posing for tourists and riding parade floats wearing feathers and buckskins, as well as providing a place for other Natives who came to New York to dance at the fair or perform in rodeos.[76] Mojica concludes her article by mentioning that she attended an opening for an exhibit at the Smithsonian National Museum of the American Indian called "New Tribe New York," a retrospective of Spiderwoman Theater, and expresses her pride at dancing on stage with her brother, her brother-in-law and cousins, and her niece, who represents the fifth generation of performers in her family line.[77]

1993: CHARMING AND ROSE: TRUE LOVE

Nightwood's 1993 production of *Charming and Rose: True Love* serves as another example of how cultural and materialist elements co-exist and can be problematized in feminist theatre. After premiering at the 1992 "Winnipeg Fringe Festival," Kelley Jo Burke's play was given a staged reading at "Groundswell" that fall, and then a full production at the Theatre Centre West, directed by Kate Lushington. The play articulates a discourse of natural identity that fits in with the cultural feminist model, and yet maintains a parallel critique of the constructed nature of identity that is more materialist. An opposition is set up between nature and culture, allowing an alternative reading and a route away from what could be considered a problematic essentialism.[78]

Like *This is For You, Anna, Charming and Rose* uses the fairy tale as a potent device for feminist revisioning. In the 1993 production, the character of Melisande the fairy godmother was played by Djanet Sears. In an interview with *NOW* magazine, Sears comments:

> Myths hold a special place in any society — they are maps of ways to live ... Like everyone else who has grown up in western culture, I've internalized myths ... the whole romantic fairy-tale myth is within me.[79]

In her book *Simians, Cyborgs, and Women: The Reinvention of Nature*, Donna J. Haraway calls myths "meaning-laden public knowledge," and illustrates the ongoing battle for mythological currency by arguing that

> feminism is, in part, a project for the reconstruction of public life and public meanings ... a search for new stories, and so for a language which names a new vision of possibilities and limits. That is, feminism, like science, is a myth, a contest for public knowledge.[80]

These quotations outline two particular uses of the term "mythology": first, the fairy tale as popular lore passed on for entertainment and instruction; and second, the notion of mythology as ideological explanation — the "stories" about sexuality, gender, and race, for example — through which understanding is constructed in a culture. In her introduction to *A Feminist Companion to Mythology*, Carolynne Larrington argues that myths are "at the centre of a web of meanings, drawn out of the body of the myth by different interpreters for different purposes."[81] Myths, here being used in the sense of legends or fairy tales, may have a plurality of meanings at successive stages in their existence; this is particularly the case when mythology becomes the source for artistic creation.

The translation of traditional mythology into the language of contemporary feminism has been considered a powerful tool, both politically and artistically. In her article "Psychic Activism: Feminist Mythmaking," Jane Caputi argues that part of the agenda of the feminist movement is to "reclaim the symbolizing/naming power, to refigure the female self from a gynocentric perspective, to discover, to revitalize and create a female oral and mythic tradition and use it, ultimately, to change the world."[82] Caputi defines this as a twofold process, involving both the repudiation of what she calls patriarchal mythology, and the active reinterpretation "of ancient myth, focusing attention on female divinities, supernaturals and powers that have been repressed and silenced"[83] — clearly part of a cultural feminist project.

Is it possible to rework a patriarchal myth (or even one believed to reflect pre-patriarchal beliefs) to feminist purposes without being undermined by its accumulated baggage? Part of the answer lies, of course, in the appeal of the stories themselves. Lena B. Ross, editor of *To Speak or Be Silent: The Paradox of Disobedience in the Lives of Women*, believes that women in mythology are always associated with disobedience in some way, and speculates that disobedience has "a special and specific value in connection with the feminine archetypes, possibly playing some vital and necessary role in the drama of human life and relations."[84] Ross suggests that hearing tales of female disobedience may serve a psychological or spiritual need for recipients of the myth.

The feminist storyteller attempts to reclaim female figures from mythology and fairy tale, and to reward them within the context of feminist reinterpretation — not unlike Ann-Marie Mac-Donald's agenda in rescuing Shakespeare's heroines in *Goodnight Desdemona (Good Morning Juliet)*. The choice of mythological characters raises particular problems and resonance within a feminist agenda, which are further complicated by theatrical considerations. How does the actor portray a fairy godmother, for example? The presence of the actor's body serves to naturalize her portrayal, but the purpose of introducing the fairy-tale figure onstage remains complex. The spectator identifies with the creature as something tangible, corporeal, demystified (especially in the case of the gin-swilling fairy godmother in *Charming and Rose*), but at the same time senses a desire on the part of the playwright to retain some of the potency and promise of the traditional figure — the fairy-tale magic, as it were. The playwright creates a role model, but one with a magic wand up her sleeve; a materialist critique and a cultural transcendence at the same time. Interestingly, casting a woman of colour in this role served to foreground the issues of convention and expectation, heightened further by Sears's choice to play the character with a West Indian accent.[85]

In *Charming and Rose: True Love*, the potential for an essentialist interpretation is most closely associated with Rose, a character defined by her sexuality and fertility, who becomes truly herself only when she returns to her natural state as a "wolf-woman" — an uncomplicated state of pre-patriarchal grace. Rose's identity as half-wolf and half-human provides a stark contrast to her role in the confines of the castle and court society. The play presents Rose as deeply marked by her experience being raised by the wolf White Paws. Her unfettered "naturalness" attracts Prince Charming to Rose: she is so different from all the other women he knows, so unselfconscious and sexually free. Later, her natural instincts, or "wolf morals," compel Rose to kill Charming when he poses a threat to her pregnancy. At the end of the play, Rose returns to live with the wolves, clearly indicating that it is within a natural, animal realm that she will find her true self, away from the false constructions and alien requirements of patriarchal culture. The natural realm was represented onstage by a film shown at the beginning of the play, a montage of images of wolves in the wild that provided a highly resonant, imaginative reference for the offstage world Rose felt drawn toward.

Yvonne Hodkinson has explained the cultural feminist identification with nature as a reclamation of female power: "The female loss of identity becomes the struggle to regain the ancient correlation with nature in pre-patriarchal society, 'when Goddess-worship prevailed, and when myths depicted strong and revered female figures.'"[86] In direct opposition to this positive view, Diane Purkiss has argued against "Romantic" feminism, defining it as an over-determination of woman's instinctual relationship with nature and "an essentialist notion of a bodily femininity assumed to be reflected in — rather than produced by — the myths they elaborate."[87] Purkiss objects to the blurring of differences between goddess figures from different cultures and expresses apprehension about an ideal of femininity that becomes a kind of transhistoric essence, located in maternity and reproductive capacity. Purkiss argues instead that femininity is itself a product of the culture and language that represses it: "Femininity is, precisely, that which is excluded from patriarchal representations and can only be glimpsed in their gaps and silences."[88] In her view, myths arising from patriarchal culture can only point to the absence, rather than the essence, of the female.

Yet in *Charming and Rose*, while Rose is assumed to have a natural identity, the image of the princess is deconstructed. The role of any "princess" (read: ideal model of femininity) is explicitly revealed as a construction, a constant deception revolving around appearances. Princess Rose complains, "Princesses don't swear. Princesses don't burp. Princesses don't pass wind, sweat, shit, zit or drool," to which her fairy godmother, Melisande, replies: "Princesses don't *appear* to swear, burp, etc. etc. I never could get you to grasp the finer points of that principle."[89] The dress that Rose wears serves as a visual theatrical symbol for this deception. The stage directions tell us, "The Dress stands by itself...a construct of wire and fabric."[90] The role of the princess is similarly free-standing and artificially constructed, quite separate from the "reality" of Rose as a girl raised by wolves, and something which, in performance, she was both literally and metaphorically "strapped into." This is an example where the signifier, the dress, relates to the onstage reality of the play, but also bypasses this intermediary step to signify its meaning to the audience directly by announcing itself as a symbol; placed upstage centre for most of the performance, it loomed over the action as a constant reminder of the social roles constricting Rose and Charming and deforming their relationship. The dress, as a metaphor for the social influences on individual circumstances, can also be seen as evidence of the play's materialist feminism.

It is possible to reconcile the cultural and materialist readings of this play through another model: the suggestion that the attraction mythological figures hold for feminist playwrights and audiences comes not from their "naturalness," but from their evocation of "monsters." After all, part of the appeal of the female character lies in her disobedience, even in the ways in which she is transgressive.

The movies are an obvious source to consider for strange and monstrous characters. In her essay "When the Woman Looks," Linda Williams maintains that the monster in the classic horror movie should not be interpreted as the eruption of repressed male sexuality, but rather as the feared power and potency of the woman — as her double. As Williams explains: "The female look ... shares the male fear at the monster's freakishness, but also recognizes the sense in which this freakishness is similar to her own difference. For she too has been constituted as an exhibition-object by the desiring look of the male."[91] The woman's look at, and identification with, the monster is a recognition of their similar status as threats to male power. The monster and the woman are both "biological freaks with impossible and threatening appetites that suggest a frightening potency."[92] Princess Rose fits this description with her remarkable sexual appetite, for example. Williams argues that this is the reason for the strange affinity that often exists between the woman and the monster in the classic horror film; the surplus of danger and excitement when the two are together; and the woman's sympathy at the monster's death. For the woman, the monster has been a horror version of her own body, one of the many mirrors held up to her by the patriarchy in which she may view her difference. With Williams' model, femininity is still located in "difference," but she switches the focus from a femininity assumed to be natural and biological to one constructed in opposition to, and repressed by, the male norm, and therefore threatening to patriarchal order. In this sense, rather than locating a woman's power in her reproductive capacities alone, Rose's relationship with White Paws is seen on the level of woman and monster, with the woman recognizing their common status as dangerous "others." Throughout the play, Rose is acutely aware that she poses a threat to Charming and his world.

Donna Haraway argues that the search for political identity can lead to "endless splitting and searches for a new essential unity. But there has also been a growing recognition of another response through coalition — affinity, not identity."[93] Thus, an affinity with the natural world need not lead to a totalizing essentialism, but rather, as with the woman and the monster, to an affinity based on recognition and responsibility, and a rejection of the false dichotomy between nature and culture. In this sense, the female character embodies the monster as part of herself.

For Haraway, women are monsters because they are boundary creatures, holding a destabilizing place in the great Western evolutionary, technological, and biological narratives. Viewed in this light, *Charming and Rose* is about boundary creatures who, in their status as neither one nor the other, represent a potent threat to the dominant order: Rose is a wolf and a woman, a princess and a murderer, while White Paws is both wolf and mother figure, Melisande is both fairy tale and earthy reality, and even Prince

Charming is both loving and abusive husband. As Haraway argues, "A concept of a coherent inner self, achieved (cultural) or innate (biological), is a regulatory fiction that is unnecessary—indeed, inhibitory—for feminist projects of producing and affirming complex agency and responsibility."[94] The play is about the search for identity, but concludes that a single identity does not suffice. This is certainly part of the appeal of mythology, in both senses, for the feminist playwright.

Charming and Rose: True Love was written ten years after *This is For You, Anna*, benefiting from the intervening years of feminist thought and an increasingly complex relationship to all feminist issues, even the issue of violence against women. *This is For You, Anna* explores the impulse toward revenge, touching upon Marianne's victimhood and culpability in a way that is both challenging and emotionally direct. *Charming and Rose* problematizes the abusive relationship in a more ambivalent way, looking at the couple in their (metaphorical) context and suggesting what must be sacrificed to maintain a "fairy-tale" romance.

1993: KATE LUSHINGTON LEAVES, BUT THE ISSUES REMAIN

Two newspaper items from the early 1990s serve to illustrate that, at least in the minds of some journalists, Nightwood's mandate remained strangely obscure. In 1991, Nightwood's associate director, Lynda Hill, was interviewed by reporter Malcolm Kelly about an upcoming "Groundswell Festival" for the October issue of the *Annex Town Crier*. In a subsequent letter to the editor ("Festival is proud of the feminist label"[95]), Hill complained that the resulting article had downplayed the feminist mandate of Nightwood, and of "Groundswell." The article had even contained the line, "You can't say this is a feminist festival," which obviously reflected the reporter's preconceptions rather than Hill's.

In 1993, the production of *Charming and Rose: True Love* marked Kate Lushington's final directing project at Nightwood before she left the position of artistic director, feeling that it was time for her to move on and let new people run the company.[96] An article in *eye* magazine discussed both the production and

Lushington's resignation, but also signalled an ongoing confusion about Nightwood's identity as a collective.[97] The *eye* reviewer describes Lushington as directing a farewell show for "the feminist theatre collective she helped start five years ago." Of course, on one level this is merely incorrect reporting, as the reviewer mistakes the date when Lushington began working for the company with the date the company was founded. But the use of the term "feminist theatre collective" points to the fact that, even though Lushington had been consistently dissociating Nightwood from the collective label during those five years, it was still perceived as such by this theatre reviewer, and, quite possibly, by some of the theatregoing public.

Glazed Tempera
Kim Renders and Maureen White in *Glazed Tempera*.
*Photograph by Robert Caspari. From the personal collection
of Kim Renders.*

Kelly Thornton
Kelly Thornton at the Nightwood Office
in 2006.
Photograph by Shelley Scott.

China Doll
Marjorie Chan as Su-Ling in *China Doll*.
Photograph by John Lauener. Nightwood Theatre publicity.

Mathilde
Tom McCamus and Martha Burns in *Mathilde*.
Photograph by Guntar Kravis. Nightwood Theatre website.

Age of Arousal
Clare Coulter and Sarah Dodd in *Age of Arousal*.
Photograph by Guntar Kravis. Nightwood Theatre website.

Distillery District
The Distillery District in 2006.
Photograph by Shelley Scott.

The True Story of Ida Johnson
Maureen White as Ida in *The True Story of Ida Johnson*.
This photo became the poster image.
From the personal collection of Kim Renders.

Three
New Leadership Models, 1994–2000 and 2001–2009

1994: A NEW LEADERSHIP TEAM

Despite Kate Lushington's efforts, Nightwood continued to be thought of as a collectively run organization, perhaps because of the existence of the Artistic Advisory and the presence of artists on its board, and perhaps because it was perceived by some people as a "community theatre."[1] Because of its inclusive mandate and the wide variety of women working on projects at any one time, Nightwood was sometimes dismissed as a social service agency rather than a professional company. This perception may have been inadvertently reinforced when a leadership team of three women took over from Lushington in 1994, even though each had a title and separate responsibilities. Alisa Palmer and Diane Roberts were named as artistic co-directors, and Leslie Lester was named as producer.

The search committee had actively looked for a new management model, a way to spread the responsibility beyond just one artistic director. While the idea of a triumvirate was appealing and effective in terms of dividing the labour, practically speaking it necessitated a financial sacrifice, since the three women had to share two salaries.[2] Diane Roberts had worked with Lushington as an artistic associate and had a long history with Nightwood, so she provided continuity for Alisa Palmer and Leslie Lester in their new positions. Palmer and Lester, on the other hand, already had a close working relationship as co-artistic directors, along with Baṇuta Rubess, of another small company called Froth.

As part of a Montreal-based improvisational group, Hysterical Women, Palmer had participated in the 1987 "Groundswell," and it was there that she met Mary Vingoe and Ann-Marie MacDonald for the first time.[3] She went on to direct "Groundswell" shows during Kate Lushington's tenure, and to work as a movement coach on shows like *A Fertile Imagination* (1991) and *The Wonder of Man* (1992), where she met Diane Roberts. The eventual pairing of Roberts and Palmer two years later as artistic co-directors was mutually determined. As Palmer recalls:

> When this opening came up to run Nightwood, both of us had been approached to apply, and both of us had the same thought — that we wouldn't apply without the other one. And I had initially thought that she should be the AD and I would be an Associate, because she had been with the company already, but she was positive … she wanted to go into a co-directorship. It made sense at that time politically and artistically, because I'd had more independent directing experience and she had a lot more experience with the company. And then I introduced her to Leslie.[4]

Roberts stayed on as part of the trio until the spring of 1996, and when she left, the company reverted to a more traditional model, with Palmer as the sole artistic director. Lester continued as producer, and two other women, Soraya Peerbaye and Jay Pitter, worked as their associates.

Despite the initial team approach, however, Alisa Palmer did succeed in finally shaking the inaccurate collective label. Because she had been associated with companies other than Nightwood, and because she maintained a strong profile within the theatre community as an award-winning playwright, director, and actor, she was most successful in finally establishing Nightwood as a "legitimate" theatre company — one with an artistic vision, not just a political mandate. As Leslie Lester observes, "That's sort of the funny thing about a company. A company this small, anyway, does become very personal and [defined by] who you bring in with you and what artists you attract."[5] Diane Roberts acknowledges the importance of individuals, too, when she muses, "That's always been the thing of Nightwood, projects that have gone forward have been usually driven by an individual's, or a group of women's, passion."[6] The Palmer-Roberts-Lester term was notable for the number of panels, workshops, and co-productions they sponsored, and for their concentration on "Groundswell" as a venue for new play development, which spread Nightwood's presence far beyond the mainstage shows produced during their tenure. Further, the triumvirate hosted a number of high-energy fundraising parties, produced regular newsletters, and encouraged women to become supporting members and donors to Nightwood, thereby building a sense of celebration and community.

Other, practical changes influenced Nightwood's profile as well. Nightwood moved to a multi-use, industrial building at 317 Adelaide Street West in the fall of 1990, and this was the space that Palmer, Roberts, and Lester inherited. In addition to office space, Nightwood had its own rehearsal/performance studio; renting it out to other arts groups generated some income, and also made it a busy hub of activity and interaction. In the fall of 1999, Nightwood moved again, this time to 9 Saint Nicholas Street. The space was more attractive and comfortable, with hardwood floors and another large area for rehearsals and events, which gave the company a more genteel image. But with a buzz-in entry system and no elevator, the downside to the new space was less accessibility.

The board structure evolved, too, with the board of directors taking on administrative tasks and a separate Artistic Advisory in place, but with considerable overlap between the two groups. For example, for the 1996/97 season, the board of directors was Clare Barclay, Shirley Barrie, Dawn Carter, and Dawn Obakata, and Sierra Bacquie and Ann-Marie MacDonald served as co-chairs (rather than use the title "president," the board designated one or two women to serve as co-chairs). Dawn Obakata was also part of the Artistic Advisory; of the Advisory's remaining six members (Alex Bulmer, Marium Carvell, Jani Lauzon, ahdri zhina mandiela, Sheysali Saujam, and Sarah Stanley), three had been board members in previous years. It is illegal for a person to sit on the board of an organization if she is employed by or receives remuneration from that organization. The Artistic Advisory was created to accommodate this stipulation; advisors could be paid as artists and still offer their assistance to the board without actually being on it. The Advisory was eventually phased out in 2003. Nightwood also, at various points, hired associate artists and producers, a general manager, and some combination of business managers and administrators, as well as a variety of temporary personnel, interns, and apprentices employed through various project grants, summer employment programs, and the like. A rotating roster of women — board members, volunteers, and staff — bring their energy and ideas to the company, and in turn spread awareness of Nightwood out into their many respective communities.

1994: Adjustments to the mandate

When the new leadership team took over, they inherited a specific mandate statement: "Nightwood Theatre's mandate is to develop, promote and produce original, innovative works by Canadian women theatre artists creating alternative visions of the world from diverse cultural perspectives."[7] The statement goes on to list "values we consider important," which are:

- a commitment to anti-racism as a visible and significant priority in the interpretation of our mandate;
- a determination to increase the opportunities for women from all cultural communities to work in all aspects of the creative process;
- a commitment to paying all artists to affirm that women's work is of value;
- a commitment to new voices;
- a commitment to the long range development of women artists as well as to specific plays;

- a commitment to artistic self-determination (e.g., hands-off dramaturgy);
- a desire to mount more shows in production in addition to our workshop activities;
- an interest in the international feminist repertoire, and also new feminist interpretations of the classics, in addition to the mandate to develop and promote original Canadian work;
- a firm commitment to finding a theatre space for Nightwood Theatre which we will operate as a women-run, woman-centred focus point for our own work and the work of like-minded artists.

The statement concludes with the slogan: "Unique feminist theatre from diverse cultural perspectives." The emphasis is on involving women of colour and women from diverse cultural communities, within the ongoing context of new play development and the creation of job opportunities. The word "feminist" is used, but not prominently, and not at all in the actual mandate statement.

The new leadership team placed special importance on the "commitment to the long range development of women artists," manifested in the many workshops and even training courses offered by Nightwood over the following few years. In 1995, for example, "The Female Body" series ran parallel to the regular "Groundswell" process, offering weekend-long workshops on voice, movement, dance, and performance.[8] Producer Leslie Lester acknowledged that the desire to function as something of a resource centre for women artists runs as a kind of subtext to the mandate. She also confirmed that the ongoing practice of downplaying the word "feminism" was a conscious choice, motivated in part by the desire to be inclusive, and in part by the ambivalent and somewhat contradictory feelings about feminism among the women running the company.[9]

That ambivalence reflects what was happening in feminism as a movement in the 1990s, as it was challenged by women of colour, lesbians, working-class women, and other women seeking redress for their exclusion from what was perceived as a white, middle-class women's movement. As feminism struggled to come to grips with the force of this critique, and as the structures of "institutions" like Nightwood opened up to women who had been on the outside, the terms and philosophy of feminism had to be treated cautiously; a redefinition was taking place. Part of the problem was that fewer women, especially younger ones, were calling themselves feminists. While the current resurgence of feminism in the Third Wave has allowed for a younger, hipper image, back in the mid-1990s, it was unfortunately more common to hear talk of a post-feminist consciousness.

Erica Sessle interviewed Alisa Palmer and Diane Roberts in 1995 for a university student newspaper called *The Varsity*, introducing them as Nightwood's new artistic co-directors. In the interview, Palmer explicitly addresses the complexity of their historical moment for defining feminist theatre:

> Women have disagreement as to what feminism is, what power for women is, and what equality for women is. But for these disagreements to be stifled in an attempt to present a unified feminist front is dangerous. Discourse must happen and should be encouraged. And that encouragement is the most radical thing that a woman's theatre company can do.

She goes on to admit that the word feminist is "no longer satisfying, because feminist is not a clear enough word."[10]

Sessle compliments Nightwood for being able to preserve aspects of its original mandate and still evolve within the theatre community. In response, Palmer observes, "There was a very clear need for Nightwood to have a clear political mandate 15 years ago. But things are different now and it is necessary to have a clear set of artist demands." She believes that the three women of the team at that time fit into the model of the four founders in being

> a collaborative group of women who are each interested in different areas of innovation. We have, of course, issues

in common, such as the direction of the future of Night-wood as a theatrical resource centre for women artists. But 15 years after the start of Nightwood, the context of the theatre scene in Toronto is different. Now there are a lot more women artists as recognized artistic directors and playwrights. But it is largely white women who have garnered this recognition. It's a different story for women of colour.

Palmer emphasizes that Nightwood provides a space for women of different ages and cultural and artistic backgrounds to come together and find support to do their work the way they want to, even if it is not explicitly feminist work.

Yet elsewhere — in the Nightwood newsletter, for example — the word "feminist" is used with pride and enthusiasm. In the first newsletter published after Palmer, Roberts, and Lester took over in 1994, they included a joint statement to outline their concep-tion of how Nightwood functions:

> We're enthusiastic to take up the challenge of maintain-ing Nightwood's dual role as a leading producer of femi-nist art and as an important resource for women artists ... Nightwood Theatre has provided a forum for women to explore the complexity of our relationships to each other, to society and consequently to history. Its identity today is a culmination of accident, serendipity and will-ful efforts to have a say in the development of women's culture. We are intrigued by the challenge of seeing the whole pattern, Nightwood's past, present and future, in order to support the contribution that each individual constituent, each artist or script or decision, can make to the whole.[11]

The mainstage shows produced over the next six years clearly aimed to publicly promote Nightwood's mandate as its leaders saw it. The mainstream acclaim and appeal of plays such as Djanet

Sears's *Harlem Duet* (1997) and Ann-Marie MacDonald's musical *Anything That Moves* (2000) provided a high-profile contrast to the more grassroots development work of projects like "Groundswell" and "The Female Body" series.

1995: TEN YEARS OF "GROUNDSWELL"

To mark the tenth anniversary of "Groundswell" in March of 1995 (and perhaps to receive some guidance in their roles as artistic co-directors), Diane Roberts and Alisa Palmer organized and hosted a panel presentation at the Theatre Centre called "Art in Your Face: what is women's theatre development and what should it be?" The playwright Sally Han moderated, and the panellists, all theatre practitioners, were Diana Leblanc, Sandra Laronde, ahdri zhina mandiela, Baṇuta Rubess, Judith Thompson, and Jean Yoon. Alison Sealy-Smith and Kim Renders also participated by performing short readings that panellists had selected for them.

At the panel discussion, the playwright Jean Yoon asked the pertinent question, "How do we, within a developmental process, accommodate the fact that we are living in a multilingual culture, where I can walk down the street and hear twenty different languages?"[12] ahdri zhina mandiela commented that much work had already been done in small, specific communities, but wondered, "in defining our collective experience, how do we begin to cross these borders, invisible as they may be sometimes? How do we begin to not just be community pockets of women artists producing out there... black women, aboriginal women, white women, etc ... How do we begin to amalgamate our processes into ... our collective process?"[13] These were the questions that Palmer, Roberts, and Lester continued to grapple with throughout their terms. The process of inclusion that marked Lushington's years at Nightwood became an even bigger cultural issue, as the city of Toronto grew and became increasingly multicultural; as feminism changed and lost its currency in the mainstream; and as the voices of performers spoke from ever more situated and diverse perspectives.

Shelley Scott • Nightwood Theatre

1997: HARLEM DUET

One productive aspect of multiculturalism is increased international cross-fertilization. As an example, one of the most outstanding and influential plays to appear in the United States is Ntozake Shange's *for colored girls who have considered suicide/ when the rainbow is enuf* (1975), which has in turn inspired many other theatre pieces, including Diane Roberts's *The Coloured Girls Project* at Nightwood in 1995. Another example in the same Black, North American, cross-border context is the play *Harlem Duet*. In 1995 and '96, Djanet Sears was in residency as an international playwright at the New York Shakespeare Festival, working on what was then called *The Madwoman and the Fool*, which would later become *Harlem Duet*. Her work in progress received a public reading and workshop at the Joseph Papp Public Theater. Nightwood then presented *Harlem Duet*, directed by Sears, at the Tarragon Extra Space in Toronto in May of 1997.[14] *Harlem Duet* won four Dora Mavor Moore Awards—for best production, direction, outstanding new play, and female performance (by Alison Sealy-Smith) — and was remounted at the Canadian Stage Company's Berkeley Street stage that fall. So despite the fact that *Harlem Duet* takes as its basis Shakespeare's *Othello*, is set in Harlem (at the corner of Malcolm X and Martin Luther King boulevards), features African-American characters, and draws from time periods in American history, it was received as a brilliant Canadian play and won the Governor General's Award, Canada's highest honour. In 2006, the prestigious Stratford Festival generated a second production of *Harlem Duet*—another exceptional achievement in the context of feminist (and, in this case, Black feminist) theatre. Obviously, plays — and these plays in particular — do speak across borders.

New voices were not only coming from diverse racial perspectives. At the turn of the millennium, Alisa Palmer encouraged and directed *Smudge,* another important play that came from yet another fresh direction: it addressed inclusion based not on gender, race, language, or ethnicity, but on disability.

Smudge began as a series of poems written by Alex Bulmer, a writer, actor, and teacher residing in Toronto. Bulmer had a solid history with Nightwood, beginning with her term on the Artistic Advisory from 1995 to 1999. She had input into Diane Flacks's one-woman show *Random Acts* in 1997, performed at the March 1999 "FemCab," and worked as apprentice producer with Leslie Lester in 2000. After *Smudge*, Bulmer went on to participate in events including Nightwood's 2002 International Women's Day panel, "The Hourglass Symposium: A Roundtable."[15]

When she began losing her vision as a result of a degenerative eye condition (recessive retinitis pigmentosa inversa), Bulmer chose to document the process in poetry, because, as she explained, "I needed the words to keep going. The sounds, the images, the heightened emotions and the absurdity of each day felt like a surreal epic comedy about falling down."[16] The poems eventually became a play, workshopped at "Groundswell" in 1997 and 2000, and also at a 1998 Buddies in Bad Times festival called "Under the Gun." In association with Bulmer's own company, S.N.I.F.F. Inc., Nightwood produced her play from 18 November to 10 December 2000 at the Tarragon Extra Space. It was directed by Alisa Palmer, and the cast was made up of Diane Flacks as Freddie; Kate Lynch as her girlfriend, Katherine; and Sherry Lee Hunter as Blindness and a number of other characters. The program states that the story was "developed and edited" with Flacks, Lynch, and Palmer. It was the penultimate show for Palmer and Leslie Lester before they left their positions with Nightwood.

In the course of the hour-long play, Bulmer's alter ego, Freddie, interacts with doctors, nurses, technicians, and therapists, but also with various people on the street who represent the many strange ways she is treated as an increasingly blind person. For example, in Scene Thirteen, entitled "Denise's Cane Lesson," Freddie moves through the world practicing her technique in using a white cane. She accidentally bumps into a character called Heroin Girl, who, once she realizes Freddie is blind, feels so sorry for speaking harshly to her that she makes Freddie take her cigarettes. Other people she passes give her descriptions of her surroundings or offer assistance that she does not require. The scene culminates with an elderly man on a streetcar who tells her, "Can't think of anything worse than what you got." Freddie, always quick with a witty retort, responds, "Well, maybe you're not thinking hard enough. There's death."[17]

At the same time that Freddie is dealing with the loss of her sight, the play is also about her developing relationship with her new lover, Katherine. From their first meeting in a café, their relationship is inexorably shaped by Freddie's disability. The two women meet because Freddie has a big smile on her face, pleased that she has managed to find a chair and sit down without mishap in the busy café. She does not realize that she is smiling at and staring into the eyes of a stranger, but Katherine takes these as signs of interest and introduces herself. In a subsequent scene, Katherine and Freddie watch a movie together, and as Katherine describes the sex taking place on screen, her erotic narration sparks the next step in their mutual attraction.

There are scenes in which Katherine tries to persuade Freddie to use her cane more consistently when she goes out, and another scene in which Katherine becomes more resigned as Freddie stubbornly refuses to make accommodations for her degenerating ability to manage the world. Katherine tries to comfort Freddie after a particularly awful incident in which she is harassed by a man in the street. But ultimately, there is a scene of confrontation, as Freddie tries to put some distance between them and cannot see Katherine's tears to gauge her response. The play ends on a poignant and somewhat uncertain note, as Freddie first tries to hide from her blindness, and then imagines a future in which she descends into madness, another form of disability. Finally, she is able to say goodbye to her sight.

Nominated for a Chalmers Award and three Doras, *Smudge* was published in *Canadian Theatre Review*.[18] It toured to Halifax in September of 2001, and then to Vancouver the following spring. The play received mostly excellent reviews. Entitling his assessment "Smudge has Clarity,"[19] the influential *NOW* reviewer

Jon Kaplan characterizes the play as episodic. Kaplan explains that the sound, set, and lighting for *Smudge* gave the audience a sense of Freddie's fragmented world; describing it as an "almost surrealistic setting," he writes that at times, "characters are indistinct behind a hazy backdrop." In her review, "Lifting the blind," Elisa Kukla reports:

> Bulmer chose Nightwood Theatre as the appropriate place to produce *Smudge* because the feminist company is committed to giving more than just lip service to the artistic value of diversity. The playwright was not interested in a moralistic or didactic mounting of her script. Bulmer's goal, rather, is to incorporate diversity into the artistic process as opposed to simply showcasing it ... When someone's difference is a given instead of the subject matter of a play, their identity becomes normalized.[20]

Kukla makes an excellent point, in that not only Freddie's disability, but also her lesbianism is taken as an integral aspect of her experience. The play may be said to display a materialist feminism in the way it highlights the differences between women's experiences. For Freddie, her blindness is as much a part of her identity as her gender and sexuality—each are the "givens" of how she must deal with the world.

Alex Bulmer could usefully be defined as part of the growing international movement of activist, disabled artists. According to Kelly Thornton, there has been interest in *Smudge* from arts and disability groups in other countries, such as England and Australia. But as Kukla points out, Bulmer's play also fits in with Nightwood's commitment to facilitating diverse women's voices. *Smudge* is a great example of the complicated intersection of identities and identifications—disabled, lesbian, artist, feminist, and much more—that are relevant to that mandate.

2001: CURRENT MANAGEMENT

Artistic director Kelly Thornton took over at Nightwood in 2001, along with Nathalie Bonjour as the new producer. Bonjour left her position in October of 2005, and Monica Esteves became the artistic producer in 2006. (In 2007, Thornton took a year of maternity leave, and was temporarily replaced by Maja Ardal as the interim artistic director).

As is common for new artistic directors, Thornton took over a 2001 season already in place, dominated by an ambitious production of Djanet Sears's play *The Adventures of a Black Girl in Search of God* at the duMaurier Theatre at Harbourfront—a production with a cast of twenty-one and a quarter-million-dollar budget. It was a risky venture, but one that paid off with packed houses and six Dora nominations. Thornton's own first contribution was to initiate a strategic planning phase by employing a fundraising consultant and a board-restructuring consultant, and to build a three-year plan.

Thornton's tenure since 2001 has been marked by a number of such bold strategic moves, designed to position Nightwood not as an alternative or marginal company, but as Canada's "national women's theatre." One of the most important of these manoeuvres was, literally, a move—in March of 2003, Nightwood transferred to its current location and, for the first time since leaving the Theatre Centre, is once again situated within a specifically cultural space. The Case Goods Building is part of Toronto's new Distillery District, an enclave of beautifully renovated historical buildings that has been conceived as a dynamic, upscale cultural destination, made up of theatres and other performance spaces, a college, art galleries, boutiques, and restaurants.

A letter sent to members on 20 September 2002, asking for membership renewal, made the big announcement:

> This year the leadership went into a period of Strategic Planning. In these sessions we created a 3-year Business Plan, revitalized the Board of Directors and initiated a Development Plan which strengthens our foundation, corporate and private sector support. We are also pleased to announce that we've secured a new home with Artscape in

the arts complex on the heritage site of Gooderham and Worts Distillery; we will move in February.

The Case Goods Building is run by Artscape and houses a number of other theatre organizations, including Tapestry New Opera Works; the two neighbouring companies share the Tapestry/Nightwood New Work Studio. The Distillery District is also the site of the new Young Centre for the Performing Arts, where Nightwood has begun producing some of its mainstage plays.

In the summer of 2005, Nightwood made a further announcement: that it had been "accepted to Creative Trust, a unique program that supports and strengthens Toronto's mid-size music, dance and theatre companies by assisting them in achieving organizational and financial balance, and acquiring and maintaining a fund of Working Capital." Nightwood was able to declare itself "in a debt free position."

2002–2003: FINDING REGINA

Finding Regina, by Shoshana Sperling, signals an openness of another kind for Nightwood: its willingness to produce a play in a Canadian city other than Toronto when the subject matter clearly calls for such an alliance. The play began as *The Regina Monologues* at Buddies in Bad Times' "Rhubarb! Festival" in 2001, and was then produced with the title *Finding Regina* by the Globe Theatre in Regina, Saskatchewan, in association with Nightwood and Theatre Passe Muraille. It premiered at the Globe on 8 October 2002, directed by Kelly Thornton, and then went on to a run at Passe Muraille in early 2003.[21]

The cast featured Sperling herself as Annabel, with Jeremy Harris as Josh and Teresa Pavlinek as Rae. Sperling is better known as a stand-up comedian than as a playwright, often performing character-based comedy at Toronto venues like "Fem-Cab" and on television.[22] Sperling describes *Finding Regina* as a love letter to her hometown: "this play is really an homage to Regina because I have this love for the place that I just can't quite shake."[23] In fact, the published play is prefaced with a list of acknowledgements written in the form of a letter to Regina, which begins, "I miss you so much when I'm away from you." Further along, she writes, "This play is for me and also those still finding Regina way out in Toronto, Vancouver, Calgary, Montreal."[24] Sperling has received many comments that "the play could be set anywhere in Canada as it is such an honest depiction of going home."[25] As Sperling implies, to find one's Regina is a metaphor, meaning to reconnect with where you come from and who you are, and therefore suggests the intersection of geography with gender in the construction of feminist identity.[26]

The play focuses on the fortunes of a generation that grew up together in Regina, and the disproportionate number of them who have committed suicide. High school pals Annabel, Rae, and Josh have gathered at the hospital in Regina to wait for news about their friend Clarky, who has attempted to kill himself. Through conversation and confrontation, many of the negative aspects of their high school experience are unearthed: Clarky was afraid to reveal his homosexuality; racism against the Aboriginal population is addressed; and the spectre of substance abuse and suicide comes up repeatedly. The three characters have a love-hate relationship with their hometown, blaming it for their distress, yet at the same time intensely aware of how it has shaped their identity and sense of belonging. Josh, in particular, plays the role of unofficial historian, recounting the stories of the marginalized and keeping his strong sense of community alive.

The situation does not immediately read as explicitly feminist, yet feminist concerns — particularly those of the Third Wave — underline all the themes of the play and culminate in the relationship between the two female characters. Annabel, played by Sperling, has moved to Toronto and is doing a master's degree in women's studies, "with a specialization in concepts of male and female archetypes in Western Civilization." This allows Annabel to deliver a lecture on how classics written by women have been "misinterpreted by patriarchal society."[27] She tries to explain her thesis, but the other characters are unable to follow her argument, which is dense with academic jargon, especially after they share a joint or two in Josh's car. Thus, Annabel's feminism is positioned as something that is vital to her new life in Toronto, but irrelevant once she comes back home to Regina.

The character of Rae, a pretty and popular girl in high school, has moved to Vancouver and become a wife and mother. She is now thirty and, like Annabel, she has been back to Regina a few times — often for the funerals of friends — but this is the first time in ten years that all three have been together. Rae is a proponent of self-help books to explain her troubled marriage, but Annabel cynically rejects such popular theorizing. Annabel declares, "It's all about looks. We're conditioned to believe that if we find a mate with ideal physical beauty, then we'll fall in love."[28] She argues that marriages based on looks alone will end up being empty and devoid of intimacy, concluding, "Most people who grow up being splendidly beautiful might find themselves in a relationship that might be splendidly empty."[29]

Annabel is obviously referring to Rae, and the roots of her hostility become apparent when Josh inadvertently admits that he does not remember having had sex with Annabel in high school. This prompts an angry Annabel to reveal that she was in fact very promiscuous throughout high school, "but not looking as girls should look, it was kept a secret. Boys tell their adventures. Unless they're embarrassed."[30] Unlike popular and sought-after girls like Rae, whom Annabel describes as "tall, thin and perfect," Annabel never had a "public" boyfriend, but she did have sex with many guys in secret simply because she made herself available. She explains: "Girls wanted to have sex but they were so worried for their reputations. I never worried about any of that because … No one ever told. They just came back for more. I practised this behaviour into my university years until I finally moved out of Regina."[31] By the end of the play, Rae and Annabel have managed to tentatively mend their friendship and admit how much they have missed each other, but societal ideals of beauty have clearly taken their toll on both women's lives and identities. The intensity of their high school friendship is treated seriously, as is the female competition that ultimately drove them apart. The focus on a complex and unequal relationship, and on the differences between women, marks the play as post-modern and Third Wave in its feminism.

2004: CHINA DOLL

Just as *Finding Regina* was inspired by, and produced in, Saskatchewan, *China Doll* is another example of an increasingly national outlook at Nightwood. Marjorie Chan's play was developed in a three-week intensive workshop at the Banff Centre for the Performing Arts in Alberta in the spring of 2003. In addition to its ongoing development with "Groundswell" (since 2002), *China Doll* had originally been commissioned as a CBC radio play before attaining a stage commission from Nightwood. After the Banff residency, Kelly Thornton directed a full production in 2004 at the Tarragon Extra Space, featuring Chan as the lead character, and with a cast made up of Jo Chim, Keira Loughran, and John Ng. The Toronto production was nominated for three Dora Awards in the General Theatre category, for outstanding costume design (Joanne Dente), production, and new play. It was also nominated for the 2005 Governor General's Literary Award. Nightwood's involvement with *China Doll* was prescient, as it cultivated artists from, and awareness in, the burgeoning Asian theatre community. On 8 March 2004, Nightwood presented an International Women's Day panel discussion called "First Steps: Chinese Canadian Women Leaving Their Mark."[32]

Set in 1918 in Shanghai, *China Doll* follows a young woman named Su-Ling as her grandmother attempts to find her a husband. Because her parents died in dishonourable ways, Su-Ling has few prospects. One of her only redeeming qualities is the extreme smallness of her bound feet. Marjorie Chan has explained that her play was inspired by a museum exhibit of the tiny "lotus" shoes worn by women in traditional Chinese culture, and there is much emphasis in the play on the work involved in binding, caring for, and adorning these symbols of female erotic beauty and oppression.

Another character, Merchant Li, teaches Su-Ling to read and gives her a copy of Henrik Ibsen's play *A Doll House*, which eventually inspires her to unbind her feet and walk away from the house of her fiancé. Like Nora in *A Doll House*, Su-Ling chooses to reject her fate as a woman in a patriarchal house; this direct analogy would seem to indicate a cultural feminist equivalency in women's oppression across historical periods, racial differences, and national boundaries. However, appearing ten years after *Charming and Rose*, *China Doll* presents a similarly complex intersection of cultural and materialist elements. The playwright is careful to focus on specific historical details of Su-Ling's situation—the political changes sweeping through China, the intricacies of foot binding, and the tensions between women of different classes and generations—allowing materialist elements to complicate its feminism.

Rather than mere exotica, the material specifics of Chinese culture inform the way the play makes meaning for its audience through visual layering in production. Rather than a straightforward, naturalistic telling of Su-Ling's dilemma, the play employs many theatrical effects to communicate her world. For example, there are magical stage effects, as when a carp and an orange appear when she wishes for them, or when letters and drawings are projected across the set. Her rebellion against sewing her confining shoes takes on physical reality: the script states, "A tantrum of fabric flies across the stage."[33] Most poignantly, Su-Ling's wedding dress is suspended in a manner reminiscent of her mother's suicide by hanging.[34] Cleverly, Chan finds many tools to evoke the ways that generations of women are diminished by a patriarchal society, but also the ways they find to remember and support each other.

2005: RAISING THE CELEBRITY FACTOR

Kelly Thornton has used some of Nightwood's traditions in strategic new ways. For example, the "Five Minute Feminist Cabaret" was not held in 2004, but the following year it was relaunched as a major gala fundraising event to celebrate Nightwood's twenty-fifth anniversary. The American feminist icon Gloria Steinem was invited as the guest of honour. Similarly, in 2007, Michele

Landsberg, a board member and influential feminist newspaper columnist, along with her husband, Stephen Lewis, a respected politician and activist, sponsored "FemCab." The guest speaker was Carol Off, host of the popular CBC radio program *As It Happens*. In 2008, the special guest was Eve Ensler, the celebrated creator of *The Vagina Monologues*. Thus, "FemCab" has become a new kind of event for Nightwood: entertainment from the theatre community combined with a famous feminist name to attract media attention and make money.

Thornton has done a good job of consistently emphasizing Nightwood's critical and artistic successes and working to solidify its legitimacy at a national level, to garner the company the respect and recognition it deserves. She comments, "The mandate obviously is political. It's a really strong mandate and it allows you to be very fierce and clear in your programming, but the business is theatre, and all the money that comes into this company from all the governments, that's to make theatre, and it's not about social programs. I want to bring more money into the company so I can produce more women, that's the bottom line."[35]

In 2006, Nightwood produced a sophisticated marketing brochure with a timeline of past productions and a statement regarding the structure of the season. Entitled "Delivering on our mandate," the statement is worth quoting in full to give a clear sense of where the company's priorities are placed today:

1. Mainstage productions — We produce a minimum of two Mainstage Productions each year (including premieres, touring and presenting).
2. Play development — We produce the annual Groundswell Festival of New Works by Women, for plays in development from our playwright's unit. We also commission playwrights and offer residency programs.
3. Mentorship and Youth — Our youth initiatives include Write From the Hip, for novice playwrights; the Emerging Actor's Program, training recent graduates in play development; and Busting Out!, our theatre training

program for teen girls. Each year we also support numerous young women, through mentorships in direction, dramaturgy, design, and producing.[36]

4. Special Events and Initiatives —
· On International Women's Day we celebrate with Fem-Cab: the Five-Minute Feminist Cabaret.
· We host Panel Discussions bringing communities together for lively debate inspired by our play productions.
· We are spearheading a national campaign, *Equity in Canadian Theatre: The Women's Initiative,* examining the present status of women in theatre (in partnership with the Playwright's Guild of Canada Women's Caucus and the Professional Association of Canadian Theatres).

Our Mission: Developing and producing essential theatre by women.
Nightwood Theatre forges creative alliances among women artists from diverse backgrounds to develop and produce innovative Canadian theatre. We produce original Canadian plays and works from the contemporary international repertoire. We advocate for women, provide a training ground for emerging talent, promote diversity and engage artists in play development and theatre production.

Our Vision: Putting women centre stage.
Nightwood's overriding vision is to work towards a society free of discrimination and to cultivate a Canadian theatre ecology that recognizes and celebrates the excellence of its female practitioners.

Our Values: Using theatre as a tool of empowerment.
· Nightwood Theatre promotes artistic innovation and diversity of expression.
· We operate with a firm belief in women's equality and use theatre to challenge stereotypes and social assumptions about gender, race and sexuality.

- We believe theatre is a communal experience wherein differences can be shared and celebrated.
- We are driven by creative exchange not exclusivity.
- We see mentorship as essential, sharing knowledge with emerging talent, and seeding a new generation of female artists in Canada.
- We think theatre should be entertaining but also believe in its ability to challenge society.
- At the very core, we believe theatre is a tool of empowerment, both for the individual and for the collective as a whole.

This is a fascinating document for what it says and does not say. On one hand, the word "feminist" is not used (although it is used in many other company statements), but at the same time, the document clearly and adamantly outlines a feminist vision of the world. In fact, it can be read as a culmination of all the previous mandate statements, incorporating new play development, new artist development and mentorship, commitment to diversity, political advocacy, Canadian culture, and theatre's place in the international feminist movement.

2006: CAST IRON

One thing that has remained consistent at Nightwood is the opportunity for individual movement and growth within the company's framework. *Cast Iron* by Lisa Codrington, a finalist for the 2006 Governor General's Award, provides a pertinent example of how a play (and people) may develop within various contexts and programs. *Cast Iron* grew out of Write from the Hip and was workshopped at both the 2002 and 2003 "Groundswell Festivals."[37] It received a full production in the spring of 2005, produced in association with Obsidian Theatre, directed by ahdri zhina mandiela and starring Alison Sealy-Smith, and went on tour to Barbados that fall. Not only does this example demonstrate how plays continue to flower at Nightwood, but it also illustrates the long-term commitment artists have made to the company. ahdri zhina mandiela directed, and Alison Sealy-Smith acted in, a play called *One Bedroom With Dignity*, written by Lillian Allen and produced at the 1987 "Groundswell Festival." Since that initial involvement, the two women have been involved with Nightwood in a multitude of capacities. For example, mandiela's own play, *dark diaspora... in DUB*, first appeared at the 1990 "Groundswell," and Alison Sealy-Smith has acted in and directed many Nightwood shows, including *The Wonder of Man* and *Martha and Elvira* by Diana Braithwaite, both presented as part of *The Wonder Quartet* in 1992. They each founded their own companies—mandiela's b current and Sealy-Smith's Obsidian—, which have done co-productions with Nightwood. As for Lisa Codrington, the creator of *Cast Iron*, she has become the current coordinator of Write From the Hip—another instance of artists nurturing the next generation of artists in turn.

2006: PRODUCING FEMINIST THEATRE — MONICA ESTEVES

In a 2006 interview,[38] producer Monica Esteves detailed some of the recent funding challenges Nightwood faced. Its high-profile production of *Mathilde* garnered rave critical reviews but did not reach its box-office target. Furthermore, at that time, the company was in the process of restructuring the board of directors and staff. On the upside, Esteves was pleased with the new website and other new marketing initiatives, but she expresses concern about broadening Nightwood's audience base:

> The organization has a limited amount of programming, one–two mainstage productions per year. An arts organization needs a sufficient amount of programming in order for the public to understand the breadth of work, to stay in their memory annually, and to build a kind of relationship that is meaningful—meaningful enough for them to return and support us, either as audience members, financial supports or ideally as both. It's challenging. We need to diversify our revenue base in order to move toward increased programming. For next season, we're launching season passes (subscriptions, essentially), so you buy the

tickets in series. We're going to publish season brochures, even with only one to two productions per year, so our patrons feel part of something bigger, rather than a one-off show. So they can see the scope of the company's activities, new this year is Future Femme Fridays, so that they can see the breadth of the work that we're doing and things that we have in development and "Groundswell." We need our patrons to be return patrons, to create a more reliable earned revenue base. We need them to have a relationship to all aspects of the company, not solely when they incidentally see a little ad, because that's not relationship building. Also in the mix: we're nomadic. Sometimes you want to bang your head (or their heads) against a wall when patrons continually identify our productions to the theatre venue, i.e. "it must be a Tarragon show because it's at the Tarragon theatre."

As a producer, Esteves's main concern is funding, and the first level of that support comes from the ticket-buying public:

Our first objective is to have our audience connect to Nightwood via the art. Without that, additional appeals for donations and other support are extremely difficult. Nightwood has tons of potential to significantly increase our earned revenue (box office) base. From there, we would be better positioned to increase our private sector revenue. At this time, only 11.7 percent of our annual revenues come through the box office and sales. Public sector funding is competitive and underfunded. The [arts] councils certainly won't increase our base operational funding unless our activity is also going up. At this time, Nightwood is 53 percent funded by the public sector. We need to lower this percentage, perhaps to 30–35 percent. We're ready to grow...there will be growing pains, but I think we set up a really good plan for ourselves for the next five years. It's a strong blueprint or map with many checkpoints: this is where we need to be by here, the size of our board, what kind of women are on it, our supporters, what's on our mainstage, what's in development. But all growth requires some managed risk.

Esteves's comments reflect the ongoing influence of arts councils and funding organizations, when she remarks, for example, on the requirements by the Ontario Arts Council that boards be made up of percentages representing certain sectors: artists and fundraisers.

According to Esteves, the budget for Nightwood has floated between $400,000 and $500,000 for the last few years, depending on the level of activity and production. For 2007, it was estimated to be at almost $600,000.[39] But only about $170,000 of that comes from funding sources, including foundations and the three levels of government arts councils. The remainder must be raised by Nightwood—a daunting prospect even for an experienced and energetic producer like Esteves. She relies on the success of certain high-profile shows to raise awareness of Nightwood among theatregoers and patrons. Frustratingly, that challenge has less to do with the specifically feminist mandate of Nightwood's shows, and more to do with theatregoing trends in Toronto in general; according to Esteves, when people are regularly going out to see theatre, they see all types, but when the trend falls off, the mid-sized and smaller companies suffer the most.

2006: AN INTERVIEW WITH KELLY THORNTON

Kelly Thornton has taken on a unique challenge in piloting Nightwood into the twenty-first century. The following is an interview from 2006, conducted prior to her maternity leave, and represents a bold vision of where the company is headed.

Was the move to this new location as smooth as you had hoped?

KT: Well, it's fantastic to be in this building. Certainly we felt very isolated over at 9 Saint Nicholas, six flights up. Plays like *The*

Adventures of a Black Girl in Search of God couldn't even rehearse there because it was so inaccessible and you couldn't get seventy-year-olds climbing six flights without an elevator. The [Distillery] District took about a year to wake up in terms of getting people down here, but it's been great to have our studio and our offices in an arts district, working with other arts organizations in the Case Goods Building. And the plan has always been to bring the work home to the Young Centre for the Performing Arts so that our office and performance venues are together in the same district... But ultimately I think where Monica [Esteves] and I are going, is to start talking about the possibility of actually having our own venue.

Somewhere in the Distillery District?

KT: I'll give you my big dream. When I took over I had a dream of starting a national women's cultural centre. It would have like-minded organizations, like Women in Film and Television, Toronto Women's Bookstore, female-driven recording studios, a national gallery, the gamut of women in culture. Because in every discipline we're under-represented. Monica Esteves, our new producer, was stage managing "Groundswell" during my first week at Nightwood and I told her about this little dream, and she was a very feisty stage manager at that point, and she said "Let me at it, I'll help you do that. That would be great, let's do it!" And, you know, five years later that whole dream has been reignited, and she's making a lot of headway into trying to cultivate those philanthropic relationships so that we can actually start a capital campaign.

Is part of the motivation to network, and to build Nightwood's profile?

KT: I really feel like it would be an opportunity to cross-pollinate audiences, share with people that are interested in women's stories, as I think we all have kind of existed on our own islands. It kills me, after twenty-six years, people don't know, so many women say, "Oh, I've never heard of Nightwood." Or, "I thought that was a Tarragon show." Since I started in 2001, I remember talking to the board of directors that were hiring me and saying, we just need to take up more space, we need to really put it out there. I think we've had a huge impact over the years on women's careers, and yet we aren't getting the bang for our buck in terms of our profile.

Has any of this been related to the Women's Initiative that you've been involved with, along with Hope McIntyre and the Playwright's Guild?

KT: They're not completely connected, but that's an important initiative and I was one of the people that spearheaded it. Hope [McIntyre] and I really took it on and started the national committee and the report is coming out. The numbers are now more concrete, statistically proven. I always felt like Nightwood's mandate is, in part, to develop and produce Canadian artists' work, but I also feel like we should be advocates for the status of women in Canadian theatre, that we have a bigger mandate than some [other] theatre companies. Bob Crew from *The Toronto Star* [newspaper] asked me in one of my first interviews for Nightwood, "What's the point of a feminist theatre company in the twenty-first century?" And I said, "That's right Bob, it's a done deal. Boy, this liberation's been fantastic for all of us!" It's a façade of equality that people read as part of a whole post-feminist era. They think it's passé, not something we should be focused on.

Have you been having face-to-face meetings with the national committee for the Women's Initiative?

KT: Because they're from all over Canada, we engage in a variety of things. We do a lot of email. That's generally how we communicate. And Hope is really the engine behind keeping the national committee together and organized. With the survey, for instance, the committee was trying to lobby people in their regions to make sure that the surveys were filled out. You know, Rina [Fraticelli's] numbers came out and it changed for a time and then everybody fell back to sleep and nothing really changed.

You know, they changed by five percent, small increments of success. But what we are trying to do with so little funding — we have literally carried it on our backs, Hope and Rebecca [Burton] and I — is to now try and put into place an action plan so that there are specific actions that we can take instead of just ranting about the inequity. We have to look at the trends and what they mean and how can Canadian artistic directors take it on and not let this issue fall asleep. A lot of it has to do with mentorship and getting women into training positions in those theatres and giving them opportunity in the theatres where they haven't previously enjoyed opportunity. You'll see that there's different regions that the women's profile is higher, but often it still is rooted in companies that have women artistic directors, that were founded by the female artistic directors. The numbers show: the richer the theatre, the less women there are. Where there's more money, for instance in the big regionals, there's not as much presence. And it's got to change in a way that our male peers don't feel like they're under attack and they don't spend all their energy being defensive, and they actually engage in the process of changing the landscape. I'm just saying, look at these numbers, and look at last year's numbers. People know that they have to wake up and recognize the rest of Canada's population. I think we have to start talking to the granting bodies about discussing gender as an issue, because it IS an issue and these numbers can now prove our point.

What have you determined through your strategic planning process?

KT: We were strategic planning the year of the second ["Hysteria"] festival, and we were looking at our centers of activity and suddenly realized that "Hysteria" didn't quite fit. What we determined was that, given our resources, our two main centres are play development/production, and youth initiatives. The youth initiatives actually feed into play development because many of the graduates from the youth programs move into "Groundswell." That's generally the idea, to develop young artists so they can enter the professional field. Ultimately, if I have more resources, I'm going to grow the company, I would prefer to produce more plays.

What is the mandate now of "Groundswell"?

KT: I made it into a playwrights' unit, so it's six plays in development yearly. They sit in a playwrights' unit from January to August and we give them very clear attention dramaturgically for those six months and then we hold a festival of play readings. And they're music-stand play readings. Unless they're a collective creation and then we do it differently. Generally, each playwright produces at least two or three drafts. I accept scripts at different levels of development, but if it's a full-length play, you want an intensive dramaturgical relationship for eight months. So, that is about going through the process of page to stage. The playwrights get a thousand dollars each.

Speaking of moving from Write From the Hip to "Groundswell" to doing a production, can you talk about Cast Iron? That seems like a really good example.

KT: Lisa Codrington was still a student at Ryerson going to theatre school, and when we outreached for Write From the Hip, we outreached to all the schools as well. And so Lisa submitted and she got in, and she was developing this piece, I think she started it as a monologue exercise for theatre school. She performed it herself in the "Fringe Festival." So basically what had happened is, she developed it in "Hip." And Lisa Silverman, who started Write From the Hip, said, "This writer's incredible...!" ahdri zhina mandiela directed the "Hip" play, which was a fifteen-minute excerpt, but Lisa continued to develop it and then produced it in the "Fringe Festival," acting in it. And then she submitted it to "Groundswell" and I immediately programmed her in "Groundswell" because I thought it was pretty powerful. During the development in "Groundswell," at one point she started talking about mak[ing] it a multi-character play. She was going to go forward, but then she kind of hit the wall when she started writing; she said, "I really think it's Libya's story in the nursing home." And then, as we got closer to "Groundswell," we started talking about the authenticity of the character. Lisa's only in her early twenties and maybe the weight of having an older actor play that role might be good. So we thought about a variety of different actors, and came upon Alison Sealy-Smith, who's Bajan-Canadian. That was fantastic, and we decided to cast her in "Groundswell," and the audience was in awe. She sat in a chair with a music stand to her right and went into multiple characters just by the twist of her body. She did a brilliant job and people loved it. Strangely enough, after several public workshops, where nobody ever said a word about dialect issues, some of the reviews for the production [were quite harsh]: how dare we put a play in dialect on stage, you can't understand a thing. Other reviewers retorted, if you're willing to listen, you can understand completely. We had big discussions around this and cited the challenge of comprehending Shakespeare as an audience member when one has a virgin ear, yet no reviewer would implore boycotting that.[40] But the central focus was definitely for a community that was not necessarily the predominant community.

And did that community come?

KT: The Black community did come. And basically, both dailies, *The Toronto Star* and *The Globe and Mail*, directly said, "Don't go." The theatregoing audience that is predominantly white didn't attend the way they should have, I think, and that's kind of tragic. And I kept running into people during the run who said, "I went to it last night. I understood everything!" So, you know, that's the challenge, and that's the risk. I think that one thing Nightwood is known for is taking risks and putting difficult work on stage and challenging its audience. So in that way I was incredibly proud to do it. We did a panel during International Women's Day called "Talking Black: Canadian women speak out on the politics of language." It was made up of a powerhouse cast of Canadian women and they all had a very, very exciting discussion. Lisa's play then went on to Barbados this year. I think it's an important piece of Canadian theatre because it broke ground. [There is a] huge Caribbean population in Canada and certainly they deserve theatre that's focused toward them.

Nightwood seems to be developing a relationship with the Banff Playwrights Colony [play development program]?

KT: I applied to Banff with *China Doll* and we got in, and then the same thing happened with *Cast Iron*. With *Cast Iron*, I thought the best person to go is Alison, because she can speak [the dialect, and] Alison also has dramaturgical skills and she certainly contributed to the dramaturgical process of that play's development. So she and Lisa went, but it was under the banner of Nightwood. I think Banff respects Nightwood and sees that we're developing good work and they want to help support that work. And certainly *Mathilde* came out of Banff too. I was there with *China Doll*, and *Mathilde's* author, Véronique [Olmi], was brought in through Canada Council. There's a France–Canada cultural exchange that they do at Banff, where they bring writers from France and get Canadian translators to translate them. So Morwyn Brebner was out there with Véronique and I was there with Marjorie, and you're allowed to go and sit in on other readings and so I sat in on a reading and I was amazed at what an intense play it was. It was several years later, when I took *The Danish Play* to Edmonton for the "Magnetic North Festival," that On the Verge [a play development program at the "Magnetic North Festival"] asked me to direct *Mathilde*.

So after Mathilde *in 2006, what's next in 2007?*

KT: [Because some shows in development are not ready] what we're going to do is plays in advanced development as showcases on our mainstage. We're also going to remount *The Danish Play*. It was supposed to come back to Toronto. It played a hundred-seat theatre in 2002 and sold out and people couldn't get in. People all along have said, "What happened to *The Danish Play*, we wanted to see it." So now, almost five years later, we've decided we're going to bring it back to Toronto, also because we're trying to build an audience for a two-hundred-seat house. And it's challenging, like, *Mathilde* is not—surprisingly enough—not selling as well as you think it should. We're trying to build that venue for ourselves and build an audience for it. I think *The Danish Play* is a great Canadian play—it kind of breaks my heart that nobody picked it up across Canada. [And] we're also going to do *Crave* by Sarah Kane.

And what about the play development work?

KT: We're calling it "Future Femme Fridays," where we take one [Friday] during *The Danish Play* and two during *Crave* and present advanced plays in development that are previews of our following season. Because we have three plays that are in development that we just want to take a little bit longer with, and show our audience, in a theatre setting, what's coming down the wire.

Thornton touches on a number of themes here, and the examples of *China Doll, Cast Iron*, and *Mathilde* are illuminating in terms of the play development process, the objective to reach new communities of audiences, and the frustrations of unsupportive critical response. As both Esteves and Thornton acknowledge, their challenge is to produce enough work and generate enough notice that Nightwood remains consistently in the public eye. The audiences and practitioners who have discovered and remained loyal to Nightwood over its long and fascinating history will continue to look forward to whatever is coming next, but the challenge is to broaden and strengthen that base of support and influence.

2007: "EXTREME WOMEN"

In 2007, the "Extreme Women" reading series introduced Toronto audiences to an array of plays by women writers from outside of Canada: *Bites* by Kay Adshead, and *Behzti (Dishonour)* by

Gurpreet Kaur Bhatti, both from the United Kingdom and both directed by Maja Ardal; and *The Princess Dramas* by the Austrian writer Elfriede Jelinek, directed by Bea Pizano. The series harkens back to "Transformations" in 1985 — staged readings at the Theatre Centre that included *Masterpieces* by Sarah Daniels, directed by Mary Durkan; *War Babies* by Margaret Hollingsworth, directed by Mary Vingoe; *Portrait of Dora* by Hélène Cixous, directed by Baṇuta Rubess; and *Signs of Life* by Joan Schenkar, directed by Svetlana Zylin.

Nightwood took the inclusion of international work further by producing Sarah Kane's *Crave* in the 2007 mainstage season. Thornton justified the mounting of a British play by arguing, "Nightwood's mandate actually is new Canadian plays as well as works from the international contemporary repertoire, work that would otherwise not be done."[41] There was one precedent: Alisa Palmer had directed *One Flea Spare* by Naomi Wallace, an American, as part of Nightwood's 1998 season. Furthermore, Thornton points out that, even when staging a non-Canadian work, the company's focus is still on women's writing, and that, to compensate, more emphasis can be placed on the Canadian woman director — and/or the translator, as in the case of Morwyn Brebner's translation of *Mathilde*. With Sarah Kane's *Crave* in 2007, as with *Mathilde*, there were no other professional Canadian companies at that time tackling non-Canadian plays that were also feminist, contemporary, challenging, and risky. As Thornton observes, Kane is a celebrated female playwright, and while her provocative work is produced in Europe, her profile has remained relatively low in North America — so it was up to Nightwood to take her on.

2007: Age of Arousal

Age of Arousal is another unique example to consider within Nightwood's production history, as it is one of few plays that actually takes the history of the women's movement as its subject matter. Written by Linda Griffiths, *Age of Arousal* premiered in Calgary at Alberta Theatre Projects' "playRites Festival" in February 2007, and was quickly picked up by Nightwood for a production in Toronto in November and December of that year. Griffiths had previously participated in "FemCab" in 1987 and "Groundswell" in 1990, and *Age of Arousal* was read as part of the "Future Femme Fridays" reading series in March 2007 before Nightwood's full production.[42]

The play is set in London, England, in the year 1885, although according to Griffiths, the action does not happen "in historical reality but in a fabulist construct — an idea, a dream of Victorian England."[43] Although she was first inspired by the novel *The Odd Women* by George Gissing (published in 1893), Griffiths says that her "own research on the women's suffrage movement and the Victorian age took precedence over the novel."[44] The central character is Rhoda, a New Woman who runs a secretarial school with her lover, Mary, a heroine and martyr of the suffrage movement. While the play takes place over a single year, Griffiths notes that it encompasses "important points in Britain's struggle for women's rights" that happened over a period of forty-five years, from 1869 to 1914. An outstanding experimental device is a technique that Griffiths calls "thoughtspeak," the external vocalization of subtext: in the midst of otherwise realistic dialogue, suddenly "characters speak their thoughts in wild uncensored outpourings."[45]

In the extensive notes and essay that accompany the published version of *Age of Arousal*, justification is provided for considering its Victorian subject matter through the lens of contemporary concerns. In his foreword, Layne Coleman suggests, "Linda has chosen the Victorian age as the ship that will carry her richest cargo, and she has chosen well. This age is the one Linda would be most comfortable in. But this is not a look back in time. This play is a cry to race towards the present."[46] The play may be about another era, "but inside it is an age remarkably like your own, an age when women have to fight for everything."[47] After conducting research into the early women's movement and reading books by Betty Friedan, Germaine Greer, and Kate Millett for the first time, Griffiths concluded, "Above all, I saw that the suffragettes were frighteningly contemporary."[48]

The suffrage movement is considered to be the First Wave of feminism, while the 1960s through the early 1980s was the Second Wave, and we are currently in the Third. As we have seen, identity, representation, and cultural production are issues particularly pertinent to Third Wave feminism, a movement sometimes criticized for its preoccupation with personal choice, popular culture, and sexual freedom. In this construction, a supposedly unified feminist agenda of the earlier Waves has been fragmented by an individualized feminism, nearly unrecognizable to those earlier, more serious struggles. But *Age of Arousal* refutes this construction. What Griffiths accomplishes in *Age of Arousal* is a kind of reversal, taking us back to the First Wave with a cast of characters who are as passionate, contradictory, rebellious, and sexually aware as we might imagine ourselves to be in the Third Wave. *Age of Arousal* reminds us of earlier incarnations of contemporary feminist problems, and asks us how far we have come.

As its title suggests, *Age of Arousal* concentrates more on the struggle for women's sexual liberation than on the right to vote. Griffiths writes, "The themes and characters of that age came bursting out of the keyboard, not as dry historical figures, but sexual and lubricious, explosive and contradictory."[49] Griffiths's preoccupation with sexuality works especially well onstage in production, embodied in her actors. The characters they play struggle to reconcile their biology with their newly won freedom to pursue education, careers, and independence. All of the characters are grappling with their sexuality in one way or another. The main character, Rhoda, is caught between her love for Mary and her attraction to the male doctor, Everard. One of the secretarial students, Virginia, embraces her celibacy gladly, while her sister Alice chooses to travel to Berlin and dress as a man. But it is their youngest sister, Monica, for whom sexuality is the greatest key to political awakening; Griffiths uses Monica to voice the philosophy of emancipation through sexual freedom, or "free lovism," as the character calls it. To her first lover, Everard, Monica proclaims, "Physical liberty is the personal expression of revolutionary change" and then continues in the "thoughtspeak" subtext: *"I know the glory of my quim."*[50] To her rival, Rhoda, Monica is unabashed: "Physically awakened women are a force to be reckoned with — I am beginning to see this power, to know its strength, its reality."[51] Her sister Alice takes a much dimmer view of the value of sexual liberation: "This is the future, emancipated women claiming their bodies in order to frig as many men as they possibly can."[52] But Monica is as much a pioneer in her way as the suffragists, reforming her culture and, ultimately, our own, through her political promiscuity.

Each Wave of feminism has been about choices for women, often won through the pleasures and hazards of female friendship. As Alice says, "The bonds between women are laughable to the world, but they are marriages in a sense, and they may be betrayed."[53] Most explicitly, Third Wave feminism has not been afraid to address questions of conflict between women, particularly when conflict arises over differing opinions of what constitute good choices. This is summed up in an interesting way between Mary and Rhoda, as they debate bringing in new pupils to their school:

> **Rhoda**: I shouldn't have invited them. Suddenly I hate them —
> **Mary**: Then you hate women, then our struggle is for nothing.
> **Rhoda**: So sick of prompting and praising, only to have them put the shackles back on their own wrists.[54]

Griffiths acknowledges an acute awareness of these issues when she writes of her subject matter: "Here were the contradictions, hypocrisies and bizarre scenarios of the sex war. I felt it was a good time to admit all the flaws of the struggle while still popping the champagne."[55] What makes this play most exciting for Nightwood's audience is Griffiths's understanding of the way issues continue to resonate, still unresolved, from the awakening Victorians to the conflicted couples of today: "These are our ancestors. These long-forgotten laws continue to have an impact on us. Behaviours and beliefs echo for generations after, reverberating into the perfect condos of young married couples, sneaking into the air systems of family homes, polluting the atmosphere as we all attempt the oh-so-delicate balance of love, sex and the outside world."[56]

2008: EXPANSION, REFLECTION, MENTORSHIP

As we have seen, Nightwood has always aimed to reach a wide audience. *Mass/Age* was performed in a tent at Harbourfront; *Goodnight Desdemona (Good Morning Juliet)* went on a national tour; "Groundswell" has nurtured playwrights from coast to coast; and recent shows like *Cast Iron* and *The Danish Play* have even gone international. Thirty years into its history, the language used by Nightwood's producer and artistic director continues to articulate a desire for growth and expansion.

In the 11 March 2008 newsletter, Monica Esteves wrote, "At a time when Nightwood has been growing in every direction, I'm delighted at this opportunity to broaden our reach, and expose a new audience community to bold theatrical excellence by women."[57] She was referring to a partnered production of *Wild Dogs*, part of a "Berkeley Street Project" in which Nightwood and two other contemporary theatre companies—Studio 180 and Necessary Angel—would each produce a play as part of the Canadian Stage Company's subscription season. There is a nice sense of history behind this announcement, since Necessary Angel was one of the companies that founded the original Theatre Centre with Nightwood. *Wild Dogs* was produced in association with the Canadian Stage Company at the Berkley Street Theatre, in October and November 2008.

In fact, Esteves announced in the same newsletter, all of Nightwood's 2008/09 programming activity would be "presented within the Berkeley Complex—a comfort to our nomadic company until we get a home of our own." Despite its relatively new office and studio space in the Distillery District, and easy access to the Young Centre for the Performing Arts, located in the same complex, Nightwood clearly feels the need to bring its shows out into the larger city, to theatres with a subscription audience and a national profile. After producing *Mathilde, Crave,* and *The Danish Play* at the Young Centre, *a nanking winter* and *Age of Arousal* went offsite to the Factory Theatre, and *Wild Dogs* went to the Berkeley.

In his 2007 book *City Stages: Urban Space in a Global City,* Michael McKinnie argues that for a theatre company to own a building, or at least to occupy one for a long period of time, is an important sign of authority and maturity.[58] Interestingly, McKinnie uses the examples of Buddies in Bad Times and Necessary Angel, two companies that started out with Nightwood at the Theatre Centre. While Buddies in Bad Times only leases its space at 12 Alexander from the city, the proximity of that address to Toronto's Gay Village establishes a strong sense that the company is in its natural home, and this in turn gives the theatre legitimacy.[59] McKinnie also cites Necessary Angel, in that the company has cleverly created theatre spaces where none existed, converting buildings in order to stage site-specific, environmental productions — *Tamara* at Strachan House, for example, or *Coming Through Slaughter* at the Silver Dollar Tavern — and making that innovative use of location integral to its identity.[60] Since the 1980s, when Women's Cultural Building initiated the "Five Minute Feminist Cabaret," feminists in Toronto have wanted a building, too. But unlike the example of Buddies and the Gay Village, no neighbourhood was an obvious natural home for a women's company. And unlike Necessary Angel, Nightwood did not require such innovative spaces for its shows. Particularly since Nightwood markets itself as a "national" company, it needs a mainstream, accessible, reasonably comfortable location. In the Distillery District, Nightwood has an office space, but no claim to any one theatre space — it shares its studio with Tapestry, and the Young Centre with George Brown College, Soulpepper, and others. One could argue that the Distillery District itself — with its retail shops and restaurants, a brewery, and so on — is too diverse and maybe even too "entertainment"-focused to be a place for political theatre. Maybe Thornton and Esteves are right to suspect that true recognition and authority will only come with owning and inhabiting one visible property, exclusively mandated for women's art.

Another document from March of 2008 marked the first time that Nightwood had released an "Artistic and Financial Mid-Season Review." In the accompanying letter, Thornton and Esteves write, "We have experienced a 27% growth in our annual operations over the past three seasons" and project that the collaboration with the Canadian Stage Company "will further raise our profile and contribute to a 44% increase in our earned revenue (box office)."[61] The review includes a graph that shows the increase in fees to artists against programming expenditures: in 2005/2006, fees to artists were just over $100,000, with programming expenditures coming in just under. In 2008/2009, the programming expenditures are shown at just over $100,000, while artists' fees have shot up to over $200,000.

Another graph shows the percentage of revenue from box office, private sector fundraising, public support, and other earned revenue. A related chart explains that the 2008/2009 "Organizational Priorities" include a triad revenue formula, comprised equally of private, public, and earned revenues; the chart predicts a forty-five percent increase in box-office revenue (accomplished through the collaboration with the Canadian Stage Company and a focused passholder campaign), a twenty-nine percent increase in corporate sponsorship, and a nine percent increase in overall private support. This same chart explains that another objective is to expand governance and resources structures to include broader community representation, which is to be accomplished by increasing the board membership to ten or twelve; establishing an advisory council of five to seven; and establishing an Emeritus Board of Directors, which would include Maja Ardal, who served as interim artistic director during Thornton's maternity leave. Again, the chart articulates the priority of increasing Nightwood's profile among larger and broader communities through increased attendance and partnerships with other organizations.

On the last page of the review, further graphs provide comparative statistics from the 1982 and 2006 national studies on women in Canadian theatre, and a pie chart on how Nightwood combats the under-representation of women through mentorship programs. The review observes, "Every week, we receive inquiries about internship opportunities and there is rarely a day when an intern is not in the office or studio. In 2007, over 35 young women participated in an internship or mentorship at Nightwood for periods spanning one to twelve months in various fields"—direction and performance; playwrighting; production and management; and others.

To put a public face on some of the young women it has mentored behind the scenes, Nightwood has offered profiles in newsletters and in fundraising letters. Of course, Lisa Codrington is a success story—someone who began in a mentoring program, which she now runs. Another example is Ruth Madoc-Jones, profiled in the 7 December 2007 fundraising letter. Madoc-Jones enthuses, "I began my relationship with Nightwood Theatre as an artist, as a feminist, and as a fan." She was the associate festival coordinator for the 2002 "Groundswell," funded by a Theatre Ontario grant. She was then an associate artistic director to Kelly Thornton, assistant directing *The Danish Play* and *Finding Regina*, this time through a Canada Council grant. Madoc-Jones "worked as a dramaturge with the playwright's unit and was the associate producer for Groundswell that year." Finally, she took on the task of directing *a nanking winter*. This progression illustrates the careful way that Nightwood helped her develop her professional skills. As Madoc-Jones sums it up, "The support I received early in my career from Nightwood was immeasurable," and in turn, she is committed to providing mentorship as a workshop leader for Nightwood's youth programs.[62]

Another example of this increased emphasis on mentorship comes in the form of new plans for "Groundswell." According to the review, in 2009, "Groundswell" would take on a greater focus: "double the amount of workshop time with actors, a production designer, focused marketing, and six additional months of dramaturgy leading up to the staged readings."[63] In the mid-season review, Thornton and Esteves speak of a desire to maximize the annual investment in new work and to provide playwrights with a more public context for the readings. The playwrights represented at the 2009 "Groundswell" would come from Vancouver, Calgary, and Saskatoon, as well as Toronto. Again, the emphasis at Nightwood is clearly on raising profiles—of the women they mentor, the playwrights they produce, and of the company itself. Esteves and Thornton project an ambitious and energetic optimism, an attitude that takes credit for their past accomplishments and insists that Nightwood will be recognized for all of its initiatives in the future.

SELECTING THE PLAYS; COMING FULL CIRCLE

If expansion and profile-raising have been ongoing administrative concerns for Nightwood since the beginning, the concomitant artistic challenge has been to create or select plays that will promote women's views and experiences of the world. Creating theatre from other sources, such as poems, visual art, and even newspaper articles, has been a recurring thread in Nightwood's history—a way to connect theatre to discoveries by women artists and activists in other fields. Nightwood is not alone in turning to literary adaptation: England's Shared Experience, for example, is a company run by two women (Nancy Meckler and Polly Teale), who stage adaptations of novels. Nightwood's very first production was an adaptation of a novel, and *Wild Dogs* is the latest example. Described as being "arranged for the stage" by Anne Hardcastle, the play was adapted from the Canadian novel by Helen Humphreys, and was directed by Kelly Thornton.

Wild Dogs also highlights Nightwood's commitment throughout its history to experimenting with form. In the company newsletter, *Wild Dogs* is described as following in the footsteps of *Crave* because of its experimentation: "When Nightwood produced Sarah Kane's *Crave* last season, we were inspired in the departure from a traditional narrative form." Playing with form and presentation began with Nightwood's first collectives; in a way, an eagerness to embrace innovative form has been a way for the company to distance itself from the "social issues only" stereotype that could accrue to the feminist mandate. So while the content might come from a factual source, it is equally important that the substance be transformed into art. As one of Nightwood's most recent productions, *Wild Dogs* is a particularly nice amalgam and illustration of all these concerns: the desire for a wider audience base (through staging the play at the Berkeley Street Theatre); the connection to literary adaptation; a willingness to experiment with form; and, of course, a commitment to promoting women's work and exploring feminist ideas.

Four
Nightwood and Feminist Theory

CHARACTERISTICS OF FEMINIST THEATRE

As we have seen in previous chapters, at its inception Nightwood participated in a widespread English-language women's theatre movement that had already been well established in the United States and Britain. As Phyllis Mael points out in an article about American feminist theatre published in *Chrysalis* magazine in April 1980, over two hundred plays by women were published between 1960 and 1980, and many more unpublished works were produced by the dozens of active feminist theatres throughout the United States.[1] Mael describes the wide variety of plays found within this movement, observing that "the voices of the resisting writers reflect — in both content and form — the broad spectrum of opinion and expression of women's culture." She specifically highlights the difference between feminist theatres that wish to portray women in positions of strength and those that refuse to show only positive images because they want to spur their audience toward social change. She also categorizes the difference between women writers who embrace the feminist label and those who reject it; those who espouse the unique perceptions of women and those who deny the existence of a specifically female sensibility; those who state that their goals are primarily aesthetic and those who insist that all aesthetic choices are also political; those who wish to depict the female condition and those who want to change it; and those who want to speak only to women and those who seek an audience of both men and women.[2]

By 1980, scholars studying the phenomenon of feminist theatre were already well aware of the diversity within the genre, although perhaps reluctant to start labelling those divisions as such for fear of undermining what was still a new movement. The emphasis was instead on celebrating the quantity of plays being created by women and noting the emergence of common themes that had previously been ignored, such as the exploration of various kinds of relationships between women.

In Part Two of the same *Chrysalis* article, Rosemary Curb focuses on some characteristics of the feminist theatre companies she surveyed, claiming that "all across this continent, there are probably forty or fifty theaters that call themselves 'feminist' rehearsing and performing right now."[3] Like Mael, she points out that not all these companies necessarily use the feminist label publicly, some preferring "anti-sexist" or "humanist" or "lesbian," and so on.[4] She also observes that some of the companies sprang up to do one show and dissolved afterwards, while others became well established. An interesting distinction is made between theatres that grow out of consciousness-raising efforts, which tend to see their aims as more political than theatrically ambitious, and those "formed in response to the artistic frustrations of women, and which serve as showcases for female talent in the performing arts."[5]

Nightwood clearly belongs in this second category, but also illustrates Curb's belief that there is considerable overlap between the two kinds of theatres, especially once a company has been around for a while; she claims that "feminist theaters which have been thriving for more than two or three years see artistic and political commitments as interconnected and interdependent." Certainly, Nightwood's awareness of itself as a voice for women developed alongside its establishment as an artistic presence in the Toronto community.

Curb goes on to enumerate other traits common to the theatre companies she surveyed, all of which are also applicable to Nightwood at this early stage. She points out that at least half of the feminist theatres in operation were run as collectives, with members taking turns fulfilling various roles and functions: "About two-thirds of the theaters create some plays through collective improvisation and list the theatre or all members of the collective as playwright. Most often a resident playwright provides an idea and a partial script which the group expands."[6] This is an accurate description of many of Nightwood's earliest productions and working models, from the *Glazed Tempera, Mass/Age,* and *Peace Banquet* collectives to the collective with a single author that produced *Smoke Damage.*

The companies Curb surveyed showed a marked similarity in the kinds of plays they produced, even in collective creations. For example, retellings of Greek myths were common, as were shows that dramatized the lives of women pioneers. Nightwood fits the pattern with its productions of *Antigone* and *Peace Banquet* (subtitled "ancient Greece meets the atomic age") in 1983, and *Love and Work Enough,* which celebrated Ontario pioneer women, in 1984. *Love and Work Enough* demonstrates similarities to an American play called *Time is Passing,* the story of Minnesota women at the turn of the twentieth century, which was developed by the Minneapolis-based company Circle of the Witch to celebrate the United States Bicentennial in 1976. An hour-long documentary-drama, *Time is Passing* incorporated vignettes about women's history, historical songs, and slides, and was based on actual documents from the period, such as letters, newspaper articles, and journal entries, giving it a strong sense of historical authenticity. Like *Love and Work Enough, Time is Passing* played for a variety of groups and toured to schools, bringing a form of feminism to what might be assumed to be more conservative audiences.[7]

In her article, Curb notes that "feminist theaters which present plays on social or political issues do primary research into the problem."[8] Nightwood again follows this pattern, particularly in the case of *This is For You, Anna* and *Smoke Damage,* but also with many of its other shows, such as *Re-Production,* which was written by Amanda Hale, dealt with reproductive issues, and was performed in 1984 at an Ottawa conference for the National Association of Women and the Law. In cases where there was a single author for a collective creation, she would usually do considerable background research, which was then passed on to the actors as material to spark improvisation before taking a final written form.[9] Collective members would educate themselves on the issues and context of their project—a dramaturgical technique especially appropriate for feminist consciousness-raising.

About a quarter of the companies surveyed had men participating in the creation of works, often because they had valuable theatre skills and were personally committed to feminism. Some of the early Nightwood collectives, such as *Mass/Age* and *Peace Banquet*, included men, and men have almost always been involved in various capacities on productions throughout the years.

Like most women's theatres in the United States, Nightwood does not rely on ticket sales as its primary source of funding. Curb states that for most women's theatres, "major sources of income are grants, donations from members and friends, tours, fees, ticket sales, workshops, and classes."[10] According to Curb's study, in the U.S. in 1980, only about a quarter of women's theatres paid any salaries at all. Nightwood, however, has always insisted on paying salaries to its theatre workers. In its applications for funding, Nightwood has frequently addressed the need to pay artists a decent wage for their work and the struggle to find a balance between artists' fees and administrative costs. For example, in a 1992 application to the Canada Council for an operating grant of $60,000, artistic director Kate Lushington included a breakdown of administrative costs: artists' fees for the 1990/91 season were $50,695, while administrative salaries were $48,340; in 1991/92, the figures were $69,765 and $42,200 (plus a grant from the Ministry of Culture and Communications for an administrative intern position). For the 1992/93 season, Nightwood was projecting artists' fees of $92,079, while administrative salaries were reduced to $30,000, since there would be only two staff members, both on ten-month contracts. In 1995, the Nightwood board, in a document entitled "Values We Consider Important," declared "a commitment to paying all artists to affirm that women's work is of value." Another source of financial instability, which Curb bemoans, is the fact that most women's theatres do not have their own performance spaces and must rely on rented or donated spaces; Nightwood has always had its own space, although not always fully adequate ones, as we have seen. Nightwood has operated primarily through grants and fundraising efforts and, in some years, revenue generated from its rental facility and workshop offerings.

THE SIGNIFICANCE OF LONGEVITY

In 2009, Nightwood celebrated its thirtieth anniversary. The very fact that Nightwood has existed for so long makes it a kind of stalwart touchstone for women theatre-makers in Canada and assures its influence. In England, one of the first all-women theatre groups to gain national recognition was the Women's Theatre Group (WTG), founded in 1974. Goodman argues that groups such as WTG, Monstrous Regiment, and Siren have made a significant contribution to women's theatre simply because of their longevity. Like Nightwood, "WTG was one of the first groups to identify feminist issues as appropriate for representation in the theatre" and described itself as "a collective of six women who jointly implement the artistic and general policy of the group, to produce theatre about the many aspects of women's position in society and to create more work and opportunities for women."[11] Also like Nightwood, WTG adapted its mandate to "positively discriminate in favour of Black women and Lesbians," and struggled with the effects of government funding cuts to the arts in the 1990s.[12] It is wonderfully helpful to have companies like WTG to compare with Nightwood, to illustrate that mandates, procedures, and priorities reflect the changing time periods in which these long-standing theatres exist.

WHAT TYPE OF FEMINISM DOES NIGHTWOOD REPRESENT?

Nightwood's mandate and productions have explored and demonstrated many aspects of "feminisms," as defined by Sue-Ellen Case in her groundbreaking 1988 book *Feminism and Theatre*. Case thoroughly defines and explores three different kinds of feminist theatre: liberal, cultural, and materialist. Although much has been written about feminist theatre since Case's book was published, many theorists have adopted her categories to some degree—even if only to disagree with them—in order to define the position from which they are beginning.[13] This continues to be true despite the fact that, recently, it has become more common to distinguish between the First, Second, and Third Waves of feminism as historical periods and sites of concern.

Many feminists, including Case, will caution against seeing these categories as strictly exclusive, since they can overlap considerably, and since a feminist might find that one perspective may be appropriate in certain cases, but not in others. As Gayle Austin points out, "In compensating for a past in which political biases were generally not clearly expressed and therefore 'invisible,' there is a danger of creating a present in which political lines are too clearly drawn."[14] In fact, many feminist theatre practitioners would not employ Case's terms at all, preferring a more generalized conception of a "feminist" as anyone interested in and supportive of their work. This might be a particularly appropriate attitude in the context of theatre, which is by nature collaborative, and which draws together a variety of people for their artistic skills more often than for their politics; anyone reasonably open-minded and compatible might be considered "feminist enough." In such a practical context, the Wave model can also be seen as unnecessarily divisive. Evoking a generational divide between Waves may be especially problematic for a company like Nightwood that works hard to foreground the continuity of its lineage and longevity, especially in its publicity materials.

Still, categories of feminism are useful analytical tools for discussing Nightwood's work, how it achieves particular aims, and why those aims change. Feminism, and feminist theatre, can sound like terms that represent a monolithic, coherent belief system, rather than a broad amalgamation of many positions and creative endeavours. The development of feminism has been a process of acknowledging and embracing the differences between women as well as their common causes; using adjectives such as "liberal" or "radical" serves as a qualifying and cautionary reminder that quite differing attitudes and opinions may all claim to be feminist. Since Case's categories represent the first theorizing of feminist theatre, in the 1980s, when Nightwood was getting started, they are appropriate lenses with which to begin looking at Nightwood as a feminist company, and charting the process by which definitions become increasingly complex. The idea of process is particularly important, since the creation of theatre, the working out of feminist issues, and the act of defining oneself as an artist and a feminist are all very much ongoing. In a sense, these categories serve more to suggest the particular direction and nature of the process, rather than necessarily describing a finished product.

NIGHTWOOD AND LIBERAL FEMINISM

Many aspects of Nightwood's operations and philosophy have demonstrated a predilection for what Sue-Ellen Case has termed liberal feminism. According to Case, liberal feminism developed out of liberal humanism and stresses women's parity with men, basing its analysis on "universal" values. Liberal feminism can be defined as an attempt to alter the existing social system from the inside, without dismantling the system as a whole. Typical liberal feminist projects involve getting more women politicians elected, improving access to jobs and education for women, and working toward legal reform. The liberal feminist position emphasizes equality between the sexes and downplays difference, aiming instead for a more equitable distribution of power within the current social order. In terms of theatre, a liberal feminist approach would involve creating more job opportunities for women theatre workers and pointing out inequities between the sexes in positions of power. The Equity in Canadian Theatre report is an example of a liberal feminist approach.

Theatre that adheres to a liberal feminist philosophy might be concerned with criticizing the portrayal of women characters in plays by men, with an eye to exposing stereotypes and bias and highlighting the paucity of strong roles for women actors. The theatre historian Heather Jones writes from the liberal position when she argues that encouraging production of any and all plays by women, regardless of whether or not they could be defined as feminist, serves an inherently feminist aim.[15] Especially in its early years, Nightwood emphasized its commitment to women and women's work without highlighting the word "feminist" when describing the company. Some of its early productions, while issue-oriented, could not be described as specifically feminist, either: in 1981, for example, *Flashbacks of Tomorrow (Memorias del Mañana)* dealt with Latin American history, while the 1982 production *Mass/Age* was billed as "a multi-media spectacle of life in the nuclear age." Nonetheless, Nightwood was unique in being run by women and employing a large number of women. Kate Lushington has opined that there will only be real change in theatre when mediocre women have as many opportunities as mediocre men — her implication being that the minority of women who are employed and produced must be exceptional in every sense of the word.[16] Nightwood is significant as a place where women can find increased opportunities, including economic ones. In an article entitled "Alternative Visions," Janice Bryan, an actor involved with the 1988 "Groundswell Festival," praises feminist theatre because "it provides support for women economically and moral support. It is not necessarily political but it is economical."[17]

Mary Vingoe takes a slightly different, but still liberal, perspective when she argues that women's theatre should be judged by the same criteria as men's:

> There's a point in the continuum where you need to fund something to get it off the ground, to make it healthy, and then there's a point where you hope that it could be thrown into the mix. If it is left outside for too long, that's not good. I mean, I would hate to see Nightwood theatre go to a different [arts council funding] jury than anybody else — that would be weird.[18]

Cynthia Grant remembers, "As a group we brought together aesthetic concerns which immediately took us into the realm of a theatre of images ... we formed, through our shared concern, an innovative theatre company which would devote itself to explorations in style and content. Everyone should understand this today because our role, over time, has evolved into something quite different."[19] The accident/intention dialectic was at play from the beginning: women who considered themselves feminists, but who saw their work as part of an international avant-garde, were defined by others because of the makeup of the company, not because of the nature of their work. Through the persistence of the feminist label, and the women's own growing commitment to feminist politics, the label became a self-fulfilling prophecy. Meredith Levine has argued that Nightwood's very formation was a radical act because it "affirmed that women writers and directors did exist and that women's creative work had a right to be valued on par with men's."[20]

NIGHTWOOD AND CULTURAL FEMINISM

Some aspects of Nightwood's production record and collective structure align more closely with cultural feminism. In contrast to the liberal approach, cultural feminism bases its analysis on sexual difference and the separation of gender categories. In Case's paradigm, cultural feminism (which is also sometimes called radical feminism) addresses a "female aesthetic" and seeks a separate women's culture in order to provide feminist alternatives in theatre and other art forms, often in the belief that such a culture has existed throughout history, originating in ancient matriarchal societies. Radical feminist theatre seeks to bring women's biological and sexual experiences to the stage, allying this biology with spiritual states that are believed to bring women closer to nature than men. Radical feminist theatre often involves rituals that celebrate biological cycles, women's intuition, fertility, bonding, and nurturing. Women's experiences and qualities are cast in the spiritual arena, rather than in the context of socio-political history.[21]

Those who do not subscribe to the theories of cultural feminism charge it with being "essentialist": that is, operating under the assumption that there are such things as essentially female qualities rather than merely learned and reinforced behaviours. The differences between women and men can be interpreted in either a liberal or a cultural way. For example, Julia Miles, the founder of The Women's Project in New York, has noted that a playwright must launch a "campaign to obtain a production," then deal with a team of other artists — directors, designers, and so on — and that for a female playwright, "this necessitates aggressive behavior on her part that is alien to most women."[22] At first this appears to be a cultural argument about innately feminine tendencies. But then Miles goes on to suggest that some women's discomfort in these situations could be due to the fact that, until fairly recently, girls did not have the same opportunity to participate on school sports teams and therefore have not had the experience of operating within a competitive unit.[23] So what appears to be a cultural feminist philosophy turns out to be a liberal argument for equal opportunities for girls. Post-modern feminist theorists such as Judith Butler have adamantly rejected what they see as essentialism, arguing that "female qualities" are learned behaviours, constructed and maintained by a system of binary opposition, which cultural feminism upholds rather than dismantles.[24]

Nonetheless, certain techniques demonstrating a cultural feminist philosophy can provide powerful theatrical moments. In her study of American feminist theatres in the 1970s, Dinah Luise Leavitt has commented, "It may be premature to name ritual as an original or unique aspect of feminist theatre, yet one cannot avoid noticing the many elements of ritual in feminist drama and the many women's celebrations and rites being performed by theatre groups."[25] The element of ritual can be found in a number of Nightwood productions, most notably in the staging of *Princess Pocahontas and the Blue Spots*.

As the director of *Princess Pocahontas*, Muriel Miguel connects Nightwood with another strand in the lineage of experimental theatres. The historian Charlotte Canning has commented that many women who went on to found or work with feminist theatres started off with one of the famous American experimental companies, such as Open Theater; this certainly includes Miguel, a founder of Spiderwoman Theater. As Canning points out, the women involved with early experimental companies learned two contradictory lessons. One was the value of acting and process techniques that reject a traditional, linear, Method-based paradigm. The other was the painful realization of sexism and discrimination within these companies, prompting the impulse to work on feminist theatre instead.[26] As with Nightwood, the awareness of sexism also led to a commitment to some form of collective structure, as a conscious disavowal of the patriarchal structures that had been rejected; Curb writes that "at least half of feminist theaters in existence in 1979 were organized as collectives and over two-thirds used a collective/collaborative process to create works for performance."[27] The commitment to collectivity was an affirmation of the process of creation, on the means to an end rather than the end itself.[28] So the choice to work collectively comes out of a liberal desire for equal opportunity, but lends itself to a cultural feminist agenda of female sameness and solidarity.

NIGHTWOOD AND MATERIALIST FEMINISM

As identified by Sue-Ellen Case, the third type of feminism is materialist: a system of analysis that places an emphasis on the material conditions of women's lives, examining how factors such as race and class intersect with gender to determine the position of different women in different historical periods. While cultural feminism tends to be trans-historical (as in *Smoke Damage*), materialist feminism is very much rooted in the specific circumstances of women within their own cultural milieu. Materialist feminist theatre could include issue-based theatre that situates its debate within a specific set of references, identifying itself as socialist or Marxist-feminist, for example, or defining itself in terms of the race or ethnicity of its practitioners. Materialist feminism might also tend toward what has been called post-modern feminist performance: a style which points out and plays with questions of subjectivity and gender identity, defining them as constructs and fragmenting much of what is traditionally considered theatre. Materialist feminism, to quote Jill Dolan, "deconstructs the mythic subject Woman to look at women as a class oppressed by material conditions and social relations."[29]

There is no clear linear progression in the three types of feminism Case outlines, nor can they be equated with particular time periods in Nightwood's history. Elements of all three might be identifiable within a single Nightwood production. Because there are many people active within Nightwood at any given time, the women who make up Nightwood could easily encompass different attitudes and beliefs and never articulate that they are, in certain respects, in conflict.

APPLYING OTHER MODELS

Of course, Sue-Ellen Case is not the only theorist to propose helpful categories of feminist theatre. Gayle Austin, in *Feminist Theories for Dramatic Criticism*, identifies three models for looking at stages in feminist criticism.[30] In stage one, the emphasis is on compensatory or contribution history, devoted to the work of "notable women" and women's contributions to movements in male-written history. A Nightwood example would be the 1981 stage adaptation of *The Yellow Wallpaper*, a short story written by the pioneering American feminist writer Charlotte Perkins Gilman in 1892. Directed by Cynthia Grant and performed by Mary Vingoe, this one-woman show was one of Nightwood's earliest productions and went on to be adapted for radio. It is a good example of how a feminist theatre may recover a neglected work by a "notable woman" of the past that deals directly with female consciousness.

The Yellow Wallpaper also relates to stage two of Austin's model: an inquiry into women's actual experiences in the past, exploring such primary sources as diaries, autobiographies, and oral history. An example here is Sonja Mills, who based her 2002 hit *The Danish Play* on the journals and poetry of her great-aunt, Agnete Ottosen, a member of the Danish resistance movement during

World War II. The third stage in Austin's model challenges the basic assumptions of historians regarding the division of historical periods. For example, in both the 1983 productions *This is For You, Anna* and *Smoke Damage*, trans-historical comparisons are made as the action moves back and forth between time periods and countries, in order to suggest the parallels in women's experiences of oppression.

Another three-stage model identified by Austin follows a similar progression. Here, the first stage critiques negative aspects of men's work about women. The 1987 collective creation *The Last Will and Testament of Lolita*, which attempts to reassess the character of Lolita from Vladimir Nabokov's classic novel, is a good example. The second stage focuses on the tradition of women writers; an example is Nightwood's 1986 production of *The Edge of the Earth is Too Near, Violette Leduc* by Jovette Marchessault. The publicity and program materials for this production featured extensive information about the real-life Violette Leduc, her writings, and her relationship with Simone de Beauvoir, as well as about Jovette Marchessault as an important lesbian feminist writer from Quebec. This was not the first time Nightwood had dealt with lesbian themes (*The True Story of Ida Johnson*, its very first production, implied a lesbian relationship), but it could be viewed as the first occasion where its work was placed explicitly within a lesbian feminist literary context and marketed to the gay and lesbian community. In Austin's model, the third stage begins to look at the differences between women writers, rather than just their differences from men. This important idea — that our experiences of gender can be endlessly complicated and problematized — runs as a theme throughout feminism and feminist theatre in the twenty-first century, and forms a central principle of contemporary Third Wave feminism.

DEVELOPING A DISTINCTIVELY FEMALE FORM OF THEATRE

Practically speaking, many of the staging techniques commonly employed by Nightwood and other feminist theatres can be traced to the experimental and political theatres of the 1960s and 1970s: episodic, circular structures; the use of songs; and transformational acting techniques. However, in their discussion of Megan Terry's work, for example, Breslauer and Keyssar identify her willingness to "exploit theater's liberty with time and place to conjoin previously disconnected elements of culture and history" as a technique particularly employed by feminist theatre. They argue that by subverting conventional representations of history and chronology, the spectator is allowed alternative ways to view the past and the present. Caryl Churchill's classic plays *Cloud Nine* and *Top Girls* provide ready examples.[31]

Breslauer and Keyssar argue that these kinds of techniques — "unprecedented historical representations and explicit intertextual gestures" — constitute a kind of dangerous history. Feminist artists simultaneously address what has gone on before — the absence of women from the stage, or what they perceive as women's misrepresentation — and attempt to sort out their own positions. This means acknowledging potential collusion or resistance to perpetuating stereotypes, and a constant attempt to imagine and create a new self without the old obstacles and inhibitions.

One of the strategies frequently employed by feminist (and other types of) theatre is to allow the *actor* to emerge as the speaking subject, hence the prevalence of autobiographical or semi-autobiographical works dealing with the creation of personal identity, performed by the author. In the afterword to her 1990 play *Afrika Solo*, Djanet Sears uses a term attributed to the African-American feminist poet Audre Lorde, "autobio-mythography," in an attempt to describe the process by which she finds her place in the world through a combination of fact and fiction. The play is not strictly autobiographical, yet it is very much about Sears's struggle to define herself, and to represent this struggle and self onstage. For example, one of the specific ways the character grapples with identity is to change the spelling of her name from "Janet" to "Djanet." The submersion of self within a role could be seen as a loss of subjecthood. But when the actor is performing a statement about her own creative process and belief system, the performance becomes less a submersion than a powerful act of personal communication and an affirmation of self.

Jill Dolan concludes that "giving up the notion of theater as a place to image those who are elsewhere erased is difficult, even as feminists debate the efficacy of theater as mimesis."[32] Whether those who have been erased are lesbians, women of colour, or some other marginalized group, Dolan's point is important: those who have yet to be adequately represented onstage and who have seldom had the opportunity to see themselves as subjects in the theatre will not be willing to give this up as a goal, no matter how theoretically problematic the construction of subjecthood may be. There is both pleasure and power in seeing oneself represented. This is not to say, however, that the theatre created from these perspectives will employ a naive realism or an essentialist insistence on identity. On the contrary, the experience of women of colour, for example, as doubly or triply erased in mainstream culture, may well provide an analysis based in personal experience that at the same time takes into account the constructed nature of identity. A good example here might be Nightwood's 1992 production of *Do Not Adjust Your Set* by Diana Braithwaite, in which the theatre audience watches a day of role-reversal "television" in which all the people who are usually white are Black, and vice versa. Behind the parodic comedy is the acknowledgment that how we see ourselves represented affects how our identities are constructed.

In all of Nightwood's productions, regardless of their form, the significance of the women onstage — as performers, feminists, and members of a women's theatre company — informs the audience's experience, and the particular nuances, of the representation. The presence of a female body onstage has always been erotically charged and therefore significant — for its novelty value, the suggestion of impropriety, the implications of voyeurism, or perhaps because of the weight of collective sexual signification — but only within the context of feminist theatre does female presence become synonymous with identity and subjecthood.

Another Perspective on Feminism: Post-Modernism

In her book *The Politics of Postmodernism*, Linda Hutcheon argues that feminism has had a great impact on post-modernism, in that it has affected our understanding of aesthetic and political interactions at the level of representation. Feminism has influenced the way we understand the political to have an impact on the private and the public, changing the way we think about culture, knowledge, and art.[33] Feminism and post-modernism are most often conflated at the level of representation, especially when defining their cultural expression in art forms like theatre. The same characteristics are used to describe both feminist and post-modern theatre because both use techniques that denaturalize and question the dominant ideology.

While post-modernism is often criticized for its lack of a political agenda, Hutcheon argues that the existence of a critique is part of its very definition. She situates post-modernism as part of the "unfinished project of the 1960s" because it promotes a distrust of "ideologies of power and the power of ideologies."[34] On the other hand, post-modernism is also less oppositional and idealistic than earlier movements and must acknowledge its complicity with the values it comments upon. Post-modern art, for example, may criticize and parody popular culture, even as it depends on references to popular culture for its own substance and simultaneously celebrates them on some level. According to Hutcheon, this dual nature, containing both critique and complicity, defines post-modernism, although one is always reminded that post-modernism, like feminism, is a shifting and multifaceted condition rather than something definite and monolithic.

Post-modernism and feminism become more alike as time goes on. Just as post-modernism continues the project of the 1960s without the same idealism and oppositional understanding that characterized those earlier movements (that sense of "us versus them"), so too does feminism move on from its rebirth in the sixties with ever more complexity and fragmentation. This is most evident in the current practice of distinguishing the Second Wave feminism of the sixties from the Third Wave that is upon us now. Complicity is not full affirmation or adherence, and theorists such as Shannon Bell and Janelle Reinelt, among others, have embraced acknowledgment of complicity as a move toward opening feminism to its own "others." Bell argues that the post-modern influence, by acknowledging complicity and incorporating parts of the dominant discourse, actually "improves" feminism by allowing it to explain the ideological loopholes in patriarchy—those occasions when patriarchy enables its own subversion. It is not simply "knowing one's enemy," but rather using one's enemy against itself, or in the case of much Third Wave practice, actually embracing and reclaiming aspects of popular culture that were rejected by earlier feminists. The practice of reclaiming certain problematic labels comes to mind: embracing "girl," "lady," or "bitch," for example, as ironically affirmative identifiers, and actively celebrating and recasting denigrated aspects of traditional feminine work, such as crafts and sewing.[35]

Many of the characteristics that are defined (by Hutcheon, Reinelt, and Bell) as post-modern can also be applied to much feminist theatre, but the feminist insistence on truth, meaning, and a message of social equality tends to prevent feminist theatre from being post-modern in an uncomplicated way. Some of the most obvious post-modern qualities are the transgression of discrete boundaries between genres, and the blurring of distinctions between private and public. A good example is ahdri zhina mandiela's play *dark diaspora... in DUB*, which began as a "Groundswell" piece and was sponsored by Nightwood for the "Toronto Fringe Festival" in 1991. The play is actually a series of poems, which are spoken and danced in performance, much in the manner of Ntozake Shange's profound work *for colored girls who have considered suicide/when the rainbow is enuf* (1976). Like that earlier work, *dark diaspora... in DUB* is performed by a group of women, rather than by an individual, which serves to break up the unitary subject position. Furthermore, the play blurs public instances of racism and economic hardship with personal issues of identity and emotional development, transgressing the strict separation between public and private spheres, the personal and the political, in order to show how they are interrelated.

The work has a fragmentary, nonlinear form that seeks to communicate a vision of society from the standpoint of gender, race, and lesbian sexuality, thereby challenging a definition of feminism that does not consciously acknowledge all of these identities. It is also post-modern in the sense that it is localized, understood as an act of identity formation in progress, while it is very much feminist in its implicit call for a world in which this process can be carried out with fewer constraints and less violence. As Bell explains, "Postmodernity revalues the aesthetic as a site for the intervention of little narratives; it is in little 'ephemeral stories' that the assumptions of the great, institutionalized narrative(s) are questioned, (re)presented, challenged and undermined."[36] The performance text is a work in progress that changes with each production; the audience is drawn into interaction with the performer, and spectatorship is a part of the work.

Post-modernism is very much applicable to performances of plays like *dark diaspora … in DUB*, Djanet Sears's *Afrika Solo*, Monique Mojica's *Princess Pocahontas and the Blue Spots*, and other Nightwood-sponsored productions by women of colour. While the women onstage are not necessarily portraying themselves (or at least, not all of the time), the fact that they have written and are performing the piece, that the piece is about being a woman of colour, and that they themselves are women of colour all have a crucial impact on the piece's effect and how it is received by an audience. The very fact that a Black woman, for example, is speaking her own words onstage in Canada is charged with cultural importance: *Afrika Solo*, published by Sister Vision Press in 1990, was the first play by a Black woman to be published in Canada. Lisa Codrington's play *Cast Iron*, written in the Bajan dialect, is another example of how the authenticity of voice is integral to a play's power.

Hutcheon criticizes post-modernism for not taking the next step into political action, but this is less of a problem or a goal for feminist theatre, at least in Nightwood's case. Unlike the kind of political manifesto or document of social policy Hutcheon seems to be advocating, the plays done by Nightwood portray a situation and make it recognizable, but seldom include a direct command for specific action for fear of appearing too didactic. Part or most of the social action has already occurred in the very creation of the piece of theatre: who made it and how. The empowerment of women, whether as characters or authors, and the act of telling their stories creatively, is in itself both feminist and post-modern. Feminism is a politics and post-modernism is not, but all representation is political.[37]

THIRD WAVE FEMINISM

The difficulty of capturing definitions of feminist theatre is very apparent in the range of ways that terms are used; this is abundantly illustrated by the use of "Third Wave" and "post-feminist" to describe contemporary feminism. At one extreme, Suzanna Danuta Walters disavows the term post-feminism as being too much associated with the work of certain conservative American writers, and believes that it "encompasses the backlash sentiment … as well as a more complex phenomenon of a recent form of antifeminism."[38] Other writers, such as Sophia Phoca and Sarah Gamble, use the terms post-feminism and Third Wave feminism almost interchangeably to denote a scholarly understanding of "an alignment with postmodernist theory in destabilizing notions of gender."[39] Still others, such as Leslie Heywood and Jennifer Drake, Baumgardner and Richards, and Gillis and Munford, specifically adopt the term Third Wave in order to signal a generational shift, but one that does not entail a rejection of what has come before, insisting that "third wave feminist politics allow for *both* equality and difference."[40] Heywood and Drake, the editors of *Third Wave Agenda*, maintain that the biggest difference between Second and Third Wave feminism is a Third Wave comfort with contradiction and pluralism. They identify the Third Wave as originating with critiques of the women's movement by theorists of colour such as bell hooks, ensuring that Third Wave feminism is intrinsically pluralistic and hybridized, and that it is linked with activism and not just theory.[41]

This activist element seems to be what differentiates the use of the term post-feminist from the label Third Wave. Sarah Gamble, for example, defines post-feminism as "more theoretical than actual"[42] and argues that those calling themselves post-feminist "support an individualistic, liberal agenda rather than a collective and political one."[43] This is contrasted with her definition of the Third Wave as "a resurgence of interest in feminist activism on the part of young women who wish to differentiate themselves from the postfeminist label ... characterized by a desire to redress economic and racial inequality as well as 'women's issues.'"[44] So while Gamble defines post-feminism as an attitude that "attacked feminism in its present form as inadequate to address the concerns and experiences of women today,"[45] Heywood and Drake insist that they are not distancing themselves from the Second Wave, which they characterize as being concerned with gaining opportunities for women. Rather, they embrace "second wave critique as a central definitional thread while emphasizing ways that desires and pleasures subject to critique can be used to rethink and enliven activist work."[46] Interestingly, the points of tension seem to accrue around issues of self-definition, the relative status of popular culture, and a Third Wave insistence on pluralism. Rubin and Nemeroff argue that "though the form (personal narrative rather than group consciousness-raising) and content (examining, often celebrating difference rather than seeking commonality) of personal expression in the third-wave may differ from that of the second wave, we believe their functions are quite congruent."[47] It has been suggested, in a poetic turn of phrase, that "the third wave can come to view itself as indivisible from the ocean of feminism."[48] At the same time, feminists who may have considered themselves somehow outside of the Second Wave, by virtue of their colour, age, sexual identity, or experience, have a real interest in exploring how the shift to a Third Wave consciousness can be of benefit to them; as the Muslim feminist Sherin Saadallah writes, for her, "the pluralities embraced under third wave feminism offer a more welcoming space than previous feminisms."[49]

Any definition of Third Wave feminism must foreground its relationship with popular culture, and its emphasis on "the contradictions and conflicts shaping young women's experiences."[50] All of Nightwood's current youth programming, including support for Buddies' "Hysteria Festival," and its own Write From the Hip and Busting Out! initiatives, are clearly targeted at a new generation.[51] Most importantly, Third Wave feminists "often take cultural production and sexual politics as key sites of struggle, seeking to use desire and pleasure as well as anger to fuel struggles for justice."[52] Central to this understanding of the Third Wave is the refusal of guilt and the revolutionary acknowledgement that feminist meaning can be derived from the most unlikely of sources—including theatre. Third Wave feminism is yet another theoretical label that can, and does, shape the way that Nightwood practices art into the twenty-first century.

CONCLUSIONS/BOTTOM LINE: WHAT MAKES A COMPANY FEMINIST?

Lizbeth Goodman has written, "'Feminist theatre' is itself a form of cultural representation, influenced by changes in the geographies of feminism, women's studies, economics, politics, and cultural studies."[53] The fact that Nightwood Theatre has continued to redefine its mandate, policies, and practices over the years reflects the practical nature of feminism: it must be provisional and changeable, adapting to social forces and the evolution of thought within the movement, in order to remain relevant. A feminist theatre that did not change, evolve, and constantly work on redefining itself would not be very feminist. In addition, the collaborative nature of theatre and the large number of people and projects that have been associated with Nightwood all contribute to its direction. And finally, external forces like granting agencies and the media can have a significant influence on the way a company develops.

The potential and relative value of being considered "marginal" leads to the question of assimilation and separatism, the fear of being either co-opted or ghettoized that comes up so frequently in discussions of women's theatre. Rina Fraticelli has written persuasively about this dilemma:

> Why, we are asked, can't women simply bring their aesthetics, sensibility, vocabulary and even politics to bear on the cultural community through existing art institutions — in a non-compliant and direct way, of course? Why, when there are no longer formal barriers to full and equal participation, do we choose to ghettoize ourselves and our work in such a "restrictive manner"? ... Women's lack of authority in the Canadian theatre does not stem from our lack of positions of authority. It is the reverse: we do not hold or have no access to positions of authority because patriarchal society views women as *intrinsically* lacking in authority. And to believe that the full emancipation of women will be accomplished through the fulfilment of affirmative action quotas is a little like believing racial integration will rid the world of racism.[54]

In her view, women's contributions cannot merely be added on to pre-existing androcentric structures, since the structure will alter the work but not be reformed in turn. Women have always made, and continue to make, culture, but it is erased, suppressed, marginalized, and appropriated by a theatre industry that is overwhelmingly male-dominated.[55] The existence of a company like Nightwood, which is run by women for the express purpose of encouraging women's work in a supportive environment, allows the work to develop in a very different (and much healthier) context.

We learn something about the multiplicity of feminist theatre by extrapolating from the example of Nightwood, by drawing some conclusions about what a feminist theatre company is or might be. Some productions consistently reflect and grow out of a stated philosophy, while others might be accused of contradicting and changing the philosophy. Nightwood's artistic directors and board members see themselves as different "kinds" of feminists, which shapes the projects they choose, their working methods, and the audiences they seek. Nightwood has been a feminist theatre — or rather, a series of constantly shifting feminist theatres — throughout its history, despite its changing mandates and relative levels of commitment to the feminist label.

Feminist theorists do not intend to create monolithic categories into which all feminist work must be divided. But a company like Nightwood, which has occupied shifting positions in the definition and implementation of feminism, illustrates the importance of constantly redefining one's terms and goals. For example, a newspaper reviewer considering the significance of a particular Nightwood production might try to take into account the "kind" of feminism it most clearly espouses in order to determine how effectively it fulfills both political and aesthetic agendas. Unfortunately, critics (of all kinds) can have their own, sometimes narrow, understandings of feminism, and may then apply their definitions to any production by women without attempting to position it along a wide spectrum of possibility.

I find that speaking from the perspective of what I consider to be the most current and contemporary form of feminism (what has been dubbed Third Wave) is relevant, because this is where the company sits in 2009. Nightwood's youth programming, its embrace of mainstream visibility, and its willingness to be both bolder and, in some ways, less consistent in its programming choices are all congruent with Third Wave feminism. At the same time, the only way to look back on Nightwood's long history is with a "playfully plural" open-mindedness. There are plays that, I argue, were successful in the past precisely because they were prescient in anticipating where feminism was going. There were other plays that chanced upon potency — not so much because of their gender politics, but because of their racial politics. Still others were very much plays of their time, but I have tried to be scrupulous in not implying that they were somehow more "primitive," or that one feminist experiment led to another, better feminism.

Nightwood tends to promote its standard of excellence by highlighting the shows that have won awards. In the program for *Cast Iron* in March 2005, for example, the company description read in part: "Nightwood is the premiere professional women's theatre company in Canada. For twenty-five years it has produced, developed and toured landmark, award-winning plays about outspoken Canadian women." The statement goes on to list shows such as *Goodnight Desdemona (Good Morning Juliet)*, *Harlem Duet*, *The Danish Play*, and *China Doll*, and to describe "Groundswell" and the Write From the Hip and Busting Out! programs. It concludes, "As a feminist theatre company, from our beginnings, Nightwood has broken new ground in gender and cultural representation on Canadian stages."

As always, the "trick" is to position the company in such a way that neither downplays its feminism, nor alienates by the use of that highly charged, yet potentially galvanizing word. Just as *Age of Arousal* reminds us of the struggles of earlier generations of women, I hope that this book about Nightwood brings together material that might otherwise have remained scattered and disconnected. Articles from journals, reviews of plays, selections from interviews — much has been written about Nightwood and its work, some of it by the women artists themselves, but what I hope to have done here is to collect it all in one place and to give the subject the focused attention it deserves. So many women have worked so hard, not just at Nightwood, but in feminist theatres internationally, and in journalism, and in scholarship. All that can easily be lost, especially in the ephemeral world of theatre production or in the peripatetic nature of a nomadic theatre company. I find it fascinating to notice the recurrences of literary adaptations, for example, or of themes that come up repeatedly, or references to people who have been involved in the company over and over.

Nightwood has been around for so long that it might almost be taken for granted, but it really is a unique and remarkable company. I often feel it does not get the attention or recognition that it deserves — but then, we all tend to have short memories! If I have accomplished anything with this study, I hope it is to have taken the weight and measure of an enduring Canadian phenomenon, and to have done something to preserve its contribution.

Shelley Scott • Nightwood Theatre

Appendix
A Nightwood Chronology

1979

The B.A.A.N.N. Theatre Centre established by Nightwood, Buddies in Bad Times, Necessary Angel, Actors Lab, AKA Performance Interface, and Theatre Autumn Leaf.

6–15 SEPTEMBER

The True Story of Ida Johnson, at the NDWT Side-Door Theatre and later (18 October–11 November) at the Adelaide Court Theatre. A Nightwood Theatre production adapted from the novel by Sharon Riis. A project of the Explorations Program of the Canada Council, with supplementary funding from the Ontario Arts Council. Kim Renders, Mary Vingoe, and Maureen White in the cast (with Lee Wildgen), directed by Cynthia Grant. Nightwood Theatre Collective and Associate Members: the four founders, plus Marie Black (who did the design with Kim Renders), Kit Goldfarb (production manager), Karen Rodd (masks), Rose Zoltek (publicity), and Christa and Erna Van Daele, who were participants in the first readings.

Mary Vingoe was the only Equity member.

1980

APRIL

Self-Accusation by Peter Handke, directed and performed by Cynthia Grant and Richard Shoichet, at the Theatre Centre, co-produced by Nightwood.

MAY

Buddies in Bad Times and Nightwood Theatre present "Rhubarb! A Festival of New Canadian Plays" (this was Nightwood's first involvement; "Rhubarb!" was created in 1979, and Maureen White had been a participant in its first year). "Rhubarb! is a workshop production presented to give artists a chance to explore new works. Plays will be presented at various levels of performance from staged reading to fully mounted production." A Theatre Passe Muraille SEED Show. Nightwood's contributions: 1. *Psycho-Nuclear Breakdown* by Cynthia Grant: this "sombre little piece" involved Grant seated in a rocking chair, wearing a bathrobe and performing a monologue she had written as well as reading from *Nuclear Madness* by Helen Caldicott. Her live reading was juxtaposed with a tape-recorded voice reading from another book, "The Denial of Death" by Ernest Becker, and a videotape, produced by Chris Clifford and Videocab, showing Grant on the verge of a nervous breakdown; 2. *Gently Down the Stream* by Kim Renders, performed by Renders, Grant, and Maureen White; 3. *Soft Boiled* by Renders, performed by Renders and White.

19—28 JUNE

Glazed Tempera, inspired by the works of Alex Colville, presented by Nightwood at the Passe Muraille Backspace. The performers are Renders, White, and Peter Van Wart, with a taped reading by Jack Messinger; Grant is the director and the production is said to be "conceived by" the three women. Kim Renders also did the costumes. In the program they "acknowledge the influence of Mabou Mines' *Southern Exposure* and the films of Marguerite Duras." 45 minutes long.

NOVEMBER

Second "Rhubarb!" that year, part of the 1980/81 season at the Theatre Centre. Nightwood's contributions: 1. *The Best of Myles* by Flann O'Brien, adapted by Maureen White and Mary Durkan; 2. *Soft Boiled #2* by White and Renders as clowns Orangeade and Cellophane; 3. *G*, adapted from the novel by John Berger, directed by Renders and Grant; 4. *Ten Seconds After Closing* by Mary Vingoe, directed by Grant; 5. *Object/Subject Nausea*, a video and live performance piece by Grant.

From the "Rhubarb!" program: "Nightwood Theatre operates as a collective to produce original or adapted material in a style which emphasizes the visual, musical and literary elements of the presentation. Their adaptation of *The True Story of Ida Johnson*, and *Glazed Tempera*, inspired by the paintings of Alex Colville, were presented last season as well as Rhubarb (May 1980) and Handke's *Self Accusation* (April 80)."

1981

28 JANUARY–8 FEBRUARY

Theatre Autumn Leaf and Nightwood present in repertory (three shows daily) at the Theatre Centre: *The Audition*, a clown show directed by Dean Gilmour; *Specimens*, directed by Thom Sokoloski; and *For Rachel*, directed by Kim Renders. The latter piece had been workshopped at the Factory Theatre Lab; the performers are Shelley Thompson and Maureen White, with "dramaturgical work by Rina Fraticelli." In its second week of performance, it is accompanied by *Epilogue*, directed by Grant, performed by Lindsay Holton and Barbara Wright.

MAY

Flashbacks of Tomorrow (Memorias del Mañana), a collective presentation by Nightwood and Open Experience Hispanic-Canadian Theatre, performed at the Toronto Free Theatre (Berkeley Street) as part of the Toronto Theatre Festival's Open Stage. Grant is the director and White and Renders are in the cast. Music written and performed by Compañeros. "An original theatre production, presented in a mosaic of dance, ritual, personal experience and music, based on legends, documents and the art of Latin America."

SUMMER

Theatre Centre moves to 666 King Street West from its original location above a Greek disco on Danforth.

1–18 OCTOBER

The Yellow Wallpaper, produced by Nightwood at the Theatre Centre, adapted from the story by Charlotte Perkins Gilman and with additional text by Cynthia Grant and Mary Vingoe; performed by Vingoe and directed by Grant; music by Marsha Coffey; designed by Patsy Lang. Later adapted for radio. Kim Renders is among those thanked in the program, and Maureen White is thanked "for directorial advice." "Funded in part by the Ontario Arts Council, the Toronto Arts Council, and Metro Arts Council."

1982

1982 was the year of Nightwood's Charter.

5–21 MARCH

Hooligans, produced by Nightwood Theatre at the Theatre Centre, written by Jan Kudelka and Mary Vingoe, in collaboration with the company, from an idea by Irene Pauzer (who played Isadora), and from the diaries and writings of Isadora Duncan, Edward Gordon Craig, Sergei Esenin, Kathleen Bruce, and Robert Falcon Scott. Directed by Grant and designed by Renders. Cast: Ian A. Black, Jay Bowen, Irene Pauzer, Linda Stephen, Bruce Vavrina. Published in *New Canadian Drama* 6, edited by Rita Much (Ottawa: Borealis Press, 1993).

25–29 AUGUST

Mass/Age, a collective, multimedia spectacle of life in a nuclear age, performed by Jay Bowen, Kim Renders, Daniel Brooks, Allan Risdill, Gordon Masten, and Maureen White, directed by Grant, presented in a tent at Harbourfront Centre. Live music by Charis Polatos (a member of Compañeros); visual artist John Scott; choreographers Johanna Householder and Allan Risdill.

8 SEPTEMBER

Nightwood participates in A Concert for Peace with Compañeros and others.

NOVEMBER

"Rhubarb!" at the Theatre Centre includes *Soft Boiled* #3. Maureen White and Kim Renders return as Cellophane and Orangeade, joined by Cheryl Cashman as Mrs. Fudge. Also, *Notes on a Tumour*, "a comic look at one man's attempt at coping with the phobias of our society." Written and performed by Kim Renders and Christopher Thomas.

"Over the three-week period, 50 or 60 people are involved in short, often multi-media works" (Jon Kaplan, "Actors Make Rhubarb," *NOW*, 4 November 1982).

Another notable show is *American Demon*, "a series of poems exploring images of women in rock music." This work, part of a new play by Jan Kudelka, was directed by Kate Lushington and featured Nion, Maggie Huculak, Theresa Tova, and Svetlana Zylin.

Cynthia Grant was the master of ceremonies for the second week of "Rhubarb!"

The Saturday, 20 November show was followed by an "open stage" for the audience to perform.

1983

MARCH

Women's Cultural Building presents a "Festival of Women Building Culture" at various venues: 8 March, the first "Five Minute Feminist Cabaret" is held at Stagger Lee's (the Horseshoe Tavern). *American Demon* is produced 22–25 March, and Pol Pelletier performs *Night Cows* by Jovette Marchessault and *My Mother's Luck* by Helen Weinzweig 21–24 April. Both done as part of Factory Theatre Lab's "Brave New Works," produced at Theatre Passe Muraille. On 28–29 April there is a collective performance from *The Euguélionne* by Louky Bersianak, which had previously had a reading by Cynthia Grant on 21 January.

26–29 MAY

Women's Perspectives '83, a month-long art exhibit sponsored by Partisan Gallery, includes "Caution: Women at Work," a weekend of performances, all from Nightwood: 1. *Four-Part Discord*, an expansion of the earlier piece *Gently Down the Stream*, performed by Mary Durkan, Cynthia Grant, Kim Renders, and Maureen White; 2. *Psycho-Nuclear Breakdown* by Cynthia Grant; 3. *This is For You, Anna/a spectacle of revenge*, collectively written and performed by Suzanne Khuri, Ann-Marie Mac-Donald, Baṇuta Rubess, Aida Jordão, and Maureen White.

19–26 JUNE

Nightwood presents *Antigone* by Sophocles, dramaturged by Patricia Keeney-Smith, directed by Cynthia Grant, with a chorus of 40 actors and musicians, at St. Paul's Square (Avenue Road at Davenport). Cast includes Peggy Sample, Tracy Wright, and Aida Jordão. The Chorus was sung in Ancient Greek. Program note: "This production of *Antigone* involves a company of young people under the age of twenty-five. The backgrounds of the participants range from young people beginning professional careers in music and theatre to those for whom this has been an entirely new experience." In the press release, Cynthia Grant is referred to as Nightwood's artistic director.

18–28 AUGUST

Midnight Hags presents *Burning Times*, at the Theatre Centre, written by Baņuta Rubess with the cast (Peggy Christopherson, Ann-Marie Mac-Donald, Mary Marzo, Kim Renders, Maureen White) and the director, Mary Ann Lambooy. Renders and White are identified in the program as members of Nightwood.

30 SEPTEMBER–23 OCTOBER

Nightwood presents *Smoke Damage: A story of the witch hunts* at St. Paul's Square, 121 Avenue Road. Written by Baņuta Rubess with the cast: Peggy Christopherson, Ann-Marie MacDonald, Mary Marzo, Kim Renders, and Maureen White. Rubess and Cynthia Grant were "direction consultants." The opening night is a benefit performance for the Women's Bookstore, which had been damaged in a recent arson attempt on the Morgentaler Clinic next door. The play was published by Playwrights Canada in 1985. A note reads: "*Smoke Damage* develops several themes from the successful workshop of *Burning Times*, written by Baņuta Rubess and presented by Midnight Hags at the Theatre Centre, Toronto, in August 1983. *Burning Times* was initiated and produced by Mary Ann Lambooy. *Smoke Damage* was developed through a collective process. Although the main writer, Baņuta Rubess, gave the play its final shape, the five actors contributed largely to its content."

3–19 NOVEMBER

Peace Banquet: Ancient Greece Meets the Atomic Age, adapted from Aristophanes' *Peace*, collectively written by Micah Barnes, Sky Gilbert, Dean Gilmour, Cynthia Grant, Charis Polatos, Kim Renders, Judith Rudakoff, Philip Shepherd, and Maureen White. Produced by Grant. Presented by Nightwood at St. Paul's Square.

1983/84

Nightwood produced a season brochure for the first time. It listed a board of directors: David Heath, Rosemary Sullivan, Grant, and White. The brochure included *Smoke Damage, Peace Banquet, The Kingdom of Loudascanbe, Penelope,* "Rhubarb," and "Women Workshop Plays 1984," with a call for submissions by December 1983.

Nightwood also produced a press release–like document with press clippings, statistics from the Fraticelli Report on the Status of Women in Theatre, and the statements: "Nightwood Theatre is the only theatre company in Toronto founded by women, and it continues to be operated by women" and "Since 1978, Nightwood Theatre remains a community-oriented, politically-concerned company, striving to create original Canadian plays."

In a 1983 Toronto Arts Council grant application, Cynthia Grant is listed as artistic director. Nightwood had previously received $1,700 and was asking for $4,000. In the previous year, it had given 32 performances, with a total audience of 2,900 and an average of 91 per show. Its special audiences are listed as women's groups, the literary and visual arts community, and the Spanish-speaking community.

1984

As noted above, the 1983/84 season brochure indicated that *The Kingdom of Loudascanbe* by Kim Renders and Maureen White would be performed as a Christmas show; that "Rhubarb!" would be done at the Theatre Centre in January; that *Penelope* would be presented in February; and that an event called "Women Workshop Plays" would happen sometime in 1984. (Subsequent press releases mentioned the long delays and postponements for *Penelope*, but insisted it would be done in the fall.)

January

"Rhubarb!" at the Theatre Centre: White, Vingoe, and Grant appear in *Nancy Drew (Goes in Search of Her Missing Mother)* by Ann-Marie Mac-Donald and Beverley Cooper, which became part of a late-night series at Theatre Passe Muraille in 1984, then was given a full production in 1985, with the title *Clue in the Fast Lane*, directed by Maureen White.

Other "Rhubarb!" participants with Nightwood ties include Mary Durkan, Peggy Sample, and Amanda Hale. *Temptonga* is performed by Ida Carnevali and directed by Richard Pochinko.

22 March–1 April

Cynthia Grant and Bob Nasmith appear in a production of *La Musica* by Marguerite Duras, subtitled "an interlude in a divorce." Theatre Passe Muraille Backspace. No indication this is a Nightwood production.

Also in April, Cynthia Grant directs an anti-nuclear play by Brian Metcalfe called *Pink Flies!* intended to link Toronto with Volgograd. It runs for two performances at the George Ignatieff Theatre. The cast includes Mary Vingoe; a note in the program reads, "Director Cynthia Grant and actors Mike Hiller, Peggy Sample, Mary Vingoe and Philip Shepherd are members of Nightwood Theatre who have donated their services to the production."

June

The Theatre Centre moves to the Poor Alex Theatre on Brunswick Street; tenants are Crow's Theatre, Nightwood, and Theatre Smith-Gilmour.

Spring

The Anna Project (consisting of Suzanne Khuri, Ann-Marie MacDonald, Patricia Nichols, Baṇuta Rubess, Tori Smith, Barb Taylor, and Maureen White) tour southern Ontario, funded by Canada Council Explorations, the Ontario Arts Council, and the Floyd S. Chalmers Fund. On the publicity brochure, Maureen White is identified as a founding member of Nightwood Theatre. The brochure states, "Together we combine multi-media creative backgrounds and a range of theatrical styles, with years of community organizing and outreach. We share firm roots in the collective creation process and have worked together and with other artists for the past several years to produce and perform original theatre spectacles which are both innovative and socially challenging."

This is For You, Anna is nominated in 1984 for a Dora Mavor Moore Award for artistic excellence and theatrical innovation.

SUMMER

Love and Work Enough ("A celebration of Ontario's pioneer women"), created collectively by its five actors—Kate Lazier, Eva Mackey, Peggy Sample, Heather D. Swain, and Cathy Wendt; directed by Mary Vingoe with Cynthia Grant; musical director Anne Lederman. Shawna Dempsey is the administrator/publicist. Tours for five weeks, then tours again in fall 1984 and into '85 to 150 schools across Ontario, co-produced by Theatre Direct Canada. Funded by Summer Canada Works, Theatre Ontario's Youth Theatre Training program (funded by the Ontario Arts Council), and the Department of the Secretary of State to mark the bicentennial of Ontario. Winner of a Dora Mavor Moore Award for best production in the Children's category.

A videotape was made of one performance. It shows many common techniques of the collective creation method; for example, actors playing animals and objects, inventive staging with songs and dances, and quotations from historical documents.

The central theme was the discrepancy between the delicacy expected of women in the Old World and the resilience they had to show to survive in the New World

Began research 14–26 May, rehearsed 28 May to 16 June, and toured 18 June to 21 July to: museums, Ontario Place, seniors' homes, high schools, Harbourfront Centre, Poor Alex Theatre, hospital, Interval House, libraries, Queen Street mental health centre, café.

23 May 1984: Theatre Direct had already proposed a school tour and Nightwood agreed that, if TD commissioned it, "we will consider, even at this stage, building the script as a series of interlocking parts, some of which could be added or deleted depending on our audience."

Nightwood contributed $15,000–$20,000 and would receive royalties based on a percentage of earnings. Theatre Direct would pay salaries and production costs and book the tour.

Margaret Laurence gave the show her endorsement: "*Love and Work Enough* is a marvellous show. It is entertaining, educational and very moving. Historically accurate, it presents the lives of pioneer women in their own words in such a way that audiences of all ages learn a great deal about the stamina, the sufferings, the humour and above all the courage of our foremothers. For young audiences especially, this way of presenting our history is a rich and enjoyable experience. The four young women who act, dance and sing, taking a multitude of parts in the show, are exceptionally talented. To be able to create both laughter and tears — that is a sign of true artistry. I feel privileged to have seen *Love and Work Enough*. It's a winner."

5–23 September

Nightwood presents *Pope Joan* ("A non-historical comedy") by Baņuta Rubess, produced and directed by Cynthia Grant at the Theatre Centre at the Poor Alex. Cast: Maureen White (as Joan), Mary Durkan, Mary Vingoe, Dean Gilmour, Andy Jones, and Charles Tomlinson. Nominated for a Chalmers award. "A non-historical investigation into the 9th century legendary Pope." Coincides with Pope John Paul's visit to Toronto.

A review by Dr. Linda Beamer, aired on CJRT radio, stated, "This is the kind of theatre we had a lot of in Toronto in the '70s: imaginative, original, low-budget but high-quality entertainment. I found it fresh — in both senses of the word. It breathes vitality; it is also cheeky."

Fall

The "Theatre Centre R&D Festival." Nightwood contributions are: *The Woman Who Slept With Men to Take the War Out of Them* by Deena Metzger (adapted by Maureen White and Baņuta Rubess, invited to Playwrights Workshop in Montreal to develop further); and *The Medical Show* by Amanda Hale (actors are Ann-Marie MacDonald, Donna Bothen, and Maureen White, with Grant as director).

The 1984/85 season brochure mentions the success of *Love and Work Enough* and *Pope Joan*, and emphasizes that past shows have gone on to be repeated: *Yellow Wallpaper* on CBC Radio's Vanishing Point; *Nancy Drew* in a Theatre Passe Muraille run; and the tour of *This is For You, Anna* (referred to as a "Nightwood seed show") to The Great Canadian Theatre Company in Ottawa. Upcoming Spring productions are: *The Woman Who Slept With Men to Take the War Out of Them, Kollwitz, Penelope,* and *Before and Beyond Testubes*.

1985
FEBRUARY

Re-Production, or Testube Tots in Baby-lon by Amanda Hale, presented by Nightwood in Ottawa at a conference of the National Association of Women and the Law.

Also in February and March and again in May–June, *Temptonga: The Reddest Woman in the World*, written and performed by Ida Carnevale, is performed in venues around Toronto. Nightwood financially supported the services of Mary Vingoe as director.

Nightwood intended to show three plays in development on 19 May: *Kathe Kollwitz* by Dena Saxer, *Women Organizing*, and *Penelope*. Another proposal was for a play called *Moira* by Mary Vingoe. Nightwood also applied unsuccessfully for funding to do an "Immigrant Women" project and to expand on the *Re-Production* play.

APRIL

Nightwood sponsors a reading of *The Edge of the Earth is Too Near, Violette Leduc* by Jovette Marchessault at Factory Theatre's "Brave New Works."

MAY

Time and Space Limited from New York (8–12 May; writer and director Linda Mussman, actors Deborah Ayer-Brown, Cludia Bruce, Semih Sirinciogly, and Ingrid Reffert) and Ladies Against Women from San Francisco (15–18 May; written by The Group—Jain Angeles, Jeff Thompson, Selma Vincent, and Gail-Anne Williams—and directed by Marcia Kimell) both present evening performances at the Theatre Centre as fundraisers for Nightwood. Time and Space Limited also does a two-week workshop.

MAY–JUNE

"The Next Stage: Women Transforming the Theatre," a two-day conference as part of the Theatre Festival of the Americas in Montreal; Grant is a panellist. Other participants include Rina Fraticelli, Kate Lushington, and Pol Pelletier; international participants include Joan Schenkar, Maria Irene Fornes, Judith Malina, and Joanne Akalaitis.

SUMMER

Canadian Theatre Review 43: special issue on women in theatre includes "Notes from the Front Line" with photos and short statements by each of Nightwood's founding four, as well as a script for, and articles about, *This is For You, Anna.*

SEPTEMBER

In 1985, Christopher Bye was working on a volunteer basis as an administrator for both Nightwood and Buddies, and Louise Kee was doing fundraising. Nightwood restructured and hired a general manager, Linda Brown. Mary Vingoe was appointed the interim artistic coordinator.

Board of directors for 1985/86: Susan G. Cole, Mary Durkan, Maureen FitzGerald, Rina Fraticelli, Rubess, Grant, Renders, and White.

3–6 OCTOBER

Nightwood presents *Penelope*, a retelling of Homer's *Ulysses* with the poetry of Margaret Atwood, adapted by Cynthia Grant, Peggy Sample, and Susan Seagrove, at the Theatre Centre. Later developed by the Company of Sirens.

OCTOBER–NOVEMBER

"Transformations," staged readings at the Theatre Centre: 24–25 October, *War Babies* by Margaret Hollingsworth, directed by Mary Vingoe; 26–27 October, *Portrait of Dora* by Hélène Cixous, directed by Baņuta Rubess; 31 October–1 November, *Signs of Life* by Joan Schenkar, directed by Svetlana Zylin; 2–3 November, *Masterpieces* by Sarah Daniels, directed by Mary Durkan.

November–December

This is For You, Anna tours England; at this point, Patricia Nichols is no longer involved. The publicity states the show is produced by The Anna Project and Nightwood Theatre.

Also in 1985:

Cynthia Grant and Aida Jordão began working on *The Working People's Picture Show,* a collective creation about labour issues. It was originally produced by Nightwood, then became a production of the Company of Sirens and Ground Zero Productions

1986

Cynthia Grant left Nightwood in 1986 to co-found the Company of Sirens. Mary Vingoe continued as artistic coordinator and Linda Brown as administrator.

14–16 January

This is For You, Anna returns to Toronto after its English tour for a run at the Theatre Passe Muraille Backspace.

10 March

Fourth annual "Five Minute Feminist Cabaret" at Lee's Palace, presented by Nightwood and Women's Cultural Building; Djanet Sears presents the earliest version of *Afrika Solo.* Attendance is over 300.

13–17 March

First annual "Groundswell Festival." Nightwood had been seeking funding for a new developmental festival throughout 1985 and had support from the Laidlaw and Jackman Foundations. Thirteen shows presented, including *To Humbert Humbert* (which later became *The Last Will and Testament of Lolita*); *The Paraskeva Principle* by Francine Volker, directed by JoAnn McIntyre, performed by Volker and Annie-Lou Chester, which Nightwood later produced; and *A Classical Education,* written by Helen Weinzweig (playwright in residence) and directed by Maureen White. Also: *A Kissing Way/Quickening,* two plays adapted from their radio versions by Judith Thompson, and *Nutshells* by Diana Braithwaite, directed by Ahdri Zhina. *Jane One Woman* is presented by Théâtre Expérimental des Femmes from Montreal.

14 MAY–1 JUNE

Nightwood presents *The Edge of the Earth is Too Near, Violette Leduc* by Jovette Marchessault, translated by Susanne de Lotbinière-Harwood, directed by Cynthia Grant, at the Theatre Centre. Kim Renders stars as Violette, with John Blackwood, Martha Cronyn (as Violette's lover Hermine), Sky Gilbert (who was nominated for a Dora Award), Joan Heney, Shirley Josephs, and Ian Wallace. Sponsored by the Gay Community Appeal.

JUNE

"duMaurier World Stage Festival" production of *This is For You, Anna.*

SUMMER

Programming for "Groundswell" begins through in-house workshops and readings led by Rina Fraticelli and Johanna Householder. Nightwood attempts to establish a library of plays by women.

1986/87

Linda Brown is the general manager (full-time, 8 months per year). In an application to the Ontario Participation Investment in the Arts program, Baṇuta Rubess is listed as the president, Kim Renders as secretary, and Mary Durkan as treasurer.

Board of directors: Susan Cole, Mary Durkan, Maureen FitzGerald, Rina Fraticelli, Carlyn Moulton, Rubess, Renders, Vingoe, and White. Playwright in residence: Peggy Thompson, through the Ontario Arts Council playwright residency program.

1987

22–30 JANUARY

Nightwood presents *My Boyfriend's Back and There's Gonna Be Laundry: A Lone Woman Show,* written and performed by Sandra Shamas, at the Factory Theatre Studio Café.

22 JANUARY–1 FEBRUARY

Second annual "Groundswell" held at the Annex Theatre. Week One: *St. Frances of Hollywood* by Sally Clark, directed by Mary Vingoe; *Afrika Solo*, a staged reading by Djanet Sears, directed by Annie Szamosi; *Swindler's Rhapsody* by Makka Kleist and Monique Mojica; *Telewalk Phone Woman Man*, written and directed by Jan Kudelka, including Kim Renders in the cast; and *Hysterical Women*, a feminist comedy improv troupe from Montreal, including Alisa Palmer. Week Two: *Artists Angst: A Political Thriller* by Beverley Cooper, directed by Maureen White; *A Particular Class of Women* by Janet Feindel, a workshop directed and dramaturged by Mary Durkan; *One Bedroom with Dignity* by Lillian Allen, directed by Ahdri Zhina and including Alison Sealy-Smith in the cast; *Hersteria*, written and performed by Janine Fuller and Shawna Dempsey; and *Sex in a Box*, written and performed by Kate Lushington, directed by Johanna Householder.

26 FEBRUARY–29 MARCH

Nightwood, in association with Toronto Free Theatre, presents *War Babies* by Margaret Hollingsworth, directed by Mary Vingoe. The cast: Duncan Fraser, Bridget O'Sullivan, Don Allison, Richard Liptrot, Thomas Hauff, Nicola Lipman, Linda Goranson. Nominated for a Dora Award for Best New Play. Had also been nominated for a Governor General's Award for Drama in 1985. From the press release: "*War Babies* centres around a couple in their early forties, she a playwright, he a war correspondent, as they await the birth of their first child. Slowly they are overshadowed by their fictional doubles, characters from a play Esme is writing. As Esme creates her play within a play, the distinctions dissolve between past and present, real and imagined, private and public."

9 MARCH

At Theatre Passe Muraille, Nightwood, with Women's Cultural Building, presents the Fifth Annual "Five Minute Feminist Cabaret." *A Fertile Imagination* by Susan Cole is first presented as a monologue. Other performers are: Laurie Bell, Susan Belyea, Diana Braithwaite, The Clichettes, Holly Cole, Bev Cooper, Evelynne Datl, Janine Fuller, Louise Garfield, Linda Griffiths, Anne Healy, Hysterical Women, Cathy Jones, Makka

Kleist, Marla Lukofksy, Ann-Marie MacDonald, Tanya Mars, Monique Mojica, Baṇuta Rubess, and Djanet Sears.

MAY

Nightwood is still at the Poor Alex but is no longer part of the Theatre Centre.

2–21 JUNE

Nightwood and The Humbert Humbert Project (Project), in association with Theatre Passe Muraille, present *The Last Will and Testament of Lolita*. Subtitled "a vile pink comedy," created and performed by Louise Garfield, Baṇuta Rubess, Peggy Thompson, and Maureen White, with Jim Warren as the Sandman and a film by Peter Mettler featuring Jackie Burroughs. Peggy Thompson is also playwright in residence at this time.

AUGUST

Maureen White begins work as artistic coordinator (she had recently directed *Thin Ice* by Baṇuta Rubess and Bev Cooper, on tour with Theatre Direct, and had acted in *Pope Joan* at Concordia University. Mary Vingoe had also been working as the co-artistic director of The Ship's Company Theatre in Parrsboro, Nova Scotia). Linda Brown is still the general manager. Nightwood applies for funding to develop *Goodnight Desdemona (Good Morning Juliet)* with Ann-Marie MacDonald and Baṇuta Rubess (the play at this point is being discussed as a collective), and *The Medea Project* with Sally Clark; also considering Peggy Thompson's *Jelvis*, Joan Schenkar's *Fulfilling Koch's Postulate*, and a collective called *Les Demoiselles de Picasso*. Also applies for funding to hold a workshop by Caryl Churchill.

NOVEMBER

At the Annex Theatre, third annual "Groundswell." Week One: *Let's Go to Your Place* by Kate Lushington and The Clichettes, directed by Maureen White; *Venius Pearls* by Colleen Wagner, directed by Mary Durkan; *Idylls*, written and performed by Wanda Buchanan, Susan Coyne, and Paula Wing; *The Euguélionne*, adapted from the novel by Louky Bersianik and performed by Cynthia Grant, Aida Jordão, Peggy Sample, and Alison

Sealy-Smith; *How I Differ From the Norm*, written and performed by Mary Hawkins and directed by Maggie Huculak; *Ebony Voices*, a collective made up of Jo-Anne Atherley, Margaret Joseph, Alana McKnight, and Carolyn Harris, with Vivine Scarlett. Week Two: *The Paraskeva Principle* by Francine Volker, directed by JoAnn McIntyre; *The Herring Gull's Egg*, written and directed by Mary Vingoe; *My Boyfriend's Back and There's Gonna be Laundry* by Sandra Shamas; *The Kingdom of LoudAsCanBe*, written and directed by Kim Renders; *Settlements* by Beverly Yhap, directed by Kathleen Flaherty.

18–20 DECEMBER

The Kingdom of LoudAsCanBe, written and directed by Renders, at the Annex Theatre. Cast: Ida Carnevali, Mary Hawkins, James Kirchner, with live music by Paul Cram, and large puppets. Nightwood and Theatre Direct also take the show on a school tour.

Board of directors for 1987/88: Mary Durkan (president), Renders, White, Vingoe, Rubess, Susan Cole, Maureen FitzGerald, Rina Fraticelli, Carlyn Moulton (and Peggy Thompson listed on some documents).

1988

16–31 JANUARY

Nightwood had been intending to produce Janet Feindel's *A Particular Class of Women*, but instead produces The Clichettes in *Up Against the Wallpaper*, written by Kate Lushington and The Clichettes (Johanna Householder, Louise Garfield, Janice Hladki), directed by Maureen White. Produced at the Factory Theatre Studio Café. Nominated for Dora Mavor Moore Awards for outstanding costume design.

Special added attraction is *Too Close to Home*, written and performed by Kim Renders. *My Boyfriend's Back and There's Gonna Be Laundry* is also done as a late-night show on Fridays and Saturdays.

JANUARY

Thin Ice by Beverley Cooper and Baņuta Rubess, directed by Maureen White, wins the Chalmers Canadian Children's Play Award.

7 March

Sixth Annual "Five Minute Feminist Cabaret" held at Theatre Passe Muraille. "A Laugh a Minute," by Marusia Bociurkiw, *Rites* magazine (May 1988).

March

Maureen White is laid off.

31 March–23 April

Goodnight Desdemona (Good Morning Juliet), "a comical Shakespearean romance" by Ann-Marie MacDonald, commissioned and presented by Nightwood, directed and dramaturged by Baṇuta Rubess, at the Annex Theatre. Cast includes Derek Boyes, Beverley Cooper, Diana Fajrajsl, Tanja Jacobs, and Martin Julien. Nominated for a Dora Mavor Moore Award, wins the 1990 Governor General's Award for Drama, a Chalmers Canadian Play Award, and the Canadian Author's Association Award. Remounted and toured in 1990.

September

Kate Lushington was hired in July and begins work as artistic director in September. Linda Brown is still the general manager.

Board of directors for 1988/89: Susan Cole, Lesley Currie, Mary Durkan, Martha Leary, Kim Renders, Wendy Elliot, Djanet Sears, Sophia Sperdakos, Mary Vingoe.

1–4 and 8–11 December

Fourth annual "Groundswell" held at the Annex Theatre. Week One: *World Class City*, written and performed by Jan Kudelka; *Copper Tin Can* by Monique Giroux, directed by Djanet Sears; *Black Friday* by Audrey Butler, directed by Karen Woolridge; *Dead Honky* by Betty Quan, directed by Beverly Yhap; *Memoirs of Darkness and Light*, performance art written by Mia Blackwell and performed by Blackwell and Kim Renders; *Miss McDoon of Doonsville (The Barrel Lady)*, written and performed by Itah Sadu and directed by Ahdri Zhina Mandiela. Special events include: *No More Bimboes for Me (The Invisibility Factor)*, written by Shirley Barrie and Julie Salverson, developed using Boal's Forum method and performed by Barrie and Salverson, Brenda Bazinet, Richard Campbell, Patricia Idlette, and Susan Seagrove. Also two children's events: "Kidsplay" writing festival and a video about Native women artists called *The Spirit of Turtle Island*. Week Two: *Godhead*, written by Ann Diamond and directed by Mary Durkan; *Baby Trials*, written and performed by Lisa Karrer and Roberta Levine, directed by Marcia Abujamra; *On Earth as it Isn't Heaven*, written and performed by Michele George; *Vox Lumina*, written by Paula Wing and directed by Michelene Chevrier; *Just One Touch* by P. Afua Marcus, directed by Ahdri Zhina Mandiela; *Out for Blood* by The Clichettes, directed by Jennifer Dean.

Selection Committee for "Groundswell": Janine Fuller, Djanet Sears, Karen Woolridge, Beverly Yhap. "Groundtalk" is a feedback session for participants, including Carol Bolt, Sally Clark, Margaret Hollingsworth, Ann-Marie MacDonald, and Judith Thompson, and hosted by Susan Feldman.

1989

FEBRUARY

Kim Renders leaves the board.

6 MARCH

Seventh annual "Five Minute Feminist Cabaret" held at Lee's Palace in association with Women's Cultural Building. Performers include Meryn Cadell, Sally Clark, Holly Cole, Joan McLeod, Marlene Nourbese Philip, Itah Sadu, Hysterical Women, and Girlfrenzy.

23 MARCH—16 APRIL

Nightwood presents *The Paraskeva Principle* ("A slightly red comedy celebrating the life and art of Paraskeva Clark"), written and performed by Francine Volker, directed by Jo Ann McIntyre, at the Annex Theatre. The program credits the clowning to Richard Pochinko, art to Sally Clark and Eric LaDelpha, and dramaturgy to Margaret Hollingsworth.

4–28 May

Nightwood presents *The Herring Gull's Egg*, written by Mary Vingoe and directed by Maureen White, at the Theatre Passe Muraille Backspace. The cast is Donna Goodhand, David Kinsman, Kate Lynch, Simon Richards, and Alan Williams. At this time, Vingoe is still artistic co-director at The Ship's Company, and is also teaching at York University, and chair of the Playwrights Union of Canada. *The Herring Gull's Egg* is about a couple dealing with an unexpected pregnancy, environmental issues, and the divide between urban and rural.

7 and 8 June

Nancy Jackman hosts fundraising lunches for Nightwood, assisted by Martha Burns and Diane D'Aquila.

Fall

First issue of *Nightwords* newsletter, vol. 1 no. 1. First board retreat held 9 and 10 September.

The period 16 November 1989 to 29 April 1990 is announced as the tenth anniversary season, to include "Groundswell," the remount of *Goodnight Desdemona (Good Morning Juliet)*, *Princess Pocahontas and the Blue Spots*, and concluding with "FemCab."

16–29 November

At the Annex Theatre, the fifth annual "Groundswell" includes *A Fertile Imagination* by Susan G. Cole, directed by Kate Lushington; and *Princess Pocahontas and the Blue Spots* by Monique Mojica, directed by Djanet Sears. Also: *Spinster* by Patsy Ludwick, directed by Anne Anglin; *Transmitting an Alarming Message* by Susette Schacherl, directed by Maggie Huculak; *El Hadj Diakouma* by Issa Traore, a presentation by Theatre de l'Harmettan from Montreal; *Ella and Jennifer* by Afua Marcus, directed by Djanet Sears; *Recycling: a Restoration Comedy* by Jean Walker, directed by Pat Idlette; *Closed Visit* by Vivienne Laxdal, directed by Barbara Lysnes, associate artist at the Great Canadian Theatre Company in Ottawa; *The Stayfresh Special* by Alison Kelly and Deborah Williams, from the Rags to Rituals Co-op from Vancouver; *Medusa Rising* by Audrey Butler, directed by Kate Lushington; *Sun and Shadow* by Janis

Nickleson and Sun Gui Zhen; *One Morning I Realized I was Licking the Kitchen Floor* by Marilyn Norry and Heather Swain; *Flowers* by Deborah Porter, directed by Jennie Dean.

Board of directors as of fall 1989: Phyllis Berck, Pat Idlette (replacing Susan Cole), Lesley Currie, Wendy J. Elliot, Astrid Janson, Martha R. Leary, Djanet Sears, Sophia Sperdakos. Staff: Linda Brown, Jennifer Trant, Andrea Williams. The playwright in residence is Sally Clark (her play *Life Without Instruction* was not produced by Nightwood).

Mission statement from the board retreat: "To provide opportunities for all women to create and explore new visions of the world, stretching the concept of what is theatrical, and to hone their skills as artists, so that more of us may see our reality reflected on this country's stages, thus offering theatre goers the full diversity of the Canadian experience."

The board was asked to read: The Fraticelli Report; Kate Lushington's *Fear of Feminism*, an article from *CanPlay* (October 1988) with an update on playwright's statistics, and "When the Performer is Black" by Rita Shelton Deverell, *Canadian Theatre Review* no. 47 (Summer 1988).

Fourth annual "Groundswell" is discussed in "The Editor's Column: Alternative Visions" by Martha J. Bailey, *Queen's Quarterly* 96/1 (Spring 1989): 216–219.

1990
JANUARY

"Theatrical decade reaffirmed central role of alternatives," by Jon Kaplan, *NOW*, 4–10 January 1990. Both Theatre Centre and Nightwood are included in list of top ten "people, companies and events that have had a major impact on Toronto theatre during the past decade."

Nightwood tours *Goodnight Desdemona* to the Great Canadian Theatre Company (Ottawa), Vancouver East Cultural Centre, and Northern Light Theatre (Edmonton), then opens at the Canadian Stage Company's Berkeley Street Theatre on 28 March 1990 (runs 21 March to 15 April). The cast is the same as the 1988 production, except Tanja

Jacobs is replaced by Kate Lynch. Budget for the original production was $20,000; budget for the tour is $250,000.

WINTER

Retitled *Night Talk* newsletter, vol. 1 no. 2., includes a mid-February report from the "Desdemona Tour" by Baṇuta Rubess, a column by Lushington, and a piece about Muriel Miguel. Also announces that general manager Linda Brown is being replaced by Pegi McGillivray.

9 FEBRUARY—4 MARCH

Princess Pocahontas and the Blue Spots by Monique Mojica, a co-production with Nightwood and Passe Muraille, directed by Muriel Miguel, at the Theatre Passe Muraille Backspace. Performed by Mojica and Alejandra Nunez, with music by Nunez. A program note states, *"Princess Pocahontas and the Blue Spots* highlights a commitment to anti-racism which will be reflected throughout the next decade." The play had been workshopped in May 1989 as a co-production of Nightwood and Native Earth Performing Arts. It was read in June at the "Weesageechak Festival of New Work by Native Playwrights," and then a workshop production was seen at "Groundswell" in November 1989, directed by Djanet Sears.

12 MARCH

"No Turning Back: the Eighth Annual Five Minute Feminist Cabaret" held at Young People's Theatre. Audience of 350.

22 MARCH

"The Goodnight Gala," a party to celebrate Nightwood's anniversary and to raise funds for the "Desdemona Tour."

FALL

Night Talk newsletter, vol. 2 no. 1, announces Nightwood has moved to 317 Adelaide Street West as of October 15. Diana Braithwaite is announced as the playwright in residence for 1990/91.

Pegi McGillivray has already moved on and been replaced by business manager Kate Tucker. Other staff are associate artistic director

Lynda Hill and administrator Jennifer Trant, as well as Victoria Dawe, Elaine Lumley, and Kim Brown.

Board of directors for 1990/91: Kay Armatage, Phyllis Berck, Wendy J. Elliott, Patricia Idlette, Astrid Janson, Marion MacKenzie, Shirley Netten, Judith Ramirez, Djanet Sears, Jo Anne Sommers, Sophia Sperdakos. Described in the newsletter as "half community members and half artist members."

15–25 NOVEMBER

"Blood and Power," the sixth annual "Groundswell," held at the Annex Theatre, begins with a fundraising event on 11 November called "Write Off," where playwrights get five hours to create a play. Writers are Baṇuta Rubess, Don Hannah, Ann-Marie MacDonald, Daniel MacIvor, Sky Gilbert, Audrey Butler, and Diana Braithwaite. Also, for the first time, "Groundswell" is organized around a core troupe of actors.

Week One: *Martha and Elvira* by Diana Braithwaite, featuring Patricia Idlette and Alison Sealy-Smith; *Flowers* by Deborah Porter, directed by Lynda Hill (second time at "Groundswell"); *Mermaid in Love* by Shawna Dempsey; *Driving Dad* by Jane Wilson, directed by Kathleen Flaherty; *A Game of Inches* by Linda Griffiths, directed by Sandi Balcovske; *Tea Lady* by Cecile Belec, directed by Susan Miner; *Woman*, performed by The Toronto Women's Auxiliary; a late-night performance called *At Odds (Or The Dead Sea Squirrels)* by Siobhan McCormick, Iris Turcott, Ellen-Ray Hennessey, Melissa Graham, and Deborah Porter. Week Two: *Exhibiting Disgusting Material* by The Woomers Group, directed by Sally Han; *Chronicle of a Free Fall* by Claude Moise and *Nothing But the Truth* by Jean Morisset, both presented by Theatre de l'Harmattan; *Hot and Soft* by Muriel Miguel; *dark diaspora... in DUB* by ahdri zhina mandiela; *Premature Mother* by Deborah Kimmet, directed by Annie Kidder; *Martha and Mary* by Vivian Payne; and a late-night performance by Empress Productions (Diane Flacks, Victoria Ward, Wendy White) called *Slow Thunder*. There are also one-time play readings of: *Body Blows* by Beverly Yhap, *Flight Before Xmas* by Victoria Dawe, *Eleanor Marx* by Robin Beltisky Endres, and *An untitled work* by Colleen Wagner.

The Play Group is Martha Burns, Jennie Dean, Lynda Hill, Djanet Sears, Pat Idlette, Kate Lushington, and Astrid Janson.

1991

30 January–24 February

Nightwood presents *A Fertile Imagination* by Susan G. Cole, directed by Kate Lushington, at the Poor Alex. Cast: Kate Lynch, Robin Craig, Patricia Idlette. Associate artist and dramaturge is Alisa Palmer and the production manager is Leslie Lester. Nominated for two Dora Awards. (Remounted at Theatre Passe Muraille in January–February 1992, directed by Layne Coleman, and with Yanna McIntosh replacing Idlette.)

11 March

Ninth annual "Five Minute Feminist Cabaret" at The Great Hall (1087 Queen Street West), hosted by Susan G. Cole and Lorraine Segato. Expected to raise $2,000–$4,000.

18 April

Actor Sandra Shamas and storyteller Itah Sadu give a special benefit performance in support of Nightwood and Friends of the Shopping Bag Ladies, a social services agency that helps transient women. Held at Young People's Theatre; tickets are $65 and $100, including a gala reception. Earns about $7,000 for each organization.

May

The Second International Women Playwright's Conference, "Voices of Authority," is held at Glendon College, York University, in Toronto.

Summer

Night Talk, vol. 2 no. 3 (Summer 1991), includes an article about *dark diaspora... in DUB*. Sister Vision Press will be publishing it "along with *black/stage/women*, an anthology of scripts by Black women playwrights which ahdri zhina is currently producing as a series of workshops and staged readings at Theatre Passe Muraille during the Company of Sirens' Women and Live Words Festival." "A Word, or two, from the Artistic Director" describes the great success of *A Fertile Imagination*, the "Nightworks" in-house workshop series on work by Diana Braithwaite, ahdri zhina mandiela, and Monique Mojica, and the Sister Reach project, with associate artist Pauline Peters and resource and outreach coordinator Annette Clough. "Springwrights" is an ongoing development group for playwrights.

28 JUNE–3 JULY

Nightwood Theatre presents the b current production of *dark diaspora... in DUB* by ahdri zhina mandiela, a "Fringe Festival" show at the Poor Alex. Co-directed by mandiela and Djanet Sears; the cast is Deborah Castello, Vernita de Lis Leece, Charmaine Headley, mandiela, Junia Mason, Kim Roberts, and Vivine Scarlett. The play was developed at the November 1990 "Groundswell" and at the Company of Sirens' "Women and Live Words Festival" in May '91, and by b current. In March of 1992, *dark diaspora... in DUB* ran at Beaver Hall Studio Gallery, directed by ahdri zhina mandiela and Djanet Sears.

24 OCTOBER–3 NOVEMBER

"Hot Flashes," the seventh annual "Groundswell," held at the Tarragon Extra Space. The "Write Off" fundraising event is held again 25 November at Passe Muraille. "Black Women on Site," a meeting of Black women with an interest in theatre, held 2 November as part of "Groundswell." Week One: *The Particulars of Flora and Rosie* by Stiletto Company, performed by Catherine Hayos and Rena Polley; *Nancy Chew Enters the Dragon* by Betty Quan; *Bum Wrap* by Toronto Women's Auxiliary; *Sister Sister ME* by Lisa Walter; *The A-List* by Marcy Rogers; *Ain't That a Shame* by Vernita Leece; *Blatantly Sexual* by Bridget McFarthing (had a full production 14–31 October 1993 at Buddies in Bad Times, directed by Alisa Palmer, starring Diane Flacks and Ellen-Ray Hennessy, credited to McFarthing and also Kristyn Dunnion); *Mavis Rising* by Pauline Peters (whose *Dryland* was produced by Nightwood in 1993). Week Two: *The Sand* by Laurie Fyffe, directed by Beverley Cooper; *Fear of Lying* by Paulette Phillips; *Third Floor Women's Where*, written and performed by Heather Lord and Junia Mason, directed by Djanet Sears; *What Goes Around* by Deborah Castello, directed by ahdri zhina mandiela; *Albeit Aboriginal* by Marie Annharte Baker; *Man on the Moon, Woman on the Pill*, written and performed by Christine Taylor, directed by Janice Spence;

Love & Other Strange Things, songs by Lillian Allen performed by Djanet Sears and band.

The "Groundswell" selection committee is Jo Anne Atherley, Carol Bolt, Audrey Butler, Christine Plunkett, and Patricia Idlette.

2 NOVEMBER

The publication of Monique Mojica's *Princess Pocahontas and the Blue Spots* by Women's Press is launched as part of "Groundswell."

FALL

Night Talk vol. 3 no. 1 (Fall 1991) announces that four works by playwright in residence Diana Braithwaite will be produced in the new year, in January and February. Also announces that Monique Mojica is the new playwright in residence and that she will be working on *A Savage Equilibrium*. Lynda Hill announces that she will be leaving her position as associate director as of 13 December. Pauline Peters and Annette Clough's positions have also ended.

Board of directors: Joanne Dunbar, Astrid Janson, Shirley Netten, Teresa Przybylski, Judith Ramirez, Djanet Sears, Carol Bolt, Sally Han, Clare Barclay, Rita Deverell Staff: Kate Lushington, Kate Tucker, Jennifer Trant.

1992
JANUARY/FEBRUARY

At the Poor Alex, Nightwood Theatre presents Diana Braithwaite's "The Wonder Quartet": 1. *The Wonder of Man: A Black Woman's Trip Through the Galaxy*, 21 January–9 February, written and composed by Braithwaite, directed by Djanet Sears (with assistant Diane Roberts, and Alisa Palmer as movement facilitator), with Melissa Adamson, Lili Francks, Rosemary Galloway, Taborah Johnson, Dawn Roach, Alison Sealy-Smith, and Jean Small. *The Wonder of Man* evolved from Diana Braithwaite's 1986 "Groundswell" work, *Nutshells*, was developed through a 1990/91 playwright's residency at Nightwood, workshopped in extract as part of "black/stage/women" during the Company of Sirens' "Women and Live Words Festival" in May 1991, and further developed in workshops through a Canada Council Project Grant and donations from Levi-Strauss Canada.

2. *Martha and Elvira*, 11–16 February, directed by Alison Sealy-Smith with Taborah Johnson and Lili Francks. It grew out of a 1984 script to commemorate two hundred years of Black history in Ontario, toured with Pelican Players, and was then done at "Groundswell." Won first prize at the "Festival of African Women in the Arts" in Chicago in 1990.

3. *Do Not Adjust Your Sets*, 11–16 February, directed by ahdri zhina mandiela, with Dawn Roach, Jean Small, Luther Hansraj, and Michael Malcolm. This play came out of the Theatre Centre's Research & Development series.

4. *Time to Forget*, directed by Braithwaite, in a late-night reading of a play originated at the "Write Off!" fundraiser, about a family Christmas.

The Wonder of Man, Martha and Elvira, and *Do Not Adjust Your Set* were held over in repertory for two more weeks, 18 February to 1 March.

A Fertile Imagination by Susan G. Cole, remounted at Theatre Passe Muraille, directed by Layne Coleman, and with Yanna McIntosh replacing Idlette.

9 MARCH

Tenth annual "Five Minute Feminist Cabaret" at the Bathurst Street Theatre: "A Celebration of Women Creating Culture—Five Hundred Years of Resistance." The artistic selection committee was Lillian Allen, Maxine Bailey, Ruth Dworin, Sally Han, Lee Pui Ming, and Kate Lushington.

OCTOBER

Night Talk newsletter vol. 4 no. 1 (Fall 1992) introduces Diane Roberts as the new associate artistic director. Nightwood had taken a hiatus from May to September and rented out its office space to Fresh Elements, a summer arts job opportunity program for Black and Native youth designed by Lillian Allen, Itah Sadu, and Marrie Mumford. The general manager is now Heather Young.

22 October–1 November

Tarragon Theatre, "Making Waves," eighth annual "Groundswell." Artistic director of the festival was Diane Roberts, with committee members Monique Mojica, Alison Sealy-Smith, Susan Hogan, Dawn Obokata, Kate Lushington, and Carol Bolt. Week One: *Supreme Effect* by Kim McNeilly; *Child of the Saver* by Kim Kuhteubl, co-directed by Alison Sealy-Smith and Diane Roberts; *Clean* by Karen Kemlo, directed by Diane Roberts; *A Savage Equilibrium* by Monique Mojica, Fernando Hernandez Perez, and Jani Lauzon, directed by Floyd Favel; *Bantering the Unanswerable* by Kate Barker, directed by Lynda Hill; *Demeter and the Bird's Song* by Gail Nyoka, directed by Djanet Sears; *Emily Stowe* by Florence Gibson, directed by Elizabeth Shepherd (cast included Joyce Campion). Week Two: *Dryland: In My Village*, written and performed by Pauline Peters, directed by Diane Roberts; *Charming and Rose: True Love* by Kelley Jo Burke, directed by Kate Lushington; *Girls in the 'Hood* by young women from Metro Housing (M.T.H.A.) and Catherine Glen, directed by Diane Roberts; *Coming from the Womb* by The Red Sister/Black Sister Collective, directed by Emerita Emerencia; *Ordinary Desires* by Lisa Porter; *Pen Pals* by Lorre Jensen, directed by Michelene Chevrier. Play readings were done of: *Age of Iron* by Marie Humber (B.C.), *Heartless Disappearance into Labrador Seas* by Lois Brown (Newfoundland), *Looking for Ms. Good Dyke* by Joyce Pate (Baltimore, U.S.A.)

1993
Winter

Night Talk vol. 4 no. 2 announces that *Dryland*, a story cycle by Pauline Peters that began at "Groundswell" in 1992, will inaugurate the newly renovated Nightwood Studio space. It is described as a "showing"; showings "contain all the elements of a full production: design, lights, music; they are conceived to allow the artists to continue the evolution of their work with the audience as an integral part of the process. They form the 'missing link' between a Groundswell workshop or staged reading, and a show in a larger theatre. Budgets go to artists and materials, not rent and marketing. Risk and experimentation are encouraged; prices are kept low." Included a "FemCab" ticket order form, announcement of Theatre Resource Centre events (because *Dryland* co-incided with the fourth annual Small Theatre Trade Forum, a Small Theatre Party was held after the 13 February preview performance along with the Theatre Resource Centre, also located at 317 Adelaide Street West), and an audience survey.

FEBRUARY–MARCH

Nightwood Studio, *Dryland: A Story Cycle*, written and performed by Pauline Peters, directed by Diane Roberts. A large group of collaborating artists, including "environment" designers: Grace Channer, Bonnie Beecher, Foluké, Daya Dahl, Donald Carr, Michèle George, Jani Lauzon, Monique Mojica.

15 MARCH

Young People's Theatre, eleventh annual "Feminist Cabaret." Diane Roberts is the artistic director and Alisa Palmer the assistant director of "FemCab." The selection committee is Maxine Bailey, Ruth Dworin, Gloria May Eshkibok, Nupur Gogia, Sheila James, Lezlie Lee Kam, ah-dri zhina mandiela, Monique Mojica, Dawn Obokata, Diane Roberts, and Elizabeth Shepherd. Hosted by Dawn Roach and Cheryl Francis, with thirty-three acts. Raised $3,500.

SPRING

Night Talk vol. 4 no. 3 announces upcoming *Untitled: A Work in Progress* by Monique Mojica, Kate Lushington, and Djanet Sears, which "investigates the contradictions of race, culture and friendship.... Formerly titled The Colour Collective, the group has since dreamed up many titles: Storm Warning in Effect, Cooking Up a Storm, Seven Onion Soup, Bloodlines and Lifelines, Treacherous Remedies for Amnesia, and This Ain't the June Callwood Show. Fragments were performed at FemCab, and now the creators are joined by animators Michele George, Diane Roberts and Baŋuta Rubess, and designer Teresa Przybylski.

Cheryl Francis is production stage manager." Also announces *Love and Other Strange Things* by Lillian Allen, a musical revue to be performed by Djanet Sears at Young People's Theatre 13 and 14 June, and also *Calypsos and Coups* by M. NourbeSe Philip, in a co-production with b current at the Nightwood Studio 26 and 27 June (this did not take place, although the play was workshopped and produced in Toronto by Cahoots Theatre in 1996 and 1999).

The newsletter came with a fundraising letter, and announced other fundraising plans for a garage sale, brunch, and bingo. Also called for submissions to "Groundswell."

14–16 MAY

At the Nightwood Studio, *Untitled: A Work in Progress*, a workshop exploration of issues of race and friendship with Kate Lushington, Djanet Sears, and Monique Mojica. Animators: Michele George, Muriel Miguel, Diane Roberts, and Baŋuta Rubess; facilitator: Clarissa Chandler. Set designed by Teresa Przybylski.

13 AND 14 JUNE

Love and Other Strange Things by Lillian Allen, presented as a workshop by Nightwood at Young People's Theatre. Performed by Taborah Johnson, Djanet Sears, and Nambitha Mpumiwana.

JULY

Press release announces Kate Lushington will leave her position as artistic director as of 1 December. As Heather Young did not renew her contract as general manager, the board would begin a search for a new team to take over as of 1 January 1994. Diane Roberts continues as associate artistic director. Kate Tucker returns as the financial manager and Vanessa Gold Schiff starts as an administrative intern.

The ad specifically says, "Team proposals preferred... Visionary producing team sought... demonstrate artistic vision, producing and general management experience... innovative theatre embraces diverse cultural perspectives."

FALL

Night Talk vol. 3 no. 1: "For the first time in eight years Nightwood opens its season with a mainstage production of a finished script, while regular season's opener the Groundswell Festival of New Works is moved to a new format and new time slot." Announces *Charming and Rose: True Love* as Lushington's last show as director, and includes a statement from Kelley Jo Burke. Last full show directed by Lushington had been *A Fertile Imagination* in 1991, and after leaving Nightwood she would direct *A Fertile Imagination* again at the Grand Theatre in London, Ontario.

Also gives information about the search process, and Lushington mentions Nightwood's intention to find a new home.

9–30 OCTOBER

Charming and Rose: True Love by Kelley Jo Burke, directed by Kate Lushington, at the Theatre Centre. The cast is Kristina Nicoll, Rick Roberts, and Djanet Sears. Subtitled "A Comedy with Bite" and also "a wolf morality tale." Set and costumes by Astrid Janson, with film footage assembled by Jane Thompson. Nominated for a Chalmers Award.

On 22 October, a "Revisionist Fairy Tale Ball" fundraising party is held after the performance.

NOVEMBER

Interviews for hiring process take place. Martha R. Leary is chair of the search committee. Applicants are asked to answer the questions, "How would you allocate the resources available in order to realize your vision and that of Nightwood Theatre? What is your artistic vision of Nightwood theatre? How would you define Nighwood Theatre's community? How would you go about expanding the community?"

1994

MARCH

The new artistic team is announced: Leslie Lester is producer, and Diane Roberts and Alisa Palmer are co-artistic directors.

29 March–3 April

At the Poor Alex Theatre, ninth annual "Groundswell" — "of works in progress by women." Nine plays presented: *Mango Chutney* by Dilara Ally, directed by Diane Roberts; *Difference of Latitude* by Lisa Walter, directed by Alisa Palmer, featuring Ann-Marie MacDonald and Stephanie Samuels; *Curves Off the Gender Track* by Steph Kelemen, directed by Alisa Palmer, performed by Caroline Gillis; *Cause Unknown* by Toni Ellwand, directed by Sarah Stanley; *Forgetting to Speak Softly*, written and performed by Tanis MacDonald, directed by Marion de Vries; *Thru Her Eyes* by Anagel Saunders, directed by ahdri zhina mandiela (listed as co-creators); *Death and Renovation* by Cathy Lenihan, directed by Diane Roberts; *Black Curse* by Caroline Outten, directed by Fiona Hinds; *Mary Medusa*, co-created by Shawna Dempsey and Lorri Millan (written by Millan). Also *Growing-Up Days*, a storytelling event with Lillian Allen.

New process started with a three-day in-house workshop the previous fall.

The program included an audience feedback sheet.

August

Die in Debt presents, in association with Nightwood Theatre, *Oedipus* by Ned Dickens, derived from Seneca, directed by Sarah Stanley. Under the Gardiner Expressway between Strachan Avenue and Garrison Road at the entrance to Old Fort York. Sarah Stanley is both the co-artistic director of Die in Debt and a member of Nightwood's Artistic Advisory.

Fall

Nighttalk newsletter in new, one-page format with an introductory message from Diane Roberts, Alisa Palmer, and Leslie Lester: "We're enthusiastic to take up the challenge of maintaining Nightwood's dual role as a leading producer of feminist art and as an important resource for women artists. This year marks Nightwood's 15th anniversary!" The season is announced as *Wearing the Bone* (November/December '94), "Groundswell" (March '95), and *The Coloured Girls Project* (May '95). Also contains a report from Sarah Stanley on *Oedipus*.

Djanet Sears is playwright in residence for the 1994/95 season. Kate Tucker is still financial manager.

Board of directors: Joanne Abbensetts, Clare Barclay, Florence Gibson, Catherine Glen, Bev John, Ann-Marie MacDonald, ahdri zhina mandiela, Amanda Mills, and Elizabeth Shepherd, with Shara Stone and Linda Brown as advisors. The Artistic Advisory is formed to select "Groundswell" scripts and plan events: Dilara Ally, Sarah Stanley, Dawn Obokata, Jani Lauzon, Nadia Ross, Marium Carvell, and ahdri zhina mandiela. They are not a subcommittee of the board, but assist in the selection of scripts for "Groundswell" as well as community outreach and programming.

OCTOBER

Listing for Nightwood in *NOW* (6 October 1994) describes it: "Nightwood Theatre creates alternative visions of the world from diverse cultural perspectives by producing, developing and promoting works by women artists. Over the past 15 years, its projects have included productions, script development, collaborations and the annual Groundswell Festival of new works by women."

7 NOVEMBER

"Debutant Gala," a dance fundraiser, at the El Convento Rico Club.

15 NOVEMBER–4 DECEMBER

The first show of the new season: *Wearing the Bone*, subtitled "A revolution in paradise," written and directed by Alisa Palmer, presented by Nightwood at the Theatre Centre West. Cast: Anne Anglin, Susan Coyne, and Sandra Oh, and featuring La Orquestra de la Playa with musical director Allen Cole and vocals by Luis Mario Ochoa. Nominated for Dora Awards for lighting and sound design. "Inspired by the music of renowned Cuban composer, Ernesto Lecuona and the sonnets of celebrated contemporary poet Edna St. Vincent Millay." Dramaturgy by Diane Roberts, produced by Leslie Lester. Deborah Lambie is the assistant director.

9–11 DECEMBER

Workshops and in-house readings in preparation for "Groundswell."

17 December

Nightwood and Exploded Satellite Productions host "An Evening With JoAnne Akalaitis" in the Nightwood Studio.

1995
January

Fundraising brochure mail-out.

Nighttalk (January 1995) introduces Soraya Peerbaye as the new administrative assistant, and mentions that Diane Roberts has just returned from directing a show at Vancouver's "Women in View Festival" and that Leslie Lester has also been producing a Factory Theatre/VideoCabaret co-production. Contains a piece by Kim Renders about Nightwood's origins.

Board of directors: Joanne Abbensetts, Clare Barclay, Florence Gibson, Catherine Glen, Bev John, Ann-Marie MacDonald, ahdri zhina mandiela, Amanda Mills, Elizabeth Shepherd, and addition of Anita Lee. Djanet Sears is the playwright in residence.

13 February

Makin' Whoopi, an evening of comedy at the Factory Studio Theatre, a fundraising event organized by Marium Carvell.

24 March–2 April

Tenth Annual "Groundswell Festival" held at Theatre Centre West.

Week One: *Growing Up Suite* by Shawna Dempsey and Lorri Millan; *Dinah Queen of the Blues* by Marium Carvell, directed by Diane Roberts, cast is Dwight Bacquie, David Collins, Michelyn Emelle, Richard Greenblatt, Jackie Richardson, and Alison Sealy-Smith; *big face* by Marion de Vries, directed by Alisa Palmer and performed by Tanja Jacobs; *Glass Castles* by Lindsay Price, directed by Alisa Palmer; *The Yoko Ono Project* by Jean Yoon, directed by Sarah Stanley (went on to be workshopped at the Banff Playwrights Colony in 1995; in January '96 it received a two-week multimedia workshop and one-night "concert reading" at "Under the Umbrella"; it was produced at Theatre Passe Muraille in January 2000, directed by Jean Yoon and Marion de Vries); *Rainmaker on a Train* by Pauline Peters and Taylor Jane Green. Special event: *Late Night The Word's Out*, poetry performance hosted by Lillian Allen.

Week Two: *Controlling Interest*, created and directed by Paulette Phillips (produced at Theatre Passe Muraille in October 1995); *The Sea Woman/The Swimmer* by Sandra Laronde; *The Dissident* by Canyon Sam, a performance artist from San Francisco; *Green is the Colour of Spring* by Jay Pitter, directed by ahdri zhina mandiela and featuring the a capella group The Bush Honeys; *Dogs*, created and performed by Trisha Lamie and Kim Renders; *Mango Chutney* by Dilara Ally, directed by Diane Roberts. Special event: *Late Night Cunning Linguists*, readings by lesbian writers, hosted by Sarah Stanley.

Program contained a warning: "Pieces may contain strong language and be considered offensive by some."

29 March

Tenth anniversary "Groundswell" panel presentation, hosted by Diane Roberts and Alisa Palmer: discussion on the topic "Art in Your Face: what is women's theatre development and what should it be?" The moderator is Sally Han and panellists are Diana Leblanc, Sandra Laronde, ahdri zhina mandiela, Banuta Rubess, Judith Thompson, and Jean Yoon; Alison Sealy-Smith and Kim Renders also participate.

Documented in Peerbaye, Soraya, "Look to the Lady: Re-examining Women's Theatre," *Canadian Theatre Review* 84 (Fall 1995): 22–25.

2–19 May

Nightwood Studio, *The Coloured Girls Project*, a workshop referred to as part one of "An Explosion Project," based on Ntozake Shange's *for colored girls who have considered suicide/when the rainbow is enuf.* Written and directed by Diane Roberts. Participants: Carol Anderson, Michelle Martin, Shakura Saida, Alison Sealy-Smith, and Jane Spidell.

June

Nighttalk newsletter (June 1995) contains a report on *The Coloured Girls Project.* Catherine Glen is no longer on the board, and Amanda Mills has moved to the position of "advisor."

FALL

Nighttalk newsletter (Fall 1995) contains announcement that Soraya Peerbaye has been promoted from administrative assistant to associate artist and "Groundswell" coordinator. Playwright in residence is Kim Renders.

Board of directors: Joanne Abbensetts, Clare Barclay, Bev John, Anita Lee, Ann-Marie MacDonald, and Elizabeth Shepherd, with Amanda Mills as advisor. Artistic Advisory: Alex Bulmer, Marium Carvell, Jani Lauzon, ahdri zhina mandiela, Dawn Obokata, Pauline Peters, Sarah Stanley, Jean Yoon.

26 OCTOBER

Second annual "Fab Fall Fiesta Fundraiser" at El Convento Rico. Hosted by Elvira Kurt and featuring performances by members of The Greater Toronto Drag King Society. Documented by Romy Shiller in "Drag King Invasion: Taking Back the Throne," *Canadian Theatre Review* 86 (Spring 1996): 24–28.

29 OCTOBER

With Volcano, Nightwood hosts "short stuff": late-night soirees of new readings and music at the Nightwood Studio.

NOVEMBER

First stage of "Groundswell" workshops. In the Fall 1995 *Nighttalk*, Marium Carvell writes: "We had submissions from every province, as well as from the United States. The name of Nightwood has certainly spread."

NOVEMBER 1995 TO MARCH 1996

Running parallel to the "Groundswell" process, "The Female Body" — a series of weekend-long workshops on voice, movement, dance, and performance. Curated by Soraya Peerbaye, Alisa Palmer, and Sandra Laronde in association with Native Women in the Arts and Equity Showcase Theatre.

A. The Moving Self with Junia Mason and Charmaine Headley, 11 and 12 November 1995

B. Storytelling with Muriel Miguel, 18 and 19 November 1995 (from New York)

C. Jingle-Dress Dancing with Karen Pheasant, 23 November 1995

D. Physicalizing Text with Margo Kane, 25 and 26 November 1995

E. Indian Classical Dance with Menaka Thakkar, 2 and 3 December 1995

F. Physical Voice with Tannis Kowalchuk and Karin Randoja, 14–17 February 1996 (from Primus Theatre in Winnipeg)

G. Corporeal Mime with Denise Boulanger and Francine Alepin, 29–31 March 1996 (from Montreal)

1996

WINTER

Nighttalk newsletter (Winter 1996) announces that Jay Pitter will be returning as associate producer. Also, Diane Roberts announces that she is leaving her position as artistic co-director. Over the holidays, Alisa Palmer and Soraya Peerbaye are part of a group of Canadians, organized by Judith Rudakoff, who visit Grupo Teatro Escambray in Cuba.

Board of directors: Anita Lee, Ann-Marie MacDonald, Sierra Bacquie, Dawn Obokata.

29 FEBRUARY–17 MARCH

Wild Pig, in association with Nightwood Theatre, presents *big face* by Marion de Vries at the Factory Studio Theatre. The play originated when Marion de Vries was a member of SpringWrights, and was workshopped at the 1995 "Groundswell." DeVries and Alisa Palmer (as dramaturge) went to the Banff Playwrights Colony in June 1995.

8–30 MARCH

Mango Chutney by Dilara Ally, directed by Diane Roberts, at the Music Gallery. Cast: Elisa Moolecherry, Monique Mojica, Soheil Parsa, Simmi Raymond, and Vikram Sahay. Inspired by Kalidasa's sixth-century play *Shakuntala* and *The Natyasastra*. Originally workshopped at "Groundswell" in 1994.

24 MARCH

After a two-year hiatus, the fourteenth annual "Five Minute Feminist Cabaret" returns. Brigantine Room at Harbourfront. Produced by Dina Graser, directed by Alisa Palmer, and curated by Graser, Palmer, Leslie Lester, Soraya Peerbaye, and Jay Pitter. Hosted by Marium Carvell and Elvira Kurt. Features fifteen performers, all of whom have appeared in previous "FemCabs."

SPRING

Nighttalk newsletter (Spring 1996) contains reports on "FemCab."

Board of directors: Anita Lee, Sierra Bacquie, Ann-Marie MacDonald, Clare Barclay, Dawn Carter, Joy Lachica, Dawn Obokata.

19–21 APRIL

My Left Breast, written and performed by Susan Miller, presented at Buddies in Bad Times as a benefit fundraiser for The Alliance of Breast Cancer Survivors, in association with Nightwood and Buddies.

8–12 MAY

Eleventh "Groundswell" at the Factory Studio Café. *Fed by Fairies* by Sabina Fella, directed by Alisa Palmer; *Moist Again/Fragments for a History of…,* created and directed by Trisha Lamie; *The Gypsy Texts,* created and performed by Tannis Kowalchuk, directed by Alisa Palmer; *The Madwoman and the Fool: A Harlem Duet,* written and directed by Djanet Sears; *House of Sacred Cows* by Padma Viswanathan (from Edmonton), directed by Soraya Peerbaye and Alisa Palmer; *Visit,* written and directed by Liz Rucker, with Alisa Palmer and Theatre Fugue. Special event: *Cunning Linguists,* curated by Alisa Palmer and Sarah Stanley.

Other projects that were supported by the first phase of "Groundswell," but did not receive public performances: *Life After Death* by Bev Cooper, *Angelique* by Lorena Gale, *Raining Tin* by M.J. Kang, *Tales of the Blond Assassin* by Kate Lynch, *Yo Canada!* by Alicia Payne, *Looking for Boysland* by Christina Starr, *She Speaks Her Own* by the Wimmin of de Poonani Posse.

FALL

Mailing/announcement of 1996/97 season. The first stage of "Ground-swell" is going on. *Harlem Duet: The Madwoman and the Fool* by Djanet Sears will be produced in 1997. Volcano and Nightwood continue to present "short stuff" events on the last Sunday of every month.

Board of directors for 1996/97: Clare Barclay, Shirley Barrie, Sierra Bacquie, Dawn Carter, Ann-Marie MacDonald, and Dawn Obokata, with advisors Amanda Mills and Elizabeth Shepherd. Artistic Advisory: Alex Bulmer, Marium Carvell, Jani Lauzon, ahdri zhina mandiela, Dawn Obokata, Sheysali Saujam, Sarah Stanley. Alisa Palmer is now the sole artistic director. Playwright in residence is Alanis King-Odjig, the former artistic director of Debajehmujig Theatre on Manitoulin Island.

24 OCTOBER

"Fall Fiesta" fundraiser at El Convento Rico.

26 OCTOBER–10 NOVEMBER

At the Theatre Passe Muraille Backspace, Sugar 'n' Spice, in association with Nightwood, presents *Afrocentric: A Love Story* by David Odhiambo, directed by Maxine Bailey, with Conrad Coates and Sharon Lewis.

29 NOVEMBER–8 DECEMBER

Froth, in association with Nightwood, presents *Froth: a spectacle about shopping & hysteria* by Baņuta Rubess, performed by Janet Burke, Bonnie Kim, Susan McKenzie, and Alisa Palmer, directed by Leah Cherniak. Presented in an empty store at 318 Queen Street West. Froth, initiated in 1991, is Baņuta Rubess, Alisa Palmer, and Leslie Lester.

1997

4–11 MARCH

Creativity Cave, in association with Nightwood, presents *Green is the Colour of Spring* by Jay Pitter.

7 MARCH

"FemCab" held at the Brigantine Room, Harbourfront Centre. Hosts are Taborah Johnson and Diane Flacks. Sarah Stanley is featured, as she has recently been appointed the new artistic director of Buddies in Bad Times, to start in July. Others appearing include Barbara Hall, the Mayor of Toronto; the opera singer Measha Gosman; Judy Rebick; Djanet Sears; Sandra Shamas; and Deanne Taylor. Sold-out audience of four hundred.

SPRING

Nightwood Theatre Newsletter (Spring 1997) makes reference to recent funding cuts and points out that the recent "FemCab" "was directly allied with the International Women's Day Committee," and had "a more overtly political line-up than in previous shows." It also includes "Excerpts from *Notes of a Coloured Girl: 32 Short Reasons Why I Write for the Theatre*," by Djanet Sears, the full text of which appeared in the *Harlem Duet* program. Two honorary board members have been named: Rina Fraticelli and Patricia Rozema.

20 APRIL—18 MAY

Nightwood presents *Harlem Duet*, written and directed by Djanet Sears, at the Tarragon Extra Space. Cast: Barbara Barnes-Hopkins, Jeff Jones, Dawn Roach, Alison Sealy-Smith, and Nigel Shawn Williams. There is also a duo providing live musical accompaniment. The assistant director is Maxine Bailey, dramaturgy is by Kate Lushington and Diane Roberts, and ahdri zhina mandiela is listed as a resource artist. *Harlem Duet* won four Dora Mavor Moore Awards, for best production, outstanding new play, director and female performance for Alison Sealy-Smith, and was remounted at the Canadian Stage Company's Berkeley Street stage 27 October—29 November 1997. Winner of the Governor General's Award. It had been workshopped at the "New York Shakespeare Festival," where it received a public reading at the Joseph Papp Public Theatre.

28 MAY—1 JUNE

"Groundswell" is held at the Nightwood Studio and includes *Songs of Want* by Randi Helmers; *Hijab* by associate artist Soraya Peerbaye; *Twenty-One* by Sandy Senko; *Smudge* by Alex Bulmer; *The Inquisitor's Daughter* by Alisa Palmer; *Random Acts* by Diane Flacks; and *In the Midst of the Extraordinary* by Jani Lauzon.

FALL

Nightwood Theatre Newsletter (Fall 1997): Alisa Palmer writes, "When I first arrived at Nightwood we were barely able to put up one production in a hundred-seat theatre, with no extra personpower to even consider FemCab. Now, three years later, Nightwood is working in co-production with two of Canada's most significant theatre companies, representing the largest and most diverse audiences Nightwood has yet to access." Soraya Peerbaye announces the plays being worked on for "Groundswell": *Odawa Kwek* by Alanis King-Odjig; *Dark Room* by Beth Herst; *a cup of tears* by Sheila James; *Peter Panic* by Ruthe Whiston; *Apatride* by Abla Farhoud, translated by Shelly Tepperman; *The Aria Project* by Sandra Laronde; *IKI:Etudes* with Dawn Obokata, Joy Kogawa, and Denyse Fujiwara; *untitled* by Karin Randoja; *Fish Eye* by Ann Holloway; *Fed by Fairies* by Sabina Fella, with music by John Millard; *Hee Hee* by M.J. Kang, with music by Lee Pui Ming; *The Skriker* by Caryl Churchill, a development project with Clare Coulter.

27 OCTOBER–29 NOVEMBER

Harlem Duet remounted at The Canadian Stage Company.

27 NOVEMBER–14 DECEMBER

Random Acts, written and performed by Diane Flacks, presented by Nightwood, Mything Productions, and Buddies in Bad Times, at Buddies in Bad Times Theatre. Directed by Alisa Palmer, who is also credited with script collaboration.

Board of directors for 1997/98: Shirley Barrie, Sierra Bacquie, Diane Flacks, Jennifer Kawaja, Danielle LiChong, Ann-Marie MacDonald, Dawn Obokata, Angela Robertson, Eiko Shaul Advisor to the board: Elizabeth Shepherd Honorary board: Rina Fraticelli and Patricia Rozema Playwright in residence: M.J. Kang (her play was not produced by Nightwood) Artistic Advisory: Alex Bulmer, Karen Glave, ahdri zhina mandiela, Erin McMurtry, Sonja Mills, Melanie Nicholls-King, Dawn Obokata, and Sheyfali Saujani Apprentice producer: Jacquie Carpenter.

1998

6 MARCH

The fourteenth annual "Five Minute Feminist Cabaret," hosted by Sandra Oh and Sandra Shamas, features Alison Sealy-Smith and Sook-Yin Lee. It is held in the Brigantine Room at Harbourfront.

SPRING

Nightwood Theatre Newsletter (Spring 1998) is sent with a fundraising brochure asking for donations. Includes a report on "FemCab" and a call for "Groundswell" submissions by June 30, as well as detailed descriptions of the "Groundswell" shows being presented in May.

25—27 APRIL

"Women in Shorts," a mini-festival of Canadian women actors. At the Brigatine Room at Harbourfront, as part of the "duMaurier World Stage Festival." A showcase of excerpts from Jackie Burroughs, Allegra Fulton, Ann-Marie MacDonald, Sheila McCarthy, Karen Robinson, Alison Sealy-Smith, and Pamela Sinha.

2 AND 3 MAY

Public Presentations of *The Skriker* by Caryl Churchill, a workshop production directed by Alisa Palmer, with Clare Coulter, Jennifer Podemski, and Waneta Storms. At Theatre Passe Muraille as part of the "duMaurier World Stage Festival."

13—15 MAY

"Groundswell" 1998 at the Nightwood Studio: *The Aria Project* by Sandra Laronde, with direction and dramaturgical assistance by Monique Mojica with Susan Hookong; *Untitled* by Karin Randoja, with direction and creation assistance by Raymond Bobgan; *A Cup of Tears* by Sheila James, directed and dramaturged by Carol Greyeyes; *Hee-Hee: Tales from the White Diamond Mountain* by M.J. Kang, directed by Baņuta Rubess, with music by Lee Pui-Ming; *fish eye*, written and performed by Ann Holloway, directed and dramaturged by Moynan King; *Peter Panic* by Ruthe Whiston; and a reading of *Jaded* by Rubess.

December

One Flea Spare, "an Obie award-winning script by one of the hottest new feminist playwrights on the international scene," American poet Naomi Wallace. Directed by Alisa Palmer at Canadian Stage, Berkeley Street Theatre Upstairs. The cast is David Fox, Woody Dalrymple, Sky Gilbert, Brenda Robins, and 13-year-old Natasha Greenblatt. First production was at the Bush Theatre in London, England, in 1995.

1998 playwright in residence is Sonja Mills.

1999

March

"FemCab" features Sonja Mills, Alex Bulmer, Sook-Yin Lee, and The Delightful Divas.

Spring

Newly formatted *Nightwood Theatre Spring* 1999 *News + Events* includes a report from Diane Flacks. She and Leslie Lester had taken *Random Acts* on tour to One Yellow Rabbit's "High Performance Rodeo" in Calgary and to "Jest in Time" in Halifax.

11–21 May

"Groundswell 1999" at the Nightwood Studio in a new, expanded format, with two readings of each play: *The Gospel According to Me* by Tabby Johnson, directed by Alison Sealy-Smith; *Anything That Moves* by Ann-Marie MacDonald; *Louise and the Red River Flood* by Sheila James; *The Scrubbing Project* by Sandra Laronde, Jani Lauzon, Monique Mojica, and Michelle St. John, facilitated by Djanet Sears; *Home* by Rena Polley, directed by Trish Vanstone; *The Samba Prophet* by Padma Viswanathan; *The Danish Play* by Sonja Mills; *The White Dress* by Kathleen Oliver; *Arias* by Lynda Hill; *Smudge* by Alex Bulmer; *Brown Girl in the Ring* by Judy McKinley; and an "Excerpt of a New Work" by Djanet Sears.

Fall

Nightwood Theatre Fall 1999 *News + Events* announces Nightwood is moving to a new location: the sixth Floor of a building at 9 Saint Nicholas

Street, in the Yonge and Wellesley area. Also includes announcements for upcoming events in 2000: "FemCab," "Groundswell," and the premiere of *Anything That Moves.*

26 NOVEMBER

Nightwood's "Taking Up More Space Launch"—a celebration of the move to a new location and the launch of the twentieth anniversary season. Includes "Feminist Schmeminist," an open-mic cabaret hosted by Sonja Mills.

13 DECEMBER

Annual general meeting

Board of directors for 1999: Saniya Ansari, Shirley Barrie, Maggie Cassella, Diane Flacks, Jennifer Kawaja, Dawn Obokata, Angela Robertson, Sheyfali Saujani, Harriet Sachs, and Lisa Silverman Honorary board: Dionne Brand, Rina Fraticelli, Patricia Rozema, Sandra Shamas. Artistic Advisory: maxine bailey, Alex Bulmer, Sonja Mills, Soraya Peerbaye, Karen Robinson, and Kristin Thomson. 1999/2000 playwrights in residence: Sandra Laronde, Jani Lauzon, Monique Mojica, Michelle St. John Financial manager: Kate Tucker.

2000

Alex Bulmer is serving as apprentice producer. Leslie Lester announces her plans to move to Soulpepper as its producer, and hopes that a new hiring for Nightwood will be in place in the spring.

5 MARCH

Nightwood Theatre presents the sixteenth annual "Five Minute Feminist Cabaret" at the Bluma Appel Theatre, St. Lawrence Centre. Hosted by Sandra Shamas and Karen Robinson. Celebrated with a glossy brochure featuring photos of many of the women involved with Nightwood over the years, including Cynthia Grant; a timeline of personnel and events from 1979–2000; and a statement about the history of "FemCab" by Susan G. Cole. Some of the performers include Dionne Brand, Shirley Douglas, Sandra Laronde, Ann-Marie MacDonald, Sonja Mills, Sandra

Shamas, Swamperella, Shoshana Sperling, Sandra Caldwell, opera singer Siphiwe McKenzie, and Jackie Richardson. Mary Vingoe, Kim Renders, Alisa Palmer, and Leslie Lester blow out the candles on Nightwood's birthday cake.

25 APRIL–13 MAY

Anything That Moves: book and lyrics by Ann-Marie MacDonald, directed by Alisa Palmer, music by Allen Cole. The story is also credited to both MacDonald and Palmer. At the Canadian Stage Theatre, Berkeley Street Upstairs, as part of the "duMaurier World Stage Festival." Designed by Astrid Jansen and Andrea Lundy. Cast: Tamara Bernier, Sandra Caldwell, Dan Chameroy, David Dunbar, Judy Marshak, and Marc Richard. Nominated for Dora Mavor Moore Awards for Outstanding New Musical and Outstanding Performance in a Female Principal Role in a Musical for Judy Marshak. Program note: *Anything That Moves* began at the 1999 spring "Groundswell" with a three-week workshop.

"A Full Embrace," by Elisa Kukla, *Xtra!* 20 April 2000, 3. Cover story claims that Alisa Palmer had asked MacDonald to create something for the twentieth anniversary of Nightwood.

SPRING

Nightwood Newsletter Spring 2000 announces that *Anything That Moves* will be remounted at the Tarragon Theatre in May 2001. Also includes detailed descriptions of the plays in "Groundswell" in June, as well as a call for submissions for August.

JUNE

As it looks for a new location, the Theatre Centre temporarily locates its office and some events at Nightwood's space.

27–30 JUNE

Seventeenth annual "Groundswell Play Development Series of New Theatre by Women," at the Nightwood Studio: *The Adventures of a Black Girl in Search of God* by Djanet Sears; *Girls' Night* by Sharon Lewis, directed by Fleurette Fernando; *Smudge* by Alex Bulmer, directed by Alisa Palmer as the last stage of preparation before its premiere in the fall;

The Scrubbing Project by The Turtle Gals (Sandra Laronde, Jani Lauzon, Monique Mojica, Michelle St. John), directed by Kate Lushington; Write From the Hip—six short works by new, young women writers (Anna Chatterton, Chrystal Donbrath-Zina, Lia Foad, Goldy Notay, Punam Sawhney, Velvet Wadman). Directors: Alison Sealy-Smith, Kelly Thornton, and Fleurette Fernando, Coordinated by Lisa Silverman with Evalyn Parry and Soraya Peerbaye.

From *Nightwood Theatre Fall* 1999 *News + Events*: "For our twentieth anniversary season we are doing something unusual with our developmental programming. This year Groundswell focuses on extended workshops of projects already in development. Many of them you will recognize from previous Groundswells...At the other end of the spectrum, Nightwood offers a new program for first time playwrights..."

FALL

Fall 2000 *Newsletter (21st season/21st century).* The season is focused around four playwrights: Alex Bulmer with *Smudge* (2000), Djanet Sears with *The Adventures of a Black Girl in Search of God* (2001), Ann-Marie MacDonald with *Anything That Moves* (remounted in 2001), and Jean Yoon as the playwright in residence.

Also contains a call for submissions from women aged 18 to 29 to Write From the Hip, "a series of weekly workshops and hands-on seminars in writing skills and professional play development."

18 NOVEMBER–10 DECEMBER 2000

Nightwood Theatre, in association with S.N.I.F.F. inc., presents *Smudge* by Alex Bulmer at the Tarragon Extra Space. Directed by Alisa Palmer. Cast: Diane Flacks, Sherrylee Hunter, Kate Lynch. Nominated for a Chalmers Award and three Doras. Published in *Canadian Theatre Review* 108 (Fall 2001). The program states that the "story [was] developed and edited" with Diane Flacks, Kate Lynch, and Alisa Palmer, and mentions that this play, and *Anything That Moves*, will be the final shows for Palmer and Leslie Lester.

"Smudge has Clarity," by Jon Kaplan, *NOW*, 30 November–6 December 2000: Flacks plays Freddie and Lynch plays her new lover, Catherine, while Hunter plays multiple characters. The play is an hour long and episodic. Sound, set and lighting give the audience a sense of Freddie's fragmented world, "almost surrealistic setting, characters are indistinct behind a hazy backdrop..."

2001

"Nightwood Theatre forges creative alliances among women of diverse backgrounds in order to develop and produce innovative Canadian Theatre. A visionary producing team is sought to carry Nightwood into its next stage, replacing both the outgoing Artistic Director and the General Manager. Collaborative, innovative proposals are invited from dynamic, experienced teams and/or individuals interested in new play creation and imaginative theatre management structures. The successful candidates will have developed strong survival techniques for making challenging theatre. A progressive world-view tempered by a keen sense of humour is a winning combination for a candidate/team who will be expected to work in a very collaborative feminist context." The positions were to begin July 1, 2001.

A fundraising brochure announcing *The Adventures of a Black Girl in Search of God* and "FemCab" also states, "Last season Nightwood established an Arts Endowment Fund, an initiative of the Government of Ontario, through the Ministry of Citizenship, Culture and Recreation. Through the success of Nightwood's fundraising hyperactivity, Nightwood was able to contribute its maximum of $30,000 in one year alone. This year, we venture to add to the nest. Donations will be matched dollar for dollar."

17 AND 18 FEBRUARY

The Adventures of a Black Girl in Search of God by Djanet Sears, at the du-Maurier Theatre Centre. A work in progress produced by Nightwood and Obsidian Theatre Company (artistic director: Alison Sealy-Smith), in association with Harbourfront Centre.

4 MARCH

"Five Minute Feminist Cabaret" at the Bluma Appel Theatre, hosted by Maggie Cassella and Jennifer Podemski. Performers include Sook-Yin

Lee, Pretty Porky and Pissed Off, and COBA: Collective of Black Artists.

1 MAY–3 JUNE

Anything That Moves is remounted at the Tarragon Theatre. Wins four Dora Mavor Moore Awards in June 2002: Best Production of a Musical; Outstanding Direction of a Musical (Alisa Palmer); Outstanding Performance by a Female in a Principal Role, Musical (Glynis Ranney); and Outstanding Musical Direction (Allen Cole).

SPRING

Nightwood Theatre Spring 2001 *Events + News* contains notices on "Fem-Cab" and the remount of *Anything That Moves*. Also announces that Alisa Palmer and Leslie Lester will end their terms as artistic director and artistic producer, to be replaced by Kelly Thornton and Nathalie Bonjour. Includes detailed descriptions of the plays in the upcoming "Groundswell" and a call for the August deadline for submissions to the nineteenth "Groundswell."

10–16 JUNE

Eighteenth annual "Groundswell" at the Nightwood Studio. *On Learning Russian* by Ilene Cummings, directed by Sue Miner; *Stormbound* by Carol Anderson, directed by Alison Sealy-Smith; *Supreme Incompetence* by Karen Woolridge, directed by Kate Lynch; *The Makings of a Man* by Robyn-Marie Butt, directed by Jeanette Lambermont; *Better Safe Than Sorry* by Les Vaches (Erika Hennebury and Ruth Madoc-Jones), directed by Kelly Thornton; *Little Mercy's First Murder* by Morwyn Brebner, directed by Eda Holmes (went on to a production at the Tarragon in 2004); *Shiksas Sit Shiva* by Catherine Hayos and Melinda Little, directed by Kelly Thornton; *The Guilty Playroom* by Shoshana Sperling and Teresa Pavlinek, directed by Alisa Palmer. Also Write From the Hip, five works by young writers in Nightwood's three-month mentoring program: Dawn Dumont, Rica May Eckersley, Sarah Liss, Shannon Maguire, and Alyssa Pringle.

15 JUNE

Farewell party for Alisa Palmer and Leslie Lester, welcome for the new team: Kelly Thornton and Nathalie Bonjour. During her tenure, Leslie produced *Harlem Duet, Random Acts, Mango Chutney, Wearing the Bone,* and the "FemCabs," as well as producing for VideoCabaret from 1991–98 and for Froth since 1994.

SEPTEMBER

Smudge toured to Halifax.

8 OCTOBER

Funny Business: A Tip of the Hat to Lily, a comedy cabaret tribute to Lily Tomlin, hosted by Diane Flacks as part of the World Leaders: A Festival of Creative Genius at the DuMaurier Theatre at Harbourfront. Performers include Cathy Jones, Luba Goy, Sandra Shamas, and Shoshana Sperling.

    Board of directors: Sharlene Azam, Gigi Basanta, Gillian Calder, Diane Flacks, Sonja Mills, Kiran Mirchandani, Sheyfali Saujani. Artistic Advisory: maxine bailey, Sonja Mills, Evalyn Parry, Karen Robinson, Michelle St. John, Kristen Thomson. National Artist Advisory: Lise Ann Johnson (Ottawa), Deena Aziz (Montreal), Jillian Keilly (St. Johns), Carmen Aguirre (Vancouver). Playwright in residence: Jean Yoon.

2002

The 2001/2002 season brochure lists *Funny Business: A Tip of the Hat to Lily* (October 2001), *The Adventures of a Black Girl in Search of God* (February 2002), International Women's Day events in March, and *Smudge* on tour in fall 2001 and spring 2002. Also announces "Groundswell" in May, and a brand new Playwrights Unit for the six months leading up to "Groundswell." Sheila Heti has become the first playwright ever commissioned to write a play for Nightwood, and the Write from the Hip and new Busting Out! programs are advertised.

SPRING

Newly formatted newsletter, called *Nightwood: Defining Feminist Theatre*

(Spring 2002), contains an article about *The Adventures of a Black Girl in Search of God*: "With a chorus of 13 and a stellar cast led by Alison Sealy-Smith, this momentous production represents the largest not for profit show produced by any Toronto theatre this season." Also features interviews with Alison Sealy-Smith and Sheila Heti. More information on Busting Out! a program for girls aged 12 to 15, created by youth coordinator Lisa Silverman, for the summer of 2002.

5–23 FEBRUARY

The Adventures of a Black Girl in Search of God, written and directed by Djanet Sears, at the duMaurier Theatre Centre. Produced by Nightwood and Obsidian Theatre in association with Harbourfront Centre. Cast: Alison Sealy-Smith, Walter Borden, David Collins, Barbara Barnes-Hopkins, Lili Francks, Herb Johnson, Jackie Richardson, Michael Spencer-Davis, and a chorus of thirteen: Ingrid Abbott, John Campbell, Jennifer Dahl, Xuan Fraser, Sharon Harvey, Monique Mojica, Carlos Morgan, Alejandra Nunez, Vivine Scarlett, Lincoln Shand, Shameena Soni, Saida Baba Talibah, and Tricia Williams. It was presented as part of "KUUMBA": a celebration of Black History Month. Won a Dora Mavor Moore Award in June 2002 for Oustanding Choreography by Vivine Scarlett. Picked up and produced by Mirvish Productions.

SPRING

Smudge tours to Vancouver.

8–10 MARCH

International Women's Day Events, collectively called "Hourglass."

8 MARCH

"I'm Not Yer Little Lady" party with performances.

9 MARCH

"The Hourglass Symposium: A Roundtable" at Hart House, with Lynn Fernie, Brigitte Gall, Nalo Hopkinson, Alex Bulmer, and Mirah Soleil-Ross.

10 March

"FemCab: The Five Minute Feminist Cabaret," hosted by Kate Rigg and Shoshana Sperling, at the Bluma Appel Theatre.

20–26 May

Nineteenth annual "Groundswell" at Tallulah's Cabaret at Buddies in Bad Times. From 120 submissions from across the country, Kelly Thornton made the selections, and those playwrights became the Playwrights Unit who met from January to May. Ruth Madoc-Jones was the assistant festival director.

The Disappearance of Janey Jones, written and performed by Jennifer Fawcett, directed by Jennifer Capraru; *The Trigger* written and performed by Carmen Aguirre, from Vancouver, directed by Katrina Dunn; *You the Fortress* by Robin Sadavoy, directed by Ruth Madoc-Jones; *Four Directions* by Dawn Dumont (a previous Write From the Hip participant), directed by Marion de Vries; *The Butterfly Body* by The Butterfly Body Collective (Marjorie Chan, Catherine Bruce, Camille James, Keira Loughran, Shannon Reynolds, Nicole Stamp, and Diana Kolpak); *The Bigger World* by Lilla Csorgo, directed by Kate Lynch; *Tricycle* by Claudia Dey, directed by Daryl Cloran; *Blood* by Jean Yoon, directed by Kelly Thornton.

Also includes Write from the Hip shows by Rachel Bokhout, Melanie Hui, Anne Doelman, and Aimee Haskell, and *Cast Iron* by Lisa Codrington, directed by ahdri zhina mandiela and featuring Andrea Scott, which went on to the "Fringe" and was fully produced by Nightwood in 2005.

23 and 24 May

As part of "Groundswell," two "Playwright Slams" were held as fundraisers for Nightwood. The first was hosted by Diane Flacks and Waneta Storms, the second by Yanna McIntosh and Kristen Thomson. Featured playwrights (Carol Anderson, Morwyn Brebner, Diane Flacks, Kate Lynch, Sonja Mills, Mary Francis Moore, Teresa Pavlinek, and Mariko Tamaki) tried to create a five-minute play.

Fall

Newsletter entitled *Nightwood Theatre: Excellent Theatre by Women* (Fall

2002). Includes an introductory message from the new artistic director, emphasizing the need for an increased, national profile for women's art. The season includes Sonja Mills's *The Danish Play* (November/December 2002); *Finding Regina* by Shoshana Sperling, which would play at the Globe Theatre in Regina 8–13 October 2002, then go to Theatre Passe Muraille in February/March 2003, and to "Groundswell" in May 2003. The newsletter also promotes the www.nightwoodtheatre.net website, and includes an article by board member Maja Ardal, interviews with Sonja Mills and Shoshana Sperling, and updates on various shows and women involved with Nightwood.

A letter sent 20 September 2002 asking for membership renewal also states: "This year the leadership went into a period of Strategic Planning. In these sessions we created a 3 year Business Plan, revitalized the Board of Directors and initiated a Development Plan which strengthens our foundation, corporate and private sector support. We are also pleased to announce that we've secured a new home with Artscape in the arts complex on the heritage site of Gooderham and Worts Distillery; we will move in February."

19 NOVEMBER–15 DECEMBER

The Danish Play by Sonja Mills, directed by Kelly Thornton, at the Tarragon Extra Space.

Cast: Kate Hennig, Christine Brubaker, Dmitry Chepovetsky, Randi Helmers, Erika Hennebury, Eric Goulem, and Bruce Hunter. Special performance and reception for the Ambassador of Denmark to Canada on 28 November. Nominated for two Dora Mavor Moore Awards and invited to tour to Aveny-T Theatre in Copenhagen in May 2004.

Board of directors: Maja Ardal, Sally Han, Kelly MacIntosh, Sarah Neville, Megan Peck, Chanrouti Ramnarine, Margaret Ann Tamaki, Lascelle Wingate (Gigi Basanta and Kathleen Gallagher were leaving). Artist Advisory: Carol Anderson, maxine bailey, Sonja Mills, Evalyn Parry, Karen Robinson, Michelle St. John, Kristen Thomson. National Artist Advisory: Lise Ann Johnson, Deena Aziz, Jillian Keilly, Carmen Aguirre. Youth Initiatives Director: Lisa Silverman. Artist in Residence: Ruth Madoc-Jones. Playwright in Residence: Marion de Vries.

2003

Nightwood Theatre: Excellent Theatre by Women (Spring 2003) newsletter. Includes reports on the upcoming production of *Finding Regina* and on the highly successful run of *The Danish Play* the previous fall. Also a profile of a new board member, Barb Linds, and the lineups for "Groundswell" and Write From the Hip. There is a note from Keira Loughran, a participant in the Groundswell Playwrights Unit, and information about the upcoming move to the new Distillery location.

Nightwood Theatre's Mission Statement: "Nightwood Theatre produces excellent theatre by women artists, including original Canadian plays and works from the contemporary international repertoire, for a large broadly-based audience. We are committed to new play creation and to (inter) national creative collaborating."

Play Development — Nightwood provides opportunities for women playwrights to develop their work to the point where that work is ready to be produced on a stage.

Mentoring — Nightwood Theatre mentors women theatre artists, including actors, designers, directors and writers.

Diversity — Nightwood Theatre reflects the diversity of the women's artistic community through its Board of Directors, its staff and the artists that it hires.

Outreach — Nightwood Theatre's programs reach out to the community to cultivate an interest and a passion for the theatre arts in women. Our outreach programs also use theatre as a vehicle to empower women.

18 FEBRUARY–9 MARCH

Finding Regina by Shoshana Sperling, directed by Kelly Thornton, at Theatre Passe Muraille. Cast: Jeremy Harris, Teresa Pavlinek, and Shoshana Sperling. A co-production with the Globe Theatre in Regina, where it ran 8–13 October 2002. Published by Scirocco Drama.

"Shoshana Sperling: Funny Girl Plays with her Regina," by Glenn Sumi, *NOW*, 20–23 February 2003, 58. "In Sperling's deceptively simple piece, three former high school friends meet up in the local ICU when another friend attempts suicide. They reconnect, throw their weight around, smoke up, then bemoan their current lives and chip away at the past and each other with emotional ice picks."

Shoshana Sperling and Lisa Brooke perform character-based comedy as March of Dames, often at venues such as "FemCab" and the cabarets "Strange Sisters" and "Cheap Queers." Her play began as *The Regina Monologues* at "Rhubarb!" in spring 2001.

8 MARCH

"FemCab Remix" performed at Theatre Passe Muraille on the *Finding Regina* stage. Curated by Mariko Tamaki and hosted by Elvira Kurt.

MARCH

Nightwood moves to new location: 55 Mill Street, Suite 301, The Case Goods Building, in Toronto's new Distillery District. Building run by Artscape and also home to Tapestry New Opera Works and The Tapestry/Nightwood New Work Studio.

12 APRIL

"The Backstage Ball," a dance-a-thon fundraiser, held at Berkeley Church. Fifty dancers raised over $7,500.

1 JUNE

Strawberry and tea reception in the new location, with a reading from *Mercedes* by Marion de Vries, which would also be featured at "Groundswell."

SUMMER

Nightwood Theatre: Excellent Theatre by Women (Summer 2003) Newsletter. Announcements of "Hysteria" (October–November 2003), *China Doll* (Feb.-March 2004), "FemCab" (March 2004), *The Danish Play* on tour in 2004, "Groundswell" in June of 2004. Also reports on previous events (*Finding Regina*, "FemCab," and the dance-a-thon) and a profile of assistant producer Janice Rieger. Also details on all the "Groundswell" shows and the new location in the Distillery District.

2–8 JUNE

Twentieth annual "Groundswell Festival" at Nightwood's new location, the Tapestry/Nightwood New Work Studio. *BeBe* (Brecht's Women) by Christine Brubaker, Ruth Madoc-Jones, Keira Loughran, Camille Stubel and Erika Hennebury, directed by Jen Capraru; *China Doll* by Marjorie Chan; *Cast Iron* by Lisa Codrington (which was in the Write from the Hip program in 2002); *More* by Kate Hennig; *Privilege* by Corrina Hodgson; *Excellence, Ontario* by Emma Roberts; *Cover Her Face* by Kilby Smith-McGregor; *Mercedes* by Marion de Vries. Final night features young writers from the Write from the Hip program: Marie Breath Badian, Jane Haddad, Claire Horsnell, Katie Kehoe, Melinda Mattos, Sarah Ojamae, and Keren Zaiontz.

FALL

Nightwood Theatre: Excellent Theatre by Women (Fall 2003) newsletter introduces Lisa Valencia-Svensson as accountant, and Lisa Codrington as the facilitator of Write From the Hip. Write From the Hip runs from March to August, with weekly workshops and events, culminating in "Groundswell."

23 OCTOBER–2 NOVEMBER

"Hysteria: A Festival of Women," co-produced with Buddies in Bad Times, curated by festival directors Kelly Thornton and Moynan King. "The original founders of the Rhubarb Festival team up again to unleash a brand new multi-disciplinary feminist festival, celebrating the voices of hysterical women. Hysteria will showcase a variety of evenings which run the gamut of film, dance, theatre, performance art and music, featuring our most edgy and talented women." Held at Buddies in Bad Times, featuring a performance of *Cast Iron* by Lisa Codrington, performed by Alison Sealy-Smith, on 28 October; "Mass Hysteria" cabaret evenings, hosted by Shoshana Sperling and Mariko Tamaki; and a panel discussion on 1 November hosted by the Women's Caucus of the Playwright's Guild of Canada, entitled "Re-opening the Fraticelli Report."

Board of directors: Maja Ardal, Susan Baker, Barb Linds, Kelly MacIntosh, Trish McGrath, Sarah Neville, Lascelle Wingate. Artist in residence: Natasha Mytnowych Commissioned playwrights: Marjorie Chan and Sheila Heti (no Artistic Advisory is listed)

ALSO IN 2003:

Kelly Thornton honoured with Pauline McGibbon Award for her work as a director

2004

25 FEBRUARY

"Intimate Dinner" fundraising dinner party hosted by Michele Landsberg, Fundraising Committee Chair, along with Barb Linds, and Debbie Gray. Terry Raininger working as director of marketing and development.

WINTER

Nightwood Theatre: Excellent Theatre by Women (Winter 2004) newsletter includes article about the premiere of *China Doll,* and an interview with its set and costume designer, Joanne Dente. Notices about *The Danish Play* going in tour and the upcoming "Groundswell," and a report about "Hysteria" from fall 2003. Also an announcement that Michele Landsberg has joined the board.

17 FEBRUARY–14 MARCH

China Doll by Marjorie Chan, directed by Kelly Thornton, at the Tarragon Extra Space. Featuring Marjorie Chan as the lead character Su-Ling, with Jo Chim, Keira Loughran, and John Ng. In addition to its development with Nightwood (since 2002), *China Doll* had originally been commissioned as a CBC radio play and was then commissioned by Nightwood. It had a three-week intensive workshop at the Banff Centre for the Performing Arts in spring 2003. *China Doll* was nominated for three Dora Awards in the General Theatre category, for Outstanding Costume Design (Joanne Dente), Production, and New Play. It was also nominated for the 2005 Governor General's Literary Award.

8 March

Nightwood presents an International Women's Day panel discussion called "First Steps: Chinese Canadian Women Leaving Their Mark." It is held at the Tarragon Theatre Extra Space and features Marjorie Chan, Susan Eng, Avvy Go, Shirley Hoy, Brenda Joy Lem, Vivienne Poy, and Kristyn Wong-Tam. No "FemCab" is held in 2004.

1 May

The "Great May Day Cabaret" includes *Las Pasionarias* by Aida Jordão, developed with the support of Nightwood.

May

The Danish Play tours to Copenhagen before playing at the Magnetic North Festival in Edmonton in June and the National Arts Centre in Ottawa, 26 October to 6 November 2004.

27 June

Anna Chatterton, co-director of youth initiatives, coordinates Busting Out! a new theatre program for eight girls aged twelve to fifteen. Culminates in the performance of a collective creation on 27 June.

June

Nightwood holds three fundraising events: a yard sale at Trinity Bellwoods Park, an online silent auction, and "Strap One On," a Pride Week event fundraiser organized by Buddies in Bad Times and Nightwood.

5 and 6 July

Literary Managers and Dramaturgs of the Americas (LMDA) miniconference on dramaturgy, held at Buddies in Bad Times in Toronto. Marjorie Chan spoke about the playwriting process for her play *China Doll*, and Kelly Thornton and Yvette Nolan (artistic director of Native Earth) addressed "the status of women in Canadian theatre and the dramaturgy of work by women."

24–29 August

Twenty-first annual "Groundswell Festival" held at the Tapestry/

Nightwood New Work Studio. The "Groundswell" advisory committee was Marjorie Chan, Lisa Codrington, Jordana Commisso, Erica Kopyto (intern company dramaturg), Natasha Mytnowych (the associate festival director), Kilby Smith-McGregor, and Kelly Thornton. The plays were: *Longfellow Falling* by Celia McBride, directed by Kelly Thornton; *Blakpiggy Under* by Ann Holloway, directed by Stacey Landers; *Three Fingered Jack and the Legend of Joaquin Murieta* by Marilo Nunez, directed by Natasha Mytnowych; *The Zoe Show* by Lisa Pijuan, directed by Marjorie Chan; *Appleway* by Dian Marie Bridge, directed by ahdri zhina mandiela; and *Emergency Exits* by Jess Dobkin, directed by Erica Kopyto.

The Write from the Hip program, facilitated by Lisa Codrington, had been operating from March to August. The seven members of Write from the Hip were Carly Spencer, Mia Grace Kim, Rosemary Rose, Sarah Fenn, Becky Johnson, Asha Vijayasingham, and Elizabeth Helmers.

4–14 NOVEMBER

Second annual "Hysteria: A Festival of Women." Festival directors Kelly Thornton and Moynan King; assistant festival directors Erika Hennebury and Natasha Mytnowych. Performances include *organ-ized crime* by d'bi.young, and *Birth Rite*, the Toronto premiere of an autobiographical work by New York playwright/performer Elizabeth Hess. "Saucy: Girls with Smart Mouths," an afternoon event for girls under twenty-one, includes a performance by the participants in Busting Out! organized by Natasha Mytnowych and *Shameless* magazine, hosted by Sabrina Jalees.

12–14 NOVEMBER

"The Status of Women in Theatre: A Public Debate!" Kelly Thornton and Hope McIntyre, Chair of the Women's Caucus of the Playwrights Guild of Canada, assemble a national advisory for a three-day conference, taking place as part of "Hysteria." A public debate is held on 13 November at 2:00 pm, at Tallulah's Cabaret at Buddies in Bad Times, hosted by Elvira Kurt. "Since last year's original panel discussion at Hysteria," similar panels have been held at PACT, Magnetic North, and LMDA. Committee members: Jackie Maxwell, Jan Selman, Lousie Forsyth, Yvette Nolan, Naomi Campbell, Nancy Webster, Judith Rudakoff,

Diane Roberts, Jessica Schneider, Cynthia Grant, Kate Weiss, Aida Jordão, Susan Bennett, Denyse Lynde, and Maria Campbell, with core research by Rebecca Burton.

Board of directors, Winter 2004: Maja Ardal, Susan Baker, Kavita Joshi, Michele Landsberg, Kelly MacIntosh, Trish McGrath, Sarah Neville, Lascelle Wingate Commissioned playwrights: Marjorie Chan and Sheila Heti

Board of directors, Summer 2004: Barb Linds, Lesley Ackrill, Susan Baker, Antonella Ceddia, Michele Landsberg, Kelly MacIntosh, Trish McGrath, Sarah Neville, Helen Thundercloud Commissioned playwrights: Lisa Codrington and Sheila Heti Playwright in residence: Ann Holloway

2005

10–15 JANUARY

Workshop of *All Our Happy Days Are Stupid* by Sheila Heti, directed by Baṇuta Rubess, held at the Tapestry/Nightwood New Work Studio.

WINTER

Nightwood Theatre: Excellent Theatre by Women (Winter 2005) newsletter includes an interview by Erica Kopyto with Lisa Codrington, author of *Cast Iron*. Also notices of upcoming International Women's Day event in March and "FemCab" at a new date in May. In "A message from the Artistic Director," Kelly Thornton writes about "the advocacy work Nightwood is now doing (with the Women's Caucus of the Playwright's Guild of Canada and the Professional Association of Canadian Theatres) to address ongoing gender discrimination in Canadian theatre. This new study sees Nightwood sharing the helm of a huge national movement— "Equity in Canadian Theatre: The Women's Initiative." It is also announced that Nightwood has made two new commissions: Bev Cooper and Diane Flacks working on *The Five Stages of Womanhood* and Mariko Tamaki writing *Skim*; and Ann Holloway is the playwright in residence, working on *Mummy*. Also an announcement that Marilo Nunez has started as the new administrative assistant.

27 January

Second annual "Intimate Dinner" hosted by Michele Landsberg, Barb Linds, and Debbie Gray. With special guests Diane Flacks and Alison Sealy-Smith.

12 February–13 March

Cast Iron by Lisa Codrington at the Tarragon Extra Space, produced in association with Obsidian Theatre. Directed by ahdri zhina mandiela and starring Alison Sealy-Smith. The play began in the Write from the Hip program and was also done at "Groundswell" and at the 2002 Toronto "Fringe," produced by Back Row Theatre. It was part of the 2004 Banff playRites Colony, and the "CrossCurrents Festival" at the Factory Theatre in 2004. The program includes a "family tree" of the characters and a glossary of terms in the Bajan dialect.

4 March

Kelly Thornton and Nathalie Bonjour are honoured by The Honourable Sarmite D. Bulte, MP, at her International Women's Day breakfast.

6 March

In recognition of International Women's Day and in conjunction with *Cast Iron*, Nightwood holds a panel discussion called "Talking Black: Canadian Women Speak Out on the Politics of Language," hosted by Sharon Lewis. Panellists are Kike Roach, Denise Campbell, Marie Clarke Walker, Akua Benjamin, and d'bi young.

19 March

Mount Saint Vincent University hosts a research collaboration workshop: "Women in Theatre: The Maritime Experience." Rebecca Burton and Denyse Lynde participated in this conference as representatives of the National Committee on the Status of Women in Canadian Theatre.

2 May

"FemCab: Celebrating 25 Years of Nightwood Theatre at the Five Minute Feminist Cabaret." Hosted by Diane Flacks and Karen Robinson, and featuring special guest Gloria Steinem. Held at the Isabel Bader Theatre on the University of Toronto campus; performers include Cathy Jones, Ann-Marie MacDonald, Roula Said, Maryem Tollar, and d'bi young.

SUMMER

Nightwood Theatre (Summer 2005) newsletter. Includes a report on the "FemCab" celebration, which was attended by founders Kim Renders, Cynthia Grant, and Mary Vingoe. Notices of "Groundswell" in August and *Bear With Me* by Diane Flacks in November/December, and also "FemCab" and *Mathilde* in 2006. There is a profile of board member Leslie Ackrill, and Frances Shakov is introduced as the director of marketing and development.

Also includes a notice that Nightwood was "accepted to Creative Trust, a unique program that supports and strengthens Toronto's mid-size music, dance and theatre companies by assisting them in achieving organizational and financial balance, and acquiring and maintaining a fund of Working Capital." Nightwood "is now in a debt free position."

An article about the Write From the Hip program mentions that it is now run by Lisa Codrington, who was herself once a member. Two other former members of Write From the Hip are part of the 2005 Groundswell Playwrights Unit: Becky Johnson and Dawn Dumont. Also, a new aspect is the Emerging Actors Program, led by Natasha Mytnowych. Each of the Write From the Hip plays is matched with a professional director and cast with both professional actors and members of the Emerging Actors Program for its performance at "Groundswell."

21–27 AUGUST

Twenty-second annual "Groundswell Festival" held at Tapestry/Nightwood New Work Studio. Works presented: *The Five Stages of Womanhood* by Bev Cooper and Diane Flacks, directed by Leah Cherniak, with Cherniak, Cooper, Flacks and Janet Burke; *Love Medicine* by Dawn Dumont, directed by Marion de Vries; *Madre* by Beatriz Pizano, directed by Emma Tibaldo; *Las Pasionarias* by Aida Jordão, directed by the collective, with Paul Babiak, Rebecca Burton, Aida Jordão, and Christina Starr; *Anorexican* by Becky Johnson, directed by Cathy Gordon, with Johnson; *Skim* by Mariko Tamaki, directed by Kelly Thornton with Julie Tamiko Manning; *Horse Latitudes* by Nicola Harwood, directed by Natasha Mytnowych.

On 27 August, six short works from the Write From the Hip program, by Lena Lee, Kellee Ngan, Saidah Baba Talibah, Sylwia Przezdziecki, Karine Silverwomyn, and Kathleen Phillips. The Write From the Hip plays were matched with a professional director and a cast of professional and emerging actors from Nightwood's Emerging Actors Program, led by Natasha Mytnowych.

2 OCTOBER

Nightwood presents a panel discussion called "Ms.Conceptions: Queer Mothers and Children Tackle the Politics of Family." Moderated by Elvira Kurt, to celebrate the premiere of Diane Flacks's one-woman show *Bear With Me*. Held at the Tapestry/Nightwood New Work Studio.

OCTOBER

Cast Iron tours to Bridgetown, Barbados with Back Row Theatre Company Productions in association with Nightwood Theatre. Presented by The Nation Publishing Co. Limited at the Frank Collymore Hall.

It is announced that Nathalie Bonjour will be leaving her position as artistic producer of Nightwood as of December, to become the general manager at Queen of Puddings Music Theatre.

23 NOVEMBER–4 DECEMBER

Bear With Me, written and performed by Diane Flacks, presented by Nightwood in association with Buddies in Bad Times. Directed by Kelly Thornton. A staging of Flacks's book *Bear With Me: What They Don't Tell You About Pregnancy and New Motherhood*.

Board of directors, Winter 2005: Antonella Ceddia, Barb Linds, Lesley Ackrill, Susan Baker, Michele Landsberg, Du-Yi Leu, Kelly MacIntosh, Trish McGrath, Sarah Neville, Helen Thundercloud Administrative assistant: Marilo Nunez Commissioned playwrights: Beverley Cooper, Diane Flacks, Sheila Heti, Mariko Tamaki Playwright in residence: Ann Holloway

Board of directors, Summer 2005: Antonella Ceddia and Barb Linds (co-chairs), Lesley Ackrill, Susan Baker, Michele Landsberg, Trish McGrath (treasurer), Sarah Neville (secretary), Helen Thundercloud Administrative assistant: Christine Berg New director of marketing and development: Frances Shakov Commissioned playwrights: Bev Cooper, Diane Flacks, Mariko Tamaki Playwright in residence: Sonja Mills

ALSO IN 2005:

The third annual "Hysteria Festival" was presented 27 October–5 November 2005, curated by festival director Moynan King. After co-producing "Hysteria" for its first two years, Nightwood was not part of this third edition.

2006

Nathalie Bonjour is replaced by Monica Esteves as producer and general manager. Nightwood produces a brochure with a timeline of productions and a statement regarding the structure of the season: "Delivering on our mandate."

JANUARY

Nightwood receives a bequest of $50,000 from the late Elizabeth Szathmary, founding artistic director of Inner Stage Theatre, which was located at 9 Saint Nicholas before Nightwood took over that space.

26 JANUARY

Nightwood presents a reading of *chronicles in dub* by d'bi young, directed by ahdri zhina mandiela, at the Tapestry/Nightwood New York Studio.

27 JANUARY

The annual "Intimate Dinner" fundraising event, hosted by Michele Landsberg and Margot Franssen, with special guests Beverley Cooper and Diane Flacks reading from *Five Stages of Womanhood*.

5 MARCH

"FemCab": Nightwood distributes a factsheet of statistics about women's relative status internationally.

29 April–27 May

Nightwood presents *Mathilde* by Veronique Olmi, translated by Morwyn Brebner and directed by Kelly Thornton with Martha Burns and Tom McCamus, at the Young Centre for the Performing Arts in the Distillery District.

9 May

"Leading Ladies: Business and Culture Sharing Centre Stage": a gala reception, a performance of *Mathilde*, and post-show festivities hosted by Ann-Marie MacDonald and Phyllis Yaffe (CEO of Alliance Atlantis Communications). "Nightwood turns the spotlight on extraordinary female leaders in business communities across the GTA and Southwestern Ontario."

20–27 August

Twenty-third annual "Groundswell": *Mom's Birthday* by Tara Beagan; *A Nanking Winter* by Marjorie Chan; *The Darwinist* by Lorena Gale; *Mummy* by Ann Holloway; *Oil Man* by Sonja Mills; and *Essay* by Hannah Moscovitch. Also work from the Write From the Hip participants: Martha Schabas, Paula Schultz, Christine Harris, Ya Ya Yao, Patricia Lee, and Haley McGee; a collective creation from the Busting Out! participants; and *The B-Girl Project*, a hip-hop dance performance by girls aged twelve to sixteen, choreographed by K8 Alsterland.

Board of directors: Susan Baker, Michele Landsberg, Barbara Linds, Trish McGrath, Sarah Neville, Iris Nemani Staff: Kelly Thornton, artistic director; Monica Esteves, producer and general manager; Maggie Kwan, director of development and marketing; Marilo Nunez, administrator; Celia Philips, finance manager; Lisa Codrington and Anna Chatterton, co-directors of youth initiatives; Sonja Mills, playwright in residence.

17–21 October

Bear With Me by Diane Flacks toured to The Grand Theatre in London, Ontario.

12 December

"Ga-La-Licious," a fundraising concert headlined by Sarah Harmer, at the Courthouse Chamber Lounge.

Also in 2006

Equity in Canadian Theatre: The Women's Initiative was represented by Hope McIntyre at a forum in Calgary as part of the Alberta Theatre Projects Blitz weekend, 5 March. Findings of the National Survey were also presented by main researcher Rebecca Burton at a Playwrights Guild of Canada conference in Toronto on May 26, called "Canadian Women Playmakers: Tributes and Tribulations," co-sponsored by the Association for Canadian Theatre Research and the Graduate Centre for Study of Drama. Nightwood participants in the conference included Kelly Thornton, Kim Renders, and Diane Roberts.

2007

8 March

At "FemCab," Maja Ardal took over as interim artistic director as Kelly Thornton went on a one-year maternity leave. "FemCab" was held at the Brigatine Room, Harbourfront Centre, and featured Carol Off (host of CBC's "As It Happens") as keynote speaker. Sponsored by Michele Landsberg and Stephen Lewis, hosted by Teresa Pavlinek and Dawn Whitwell.

22 February–17 March

The Danish Play is remounted at the Young Centre for the Performing Arts.

2, 9, and 16 March

"Future Femme Fridays," staged readings of three new plays, held at the Tapestry/Nightwood New Work Studio: *Age of Arousal* by Linda Griffiths; *Oil Man* by Sonja Mills; *The Darwinist* by Lorena Gale.

26 April–19 May

Crave by Sarah Kane, directed by Jennifer Tarver, Young Centre for the

Performing Arts. Cast: Carlos Gonzalez-Vio, Michelle Monteith, Hardee Lineham, Maria Ricossa.

"Extreme Women Readings"—after three Thursday night performances of *Crave*, readings of plays by women outside of Canada: 3 May—*Bites* by Kay Adshead (U.K.), directed by Maja Ardal; 10 May—*The Princess Dramas* by Elfriede Jelinek (Austria), directed by Bea Pizano; 17 May—*Behzti (Dishonour)* by Gurpreet Kaur Bhatti (U.K.), directed by Maja Ardal.

9–15 SEPTEMBER

"Groundswell" at the Nightwood Tapestry Studio. *The Unfortunate Misadventures of Masha Galinski* by Erin Shields; *Desert Story* by Dennison Smith; *Light Swooping Through* by Stacey Engels; *a nanking winter* by Marjorie Chan; *Oil Man* by Sonja Mills; *The Corpse Bride* by Niki Landau. Also a collective creation from the Busting Out! participants and short plays from Write from the Hip.

24 SEPTEMBER

Wine-tasting and play-reading fundraising event, held by donors Margot Franssen and Margaret McCain, raises $30,000.

Board of directors: Iris Nemani (Chair), Trish McGrath, Sarah Neville, Susan Baker, Wanita Lambert, Michele Landsberg, Susan Quinn, Lorraine Rankin, Anne Tomsic Staff: Maja Ardal, interim artistic director; Monica Esteves, producer and general manager; Rebecca Peirson, director of marketing and audience development; Edita Page, director of development; Lisa Codrington, co-director of youth initiatives—Write from the Hip; Anna Chatteron, co-director of youth initiatives—Busting Out!; Beatriz Pizano, associate artistic director; Sonja Mills and Stacey Engels, playwrights in residence

23 NOVEMBER–16 DECEMBER

Age of Arousal by Linda Griffiths, directed by Maja Ardal, at the Factory Theatre. Cast: Clare Coulter, Sarah Dodd, Ellen-Ray Hennessy, Maggie Huculak, Gemma James-Smith, and Dylan Smith.

2008

23 FEBRUARY–16 MARCH

a nanking winter by Marjorie Chan, directed by Ruth Madoc Jones, at the Factory Theatre. Cast: Leon Aureued, Ella Chan, Brooke Johnson, Grace Lynn Kung, and Stephen Russell.

4 MARCH

Twenty-fifth anniversary of "FemCab," featuring Eve Ensler. Kelly Thornton officially returned from maternity leave.

MARCH

Release of "Artistic and Financial Mid-Season Review" document.

20 MAY

"Ga-la-licious" annual fundraising gala at the Courthouse (57 Adelaide Street East), featuring Mary Walsh and Women Fully Clothed.

MAY

Extreme Women readings at the Gladstone Hotel: *The Saviour of Potsdam* by Theresia Walser (Austria); *Stoning Mary* by Debbie Tucker Green (England); *In Darfur* by Winter Miller (USA).

MAY–AUGUST

Write from the Hip and Emerging Actors programs

JULY–AUGUST

Busting Out! program

6 OCTOBER–1 NOVEMBER

Wild Dogs, arranged for the stage by Anne Hardcastle from the novel by Helen Humphreys, directed by Kelly Thornton, produced in association with The Canadian Stage Company at the Berkley Street Theatre.

29 OCTOBER

An excerpt of *Wild Dogs* performed at the twenty-ninth annual "International Festival of Authors" at Harbourfront Centre; Helen Humphreys is one of the featured authors.

2009

7–24 JANUARY

Bear With Me, written and performed by Diane Flacks, at the Berkeley Upstairs Theatre. On 16 January, the show is followed by *Plan B: The After Baby Show*, featuring female comics Katie Crown, Elvira Kurt, Teresa Pavlinek, Shoshana Sperling, and Kathleen Phillips.

26–31 JANUARY

"Groundswell Festival" at the Berkeley Upstairs Theatre: *Burning In* by Natalie Meisner (Calgary); *STain* by Madeleine Blais Dahlem (Saskatoon); *Herr Beckmann's People* by Sally Stubbs (Vancouver); *Away We Go* by Maia Kareda (Toronto); *Jane* by Lisa Codrington (Toronto); *Augury* by Florence Gibson (Toronto); *La Communion* by Beatriz Pizano (Toronto/Columbia).

5 MARCH

"FemCab" at Lulu Lounge, co-hosted by Teresa Pavlinek and Shoshana Sperling. Features Dawn Langstroth and d'bi.young, with Marina Nemat (author of *Prisoner of Tehran*) as keynote speaker.

30 APRIL

"Ga-la-licious," featuring Erica Ehm and Janna Polzin; food, "fortune tellers, fire breathers, stilt walkers, magicians...and more!"

24 MAY

Public reading of *Prisoner of Tehran* by Marina Nemat, adapted by Maja Ardal and Kelly Thornton, at the Nightwood Studio.

23 AUGUST

Write from the Hip

24 AUGUST

Busting Out!

OCTOBER–NOVEMBER

"The 4 x 4 Festival," on the occasion of Nightwood's 30th anniversary. Includes a Directors' Summit running 13–20 November, as well as audience events and four productions:

26 OCTOBER–21 NOVEMBER

That Face by Polly Stenham (UK), directed by Kelly Thornton at the Berkeley Theatre downstairs.

31 OCTOBER–14 NOVEMBER

Yellowman by Dael Orlandersmith, directed by Weyni Mengesha; a co-production with Obsidian Theatre, at the Berkeley Theatre upstairs.

11–21 NOVEMBER

No Exit by Jean-Paul Sartre, conceived and directed by Kim Collier (British Columbia). An Electric Company and Virtual Stage production, at Buddies in Bad Times.

20–22 NOVEMBER

Serious Money by Caryl Churchill, directed by Eda Holmes, in partnership with Ryerson University Theatre School, at Theatre Passe Muraille.

Notes

PREFACE

1 Eco-feminism seeks to equate the oppression of women with the exploitation of nature. Donna Haraway, for example, defines eco-feminism as an insistence "on some version of the world as active subject, not as resource to be mapped and appropriated." Haraway, *Simians, Cyborgs, and Women* (New York: Routledge, 1991), 199. Interestingly, the Calgary women's theatre company Urban Curvz also uses the expression "theatre ecology" on its website.

2 Rita Much, "Introduction," *New Canadian Drama* 6 (Ottawa: Borealis Press, 1993), vii–xii.

3 Alisa Palmer, *Nightwood Newsletter,* Spring 2007, n.p.

INTRODUCTION

1 Lizbeth Goodman, *Contemporary Feminist Theatres: To Each Her Own* (New York: Routledge, 1993), 24–25.

2 Charlotte Canning, *Feminist Theaters in the U.S.A.: Staging Women's Experience* (London and New York: Routledge, 1996), 33.

3 Dinah Luise Leavitt, *Feminist Theatre Groups* (Jefferson, N.C: McFarland & Company Inc., 1980), 18.

4 Leavitt, *Feminist Theatre Groups,* 19.

5 Canning, *Feminist Theaters in the U.S.A.,* 36.

6 Leavitt, *Feminist Theatre Groups,* 67.

7 Ibid., 69.

8 Ibid., 77.

9 Amanda Hale, "Ascending Stages," *Broadside* vol. 6 no. 9 (July 1985): 10. Although At the Foot of the Mountain disbanded in 1991, Martha Boesing has continued to be an honoured and socially engaged playwright. In 1996 she wrote a play called *These Are My Sisters,* which

premiered in Minneapolis as part of the Walker Art Center's Out There Series. The play chronicles the achievements of second wave feminism through five monologues. In 2006, Boesing began writing for the Faithful Fools street ministry in San Francisco, creating *The Witness*, inspired by a famous Zen parable, and *Song of the Magpie*, which deals with homelessness.

10 Julia Miles, "Introduction," in *The Women's Project: Seven New Plays by Women*, ed. Julia Miles (New York: Performing Arts Journal Publications and American Place Theatre, 1980), 10.

11 Ibid.

12 Ibid., 11.

13 Julia Miles, *Womenswork: 5 New Plays from the Women's Project* (New York: Applause Books, 1989), v.

14 Cynthia Zimmerman, *Playwriting Women: Female Voices in English Canada* (Toronto: Simon and Pierre, 1994), 17.

15 Michelene Wandor, "Introduction," in *Plays by Women: Volume One* (London: Methuen, 1982), 8.

16 Yvonne Hodkinson, *Female Parts: The Art and Politics of Women Playwrights* (Montreal: Black Rose Books, 1991), 12.

17 Ibid., 14.

18 Rina Fraticelli also reported on her findings in an article entitled "Any Black Crippled Woman Can!" *Room of One's Own* vol. 8 no. 2: 7–18.

19 Mary Vingoe, Letter to Nathan H. Gilbert, Executive Administrator, Laidlaw Foundation, 1 March 1984, 2.

20 Chief researcher Rebecca Burton presented these statistics 26 May 2006 at a conference entitled "Canadian Women Playwrights: Tributes and Tribulations," held at the University of Toronto. She acknowledged that company revenue numbers were inflated due to the significantly larger budgets of companies reporting at the top end of the scale, and also noted a higher response rate to the survey by companies led by women.

21 Rebecca Burton, "Adding It Up: (En)Gendering (and Racializing) Canadian Theatre," *alt.theatre: Cultural Diversity and the Stage*, vol. 5 no. 1 (February 2007): 8. See also Michael Posner, "In search of a little play equity," *Globe and Mail*, 8 August 2009, R7.

22 Goodman, *Contemporary Feminist Theatres*, 9.

23 Robert Wallace, *Producing Marginality: Theatre and Criticism in Canada* (Saskatoon: Fifth House Publishers, 1990), 185.

24 Kym Bird, *Redressing the Past: The Politics of Early English-Canadian Women's Drama*, 1880–1920 (Montreal and Kingston: McGill-Queen's University Press, 2004), 5–6.

25 Roberts quoted in Catherine Glen, "On the Edge: Revisioning Nightwood," *Canadian Theatre Review* 82 (Spring 1995): 38.

26 Wallace, *Producing Marginality*, 162.

27 On the other hand, in his review of the book, Robert Nunn has argued that Wallace's definition of fringe theatre is too narrow and that companies like Passe Muraille still represent an alternative, risk-taking vision: *Canadian Theatre Review* 70 (Spring 1992): 93.

28 Rita Much, "Introduction," in *New Canadian Drama* 6 (Ottawa: Borealis Press, 1993), x.

29 Roberts quoted in Glen, "On the Edge: Revisioning Nightwood," 38.

30 Ibid.

31 These comments were made by Baņuta Rubess when speaking to a Canadian Theatre and Drama class, University of Toronto, 11 March 1993.

32 Ott quoted in Rebecca Daniels, *Women Stage Directors Speak*, excerpted in "Gender, Creativity & Power," *American Theatre* vol. 15 no. 7 (September 1998): 81.

33 For more on these distinctions, see Bruce Barton, "Introduction: Devising the Creative Body," in *Collective Creation, Collaboration and Devising*, ed. Bruce Barton, vol. 12 of Critical Perspectives on Canadian Theatre in English (Playwrights Canada Press, 2008). Barton offers the formulation: "Collective = shared purpose and motivation, *ideology*; collaboration = self-imposed framework and structure, *context*; devising = adopted strategies and rules, *process*" (ix).

34 The Anna Project, "This is For You, Anna: A spectacle of revenge," *Canadian Theatre Review* 43 (Fall 1985): 173.

35 Ibid., 170.

36 Play program, *This is For You, Anna*, Theatre Passe Muraille, January 1986.

37 Susan E. Bassnett-McGuire, "Towards a Theory of Women's Theatre," in *Linguistic and Literary Studies in Eastern Europe, Vol. 10: Semiotics of Drama and Theatre*, eds. Herta Schmid and Aloysius Van Kestern (Amsterdam and Philadelphia: John Benjamins Publishing Co., 1984), 458.

38 Ibid.

39 Ibid.

40 Monique Mojica has written something remarkably similar in discussing the absence of female stories being told as part of what she calls the "Native theatre explosion" in Toronto: "I wanted to work with other Native women who felt the void and who had the courage to tell their own stories." Monique Mojica, "Chocolate Woman Dreams the Milky Way," in *Collective Creation, Collaboration and Devising*, ed. Bruce Barton, *Critical Perspectives on Canadian Theatre in English*, Vol. 12 (Toronto: Playwrights Canada Press, 2009), 172.

41 Burning City Women quoted in Harry Lesnick, ed., "Burning City Women," *Guerilla Street Theatre* (New York: Avon Books, 1973), 389.

42 Ibid.

43 Sinfield quoted in Susan Bennett, *Theatre Audiences* (London and New York: Routledge, 1990), 4.

44 Chaudhuri quoted in Bennett, *Theatre Audiences*, 15.

45 Quoted in Bennett, *Theatre Audiences*, 17.

46 Alan Filewod, *Collective Encounters: Documentary Theatre in English Canada* (Toronto, Buffalo, London: University of Toronto Press, 1987), 19.

47 Denis W. Johnston, *Up the Mainstream: The Rise of Toronto's Alternative Theatres* (Toronto, Buffalo, London: University of Toronto Press, 1991), 225.

48 Robin Endres, "Introduction," in *Eight Men Speak and Other Plays from the Canadian Workers' Theatre* (Toronto: New Hogtown Press, 1976), xiv.

49 Bonn quoted in Jay Williams, *Stage Left: An Engrossing Account of the Radical Theatre Movement in America* (New York: Scribner, 1974), 22.

50 Ibid., 421.

51 Stasia Evasuk, "Play shows how women helped settle Ontario," *Toronto Star*, 27 October 1984, L3. "It is based on letters, diaries and books written by and about Canadian women ... The play opens with a reading of a pamphlet published in London in 1832 and addressed to those who wished to better themselves by emigrating to Canada."

52 Filewod, *Collective Encounters*, 24.

53 Ibid., 27.

54 Ibid., 30.

55 Zimmerman, *Playwriting Women*, 19.

56 Alan Filewod, "Erasing Historical Difference: The Alternative Orthodoxy in Canadian Theatre," *The Theatre Journal* vol. 42 no. 2 (May 1989): 210.

57 Pol Pelletier quoted in Amanda Hale, "Ascending Stages," 10.

58 Alisa Palmer, Leslie Lester, and Diane Roberts, "The first big word from the New Leadership Team," *Nighttalk* (Fall 1994), no page.

59 Bryony Lavery, "But Will Men Like It? Or living as a feminist writer without committing murder," in *Women and Theatre: Calling the Shots*, ed. Susan Todd (London: Faber and Faber, 1984), 27.

60 Alisa Palmer, "The Second Big Word," *Nighttalk* newsletter (January 1995), n.p.

61 Cynthia Grant, "Still 'Activist' after All These Years?" *Canadian Theatre Review* 117 (Winter 2004): 15.

62 Kim Renders, "Letter to the Editor," *Canadian Theatre Review* 119 (Summer 2005): 4.

63 Kate Lushington quoted in Diane Roberts, "Dramaturgy: A Nightwood Conversation," *Canadian Theatre Review* 87 (Summer 1996): 23.

64 Kim Renders, interview by author, Toronto, 11 May 1996.

65 Filewod, *Collective Encounters*, 35.

66 Brookes quoted in Filewod, *Collective Encounters*, 114.

67 Filewod, *Collective Encounters*, 14.

68 Ibid., x.

69 Savannah Walling, "Survival Techniques: Forces on the Artists/Artists on the Forces," *Canadian Theatre Review* 88 (Fall 1996): 12.

70 Ray Conlogue, "Squeaky floors and star turns lost the spotlight," *Toronto Star*, undated, n.p.

71 Grant, "Still 'Activist' after All These Years?" 14.

72 Ibid.

73 Ibid., 15.

74 Renders, "Letter to the Editor," 4.

75 See, for example, Susan Bennett and Alexandria Patience, "Bad Girls Looking for Money — Maenad Making Feminist Theatre in Alberta," *Canadian Theatre Review* 82 (Spring 1995): 10–13. "What Maenad is exploring is an administrative and artistic structure that makes possible a wide range of work by a diversity of women who do not or cannot, for a number of reasons, produce their theatre in the more traditional structures," 12.

76 Bennett, *Theatre Audiences*, 62.

77 Cynthia Grant quoted in Bennett, *Theatre Audiences*, 62.

78 For more information on the Company of Sirens, see *Canadian Theatre Review* 115.

CHAPTER ONE

1 www.nightwoodtheatre.net

2 Rebecca Burton assisted in compiling this information about festivals.

3 Francine Volker, "Running a Redlight," *Theatrum: A Theatre Journal* (April/May 1989): 29.

4 Ibid.

5 See Nightwood Theatre, "Notes from the Front Lines," *Canadian Theatre Review* 43 (Summer 1985): 44–51.

6 Volker, "Running a Redlight," 29.

7 Renders quoted in Jon Kaplan, "Renders goes solo in noisy kids' show," *NOW*, 17–23 December 1987, 19.

8 McKenzie Porter, "Ida: postgraduate study in wasted intelligence," *Toronto Star*, 26 October 1979, 101.

9 Grant quoted in Jon Kaplan, "Cynthia Grant Builds Images," *NOW*, August 1982, 13.

10 Kate Lushington, "The Changing Body of Women's Work," *Broadside* (August/September 1989): 21.

11 Kim Renders, *Nighttalk*, January 1995, n.p.

12 Kim Renders, interview by author, Toronto, 11 May 1996.

13 Denis Johnston, *Up the Mainstream: The Rise of Toronto's Alternative Theatres* (Toronto, Buffalo, London: University of Toronto Press, 1991), 3–4.

14 Johnston, *Up the Mainstream*, 57.

15 Johnston, *Up the Mainstream*, 219.

16 Alan Filewod, "Erasing Historical Difference: The Alternative Orthodoxy in Canadian Theatre," *The Theatre Journal* vol. 42 no. 2 (May 1989): 201–210.

17 Filewod, "Erasing Historical Difference," 209.

18 1980 "Rhubarb!" program.

19 Gilbert quoted in Jon Kaplan, "Actors make Rhubarb," *NOW*, November 1982, n.p.

20 Furthermore, Aida Jordão describes her involvement: "I was working full-time for Nightwood doubling as an actor and assistant to Cynthia Grant; since I had expressed an interest in working with Baņuta (I'd seen her wonderful work with the 1982 Theatre Company), Cynthia

'placed' me with the project as part of my work with Nightwood." Email correspondence, 24 July 2009.

21 Kate Lushington, interview by author, Toronto, 9 June 1996.

22 Patricia Keeney Smith, "Living with Risk," *Canadian Theatre Review* 38 (Fall 1983): 40.

23 Keeney Smith, "Living with Risk," 41.

24 Keeney Smith, "Living with Risk," 43.

25 Program, *Flashbacks of Tomorrow*, Toronto Theatre Festival's Open Stage at the Toronto Free Theatre, May 1981, n.p.

26 Ray Conlogue, "Triviality mars *Mass/Age*: Wit and flair don't mask unoriginal thinking," *Globe and Mail*, 30 August 1982, 11.

27 Jon Kaplan, "Cynthia Grant Builds Images," *NOW*, August 1982, 13.

28 Carole Corbeil, "Banquet full of political fare," *Globe and Mail*, 7 November 1983, 18.

29 Henry Mietkiewicz, "Peace Banquet a smorgasbord of fun," *Toronto Star*, 6 November 1983, G2.

30 Kate Lazier, "Pope Joan's Infallible Wit," *The Varsity*, 10 September 1984, 16. "Rubess' linear plot is a departure for Nightwood, whose work is usually more associative. But in typical Nightwood fashion, the transitions between scenes are smooth.

31 Banuta Rubess is quoted in Rita Much and Judith Rudakoff, eds., *Fair Play: Twelve Women Speak; Conversations with Canadian Playwrights* (Toronto: Simon and Pierre, 1990), 58. The perceived connection between Nightwood and The Anna Project was further cemented by the fact that both are featured prominently, and in an interconnected way, in the issue of *Canadian Theatre Review* where *This is For You, Anna* was first published.

32 The Anna Project, "Fragments, Afterthoughts," *Canadian Theatre Review* 43 (Summer 1985): 171.

33 The Anna Project, "Fragments, Afterthoughts," 172.

34 Ann Wilson, "The Politics of the Script," *Canadian Theatre Review* 43 (Summer 1985): 175.

35 The Anna Project, "Fragments, Afterthoughts," 173.

36 Wilson "The Politics of the Script," 178.

37 The Anna Project, "This is For You, Anna: A spectacle of revenge," *Canadian Theatre Review* 43 (Summer 1985): 158.

38 The Anna Project, "This is For You, Anna," 168.

39 The Anna Project, "Fragments, Afterthoughts," 171.

40 Regardless of whether or not this provision is legally enforceable, it does strongly convey the collective's concern that the material not be exploited; they felt that Marianne's story had been sensationalized in the German press and wanted to avoid a similar approach.

41 The Anna Project, "This is For You, Anna," 133.

42 The Anna Project "Fragments, Afterthoughts," 167.

43 See for example the use of milk as a symbol in Jovette Marchessault's play *Night Cows* in *Lesbian Triptych*, trans. Yvonne M. Klein (Toronto: Women's Press, 1985).

44 Ray Conlogue, "Cathy Jones Steals World Stage Festival Show," *Globe and Mail*, 9 June 1986, C11.

45 For example, Conlogue is incorrect in saying that Marianne Bachmeier killed her "ex-lover" who was on trial for murdering her daughter, Anna. Anna's killer was a neighbour, but nowhere in the play is it suggested that he was Marianne's lover. Conlogue writes, "It explores Anna's life history in detail [an error, he means Marianne's life history], including her various humiliations in a male-dominated society, and if it doesn't actually say her action was justifiable, it is sympathetic." He objects to the murder being portrayed as "normative" and also points out that women belittle men by calling them "wimps," which he claims suggests that they like aggressive men. These errors and irrelevant comments suggest that Conlogue was not sufficiently attentive to the actual play and was instead more concerned with expressing his own views about feminism. For further critical analysis of Conlogue's review, see Carole Corbeil, "Peeping Tom-cats: The Manly Art of Theatre Criticism," *This Magazine* vol. 20 no. 5 (December 1986/January 1987): 33–36.

46 Robert Crew, "Feminists launch festival," *Toronto Star*, 16 January 1987, D17.

47 Henry Mietkiewicz, "Lolita grows up to get last laughs," *Toronto Star*, 29 May 1987, E13.

48 Malcolm Burrows, "Perspectives in process: *War Babies'* journey," *The Varsity*, 9 March 1987, 13.

49 Susan G. Cole, "Ten Years and Five Minutes: Nightwood Celebrates a Decade of Feminist Theatre," *FUSE*, Spring 1990, 13.

50 Jeanie Forte, "Women's Performance Art: Feminism and Postmodernism," in *Performing Feminisms: Feminist Critical Theory and Feminism*, ed. Sue-Ellen Case (Baltimore and London: The Johns Hopkins University Press, 1990), 259.

51 Banuta Rubess with Peggy Christopherson, Ann-Marie MacDonald, Mary Marzo, Kim Renders, and Maureen White, *Smoke Damage: A story of the witch hunts* (Toronto: Playwrights Canada, 1985), 88.

52 Elin Diamond, "(In)Visible Bodies in Churchill's Theater," in *Making a Spectacle: Feminist Essays on Contemporary Women's Theatre*, ed. Lynda Hart (Ann Arbor: University of Michigan Press, 1989), 264.

53 Caryl Churchill, "Introduction to *Vinegar Tom*" in *Plays: One* (London: Methuen Drama, 1985), 129.

54 Program, *Burning Times*, Theatre Centre, August 1983.

55 Rubess quoted in Much and Rudakoff, *Fair Play*, 61.

56 Kim Renders, interview with author, Toronto, 11 May 1996. The dispute was resolved in Lambooy's favour, in the sense that a proposed strike by the actors was prevented by Equity's intervention.

57 Rubess in Much and Rudakoff, *Fair Play*, 62.

58 It is not clear from the correspondence that this was ever asked of her.

59 As an interesting side note, Margaret Atwood took on a very similar topic with her 2005 novel *Penelopiad: The Myth of Penelope and Odysseus*, by retelling the tale from Penelope's viewpoint. Atwood's work was adapted as a play and collaboratively produced by the Royal Shakespeare Company in Stratford-on-Avon, England, and by the National Arts Centre in Ottawa, in 2007. As part of Nightwood's thirtieth anniversary celebration, the "4x4 Festival," a concurrent directors' summit featured a week-long experimental master class, culminating in a performance on 15 November 2009 in which ten directors presented their take on Atwood's *Penelopiad*. The master class was led by Yael Farber and Josette Bushell-Mingo and involved actors from the Shaw Festival.

60 Meredith Levine, "Feminist Theatre — Toronto 87," *Theatrum: A Theatre Journal* (Spring 1987): 6.

61 Cynthia Grant, Application for a Cultural Grant from the City of Toronto, May 1983 to May 1984.

62 In her 2004 article "Still Activist After All These Years?" Cynthia Grant recalls, "Lina [Chartrand] and Amanda Hale had created lesbian performance art work that had been uncomfortably rejected at Nightwood. Partly as an act of solidarity against the homophobic undertones, I left with them to form Sirens" (15). This seems an odd claim, given that in 1986, the year Grant left, Nightwood produced *The Edge of the Earth is Too Near, Violette Leduc*, a lesbian story written by a prominent lesbian author and marketed to the gay and lesbian community.

63 Mary Vingoe, letter to Irene N. Turrin, Director of Cultural Affairs, Municipality of Metro Toronto, 13 February 1986.

64 Mary Vingoe, letter to Jeremy Long, Theatre Officer, Canada Council, 17 March 1986.

65 Mary Vingoe, letter to Nathan Gilbert, Executive Director, Laidlaw Foundation, 10 October 1986. As the quote suggests, Nightwood's collective structure allowed many women an opportunity to gain experience and exposure which later assisted them in finding work at other theatres. Rubess, for example, later became an associate artist with Theatre Passe Muraille.

66 Mary Vingoe, Internship Training Program application, Ministry of Culture and Communication, 22 October 1986.

67 Rita Much, "Introduction," *New Canadian Drama* 6 (Ottawa: Borealis Press, 1993), ix.

68 My experience of seeing this play was very different. Libra Productions presented *A Particular Class of Women,* directed by Kim Lavis, at the Alumnae Theatre in Toronto from 27 October to 6 November 1994. In this production, each character was portrayed by a different actor. Instead of admiring the virtuosity of a single performer, the audience focus was on a parade of attractive young bodies in competition with one another, undermining the intention of the playwright to emphasize female solidarity. Signs at the theatre entrance encouraged the audience to clap and cheer for the dance pieces, heightening our role as voyeurs and consumers. However, it should be acknowledged that a program note indicated that Janet Feindel was consulted on and supported the production.

69 In her 2004 article "Still Activist After All These Years?" Cynthia Grant writes that, in the early days of Nightwood, Theatre Passe Muraille's artistic director, Paul Thompson, "was a valuable ally...at least until I declined to create a show about strippers" (14). With no elaboration on the nature of that project, Grant implies that strippers are a categorically inappropriate topic for a Nightwood show, and that the very idea Thompson would suggest such a thing created a rift between them. Nightwood sponsored *A Particular Class of Women* in 1987, the year after Grant left. Feminists may hold widely variant attitudes towards sexuality, pornography, and sex-related work, with notably different degrees of acceptance between the Second and Third Waves.

70 Catherine Glen, "On the Edge: Revisioning Nightwood," *Canadian Theatre Review* 82 (Spring 1995): 39.

71 Kaplan, "Renders goes solo in noisy kids' show," 19.

72 Jon Kaplan, "Bearing the fruit of a polluted world," *NOW*, 4–10 May 1989, 47. At this point, Kate Lushington had been hired as the newest artistic coordinator. Lushington inherited a season that had already been programmed and included Vingoe's play.

73 For example, the eighth annual "Groundswell," "Making Waves," held at the Tarragon Theatre Extraspace, in October and November of 1992, featured three collective creations: *A Savage Equilibrium* by Monique Mojica, Fernando Hernandez Perez, Jani Lauzon and Floyd Favel; *Coming from the Womb* by the Red Sister/Black Sister Collective; and *Girls in the 'Hood* by Catherine Glen with young women from Metro Housing.

74 Rubess in Much and Rudakoff, *Fair Play*, 74.

75 Ibid., 61.

76 Christopher Hume, "The humour saves Lolita, but it's strained," *Toronto Star*, 5 June 1987, E19.

77 Soraya Peerbaye, "Look to the Lady: Re-examining Women's Theatre," *Canadian Theatre Review* 84 (Fall 1995): 25.

78 Levine, "Feminist Theatre — Toronto 87," 6.

79 Vingoe quoted in Levine, "Feminist Theatre — Toronto 87," 7.

80 Ibid.

81 Levine, "Feminist Theatre — Toronto 87," 7.

82 Ibid.

83 The Company of Sirens has mounted shows in more traditional venues as well, such as the Alumnae Theatre and Theatre Passe Muraille. For more information on the Sirens, see Cynthia Grant, "Still 'Activist' after All These Years?" *Canadian Theatre Review* 117 (Winter 2004): 14–16.

84 Malene Arpe, "Feminist Theatre," *Bark* magazine vol. 2 no. 8 (January 1993): 17.

85 Julie Taymor quoted in Sylviane Gold, "The Possession of Julie Taymor," *American Theatre* vol. 15 no. 7 (September 1998): 22.

86 Karen Houppert, "Ruth Maleczech: Her Life in Art," *American Theatre* vol. 15 no. 7 (September 1998): 86.

87 Michelene Wandor, *Post-War British Drama: Look Back in Gender* (London and New York: Routledge, 2001), 249.

88 Pam Brighton, "Directions," in *Women and Theatre: Calling the Shots*, ed. Susan Todd (London: Faber and Faber, 1984), 58–59.

89 Jane Wagner, *The Search for Signs of Intelligent Life in the Universe* (New York: Harper and Row, 1986), 184.

CHAPTER TWO

1 Bryony Lavery, "But Will Men Like It? Or living as a feminist writer without committing murder," in *Women and Theatre: Calling the Shots*, ed. Susan Todd (London: Faber and Faber, 1984), 28.

2 The first and only production by Mean Feet was staged in early December of 1982. Built around the theme of fathers and daughters, it included *Dark Pony* by David Mamet, directed by Padveen, and *Canadian Gothic* by Joanna McClelland Glass, directed by Lushington. It was funded by a project grant from the Ontario Arts Council. According to Amanda Hale, "It was a first class production and received very favourable reviews."

3 Nightwood Theatre, "Notes From the Front Lines," *Canadian Theatre Review* 43 (Summer 1985): 44–51.

4 Kate Lushington, interview by author, Toronto, 9 June 1996.

5 Ibid.

6 Joseph Green and Douglas Buck, "Responsibility and Leadership in Canadian Theatre," *Canadian Theatre Review* 40 (Fall 1984): 4–8. A community-based board of directors is defined as one made up of non-artists — people in the patronage and business communities. They have final legal responsibility and the authority to approve or disapprove anything. Funding agencies require that publicly funded institutions have a board.

7 Kate Lushington, letter to Ministry of Culture and Communications, July 1989.

8 Search Committee meeting minutes, 30 August 1993.

9 Sally Clark is a good example of someone who furthered her development through Nightwood. *Life Without Instruction* had a long but ultimately unfruitful history with the company; Nightwood had originally sponsored Sally Clark's application for funding to work on *The Medea Project*, a piece about women and revenge, which she was proposing for eventual production by Nightwood. This became *Life Without Instruction*, but Clark chose not to have Nightwood produce the show. Clark also developed another of her plays, *St. Frances of Hollywood*, at "Groundswell," but had it produced by the Canadian Stage Company in 1996. For further discussion of Clark's play development history, see D.A. Hadfield, *Re: Producing Women's Dramatic History: The Politics of Playing in Toronto* (Vancouver: Talonbooks, 2007).

10 Kate Lushington, "Fear of Feminism," *Canadian Theatre Review* 43 (Summer 1985): 11.

11 To suggest that Judith Thompson is marginalized in Canadian theatre seems at first a dubious statement, but Lushington is citing Thompson both as an anomaly and as someone who has encountered sexism in her rise to the position of respect she now enjoys. In Soraya Peerbaye's "Look to the Lady: Re-examining Women's Theatre," *Canadian Theatre Review* 84 (Fall 1995): 23, Thompson herself talks about the paternalistic control she had to overcome in order to get her earliest plays done to her satisfaction. Furthermore, in a larger context, even the most successful woman in our society is still the victim of sexist stereotyping, expected to behave in certain ways, at risk from male violence, concerned with reproductive issues, and so on—a common condition which forms the basis for cultural feminist solidarity among women of very different circumstances.

12 Lushington does not provide a citation for the Amos quote, but dates it 1985.

13 Vit Wagner, "By women, for everybody: Nightwood Theatre is 'very much a feminist process,'" *Toronto Star,* 17 March 1990, H2.

14 For more on the disagreement around Nightwood's earliest structure, see Cynthia Grant, "Still 'Activist' after All These Years?" *Canadian Theatre Review* 117 (Winter 2004): 14–16, and the response from Kim Renders, "Letter to the Editor," *Canadian Theatre Review* 119 (Summer 2005): 4.

15 In Alberta, where I directed the play at the University of Lethbridge in 2003, it has been done professionally in Edmonton and Calgary, and had student productions at the University of Calgary, Keyano College, and Mount Royal College.

16 Ric Knowles has maintained that *Goodnight Desdemona (Good Morning Juliet)* displays "a second-wave feminist focus on gender and genre that was very much of its 1980s context at Toronto's Nightwood Theatre." Knowles, "Othello in Three Times," in *Shakespeare in Canada: A World Elsewhere?* eds. Diana Brydon and Irena R. Makaryk (Toronto: University of Toronto Press, 2002), 377–378. But I do not think this accounts for the fact that the play continues to be so popular, far after, and in locations far removed from, its original 1980s Toronto context.

17 Peter Dickinson, "Duets, Duologues, and Black Diasporic Theatre: Djanet Sears, William Shakespeare, and Others," *Modern Drama* vol. XLV no. 2 (Summer 2002): 193.

NOTES

18 Laurin R. Porter, "Shakespeare's Sisters: Desdemona, Juliet and Constance Ledbelly in *Goodnight Desdemona (Good Morning Juliet)*," *Modern Drama* vol. XXXVIII no. 3 (Fall 1995): 365.

19 In the published text, both a quotation in the dedication, and the introduction by Rubess, emphasize the existence of a Jungian subtext. The story happens in the subconscious mind: the character Constance "stews in her office like base matter in the alchemical dish; she reaches the nigredo/nadir of her existence and this allows her to reconsider her life, her self, as if in a dream." In this interpretation, Desdemona and Juliet are archetypes of Constance's own unconscious, while Othello and Tybalt are permutations of Professor Night, and the Chorus, Iago and Yorick are all versions of her own, goading animus.

20 Shannon Hengen, "Towards a Feminist Comedy," *Canadian Literature* 146 (Autumn 1995): 99.

21 Paula Kamen, *Her Way: Young Women Remake the Sexual Revolution* (New York: New York University Press, 2000), 3.

22 Ibid., 45.

23 Ann-Marie MacDonald, *Good Night Desdemona (Good Morning Juliet)* (Toronto: Coach House Press, 1990), 76–77.

24 Porter, "Shakespeare's Sisters," 370.

25 Sophia Phoca and Rebecca Wright, *Introducing Postfeminism* (New York: Totem Books, 1999), 105.

26 Porter, "Shakespeare's Sisters," 368.

27 Ann Wilson, "Critical Revisions: Ann-Marie MacDonald's *Goodnight Desdemona (Good Morning Juliet)*," in *Women on the Canadian Stage: The Legacy of Hrotsvit*, ed. Rita Much (Winnipeg: Blizzard Publishing, 1992), 11.

28 Phoca and Wright, *Introducing Postfeminism*, 171.

29 Ann Brooks, *Postfeminisms: Feminism, Cultural Theory and Cultural Forms* (London and New York: Routledge, 1997), 157.

30 Martha Tuck Rozett, *Talking Back to Shakespeare* (Newark: University of Delaware Press, 1994), 165.

31 Ibid., 166.

32 Knowles, "Othello in Three Times," 379.

33 Natalie Fenton, "Feminism and Popular Culture," in *The Routledge Companion to Feminism and Postfeminism*, ed. Sarah Gamble (London and New York: Routledge, 2001), 112.

34 Leslie Heywood and Jennifer Drake, *Third Wave Agenda: Being Feminist, Doing Feminism* (Minneapolis: University of Minnesota Press, 1997), 4.

35 Ellyn Kaschak, *The Next Generation: Third Wave Feminism Psychotherapy* (New York: The Haworth Press, Inc., 2001), 3.

36 Ibid., 16.

37 Ric Knowles, "Reading Material: Transfers, Remounts, and the Production of Meaning in Contemporary Toronto Drama and Theatre," *Essays on Canadian Writing* nos. 51–52 (Winter 1993–Spring 1994): 285.

38 Anne-Marie MacDonald quoted in Rita Much and Judith Rudakoff, eds., *Fair Play: Twelve Women Speak; Conversations with Canadian Playwrights* (Toronto: Simon and Pierre, 1990), 142.

39 See Linda Burnett, "'Redescribing a World': Towards a Theory of Shakespearean Adaptation in Canada," *Canadian Theatre Review* 111 (Summer 2002): 5–9; Ellen McKay, "The Spectre of Straight Shakespeare," *Canadian Theatre Review* 111 (Summer 2002): 10–14; and Marianne Novy, "Saving Desdemona and/or Ourselves: Plays by Ann-Marie MacDonald and Paula Vogel," in *Transforming Shakespeare: Contemporary Women's Re-visions in Literature and Performance*, ed. Marianne Novy (New York: St. Martin's Press, 1999), 67–85.

40 Novy, "Saving Desdemona and/or Ourselves," 79.

41 Ibid., 81.

42 Hengen, "Towards a Feminist Comedy," 103.

43 Kate Lushington quoted in Vit Wagner, "By women, for everybody," *Toronto Star*, 17 March 1990, H2.

44 Jon Kaplan, "Kate Lushington: Feminism fuels director's vision for fertile comedy," *NOW*, 31 January–6 February 1991, 22.

45 Susan G. Cole, "A Very Fertile Imagination: Interview," *Night Talk* newsletter vol. 2 no. 2 (Winter 1991): 1.

46 Jon Kaplan, "Kate Lushington: Feminism fuels director's vision for fertile comedy," 22.

47 All quotes are from an unpublished, unnumbered manuscript. I thank Susan G. Cole for access to that early text. The play was published in Rosalind Kerr, *Lesbian Plays: Coming of Age in Canada* (Toronto: Playwrights Canada Press, 2007).

48 Lizbeth Goodman, *Contemporary Feminist Theatres: To Each Her Own* (New York: Routledge, 1993), 63.

49 Kate Lushington, interview by author, Toronto, 9 June 1996.

50 Stephanie Griffiths, n.p.

51 Vit Wagner, "A Shallow Look at Sexual Politics," *The Toronto Star*, 7 February 1991, B5.

52 Sandra Haar, "Breeding Ground: Dyke sensibility weeded out of play's production," *RITES*, April 1991, 15.

53 Ibid.

54 Ibid.

55 Jill Dolan,"Breaking the Code," in *Presence and Desire* (Ann Arbor: The University of Michigan Press, 1993), 140.

56 Kate Lushington, interview with author, Toronto, 9 June 1996. Lushington cites the Women's Press as an example of a feminist organization torn apart along racial lines.

57 Jill Lawless, "Djanet Sears: Deft performer unravels fairy tales' romantic web," *NOW*, 7–13 October 1993, 28–29.

58 "Groundswell's grassroots grow in new direction," *NOW*, 1–17 December 1988, 59.

59 Nigel Hunt, "Bringing the Heroine Back to Life," *Performing Arts* (March/Spring 1990): 28.

60 Kate Lushington, interview with author, Toronto, 9 June 1996. With a few exceptions, such as Diane Flacks's one-woman show *Random Acts*, and *One Flea Spare* in 1998, Nightwood avoided all-white casts in mainstage productions.

61 A shorter version was first published in *Canadian Theatre Review* 64 (Fall 1990), but my references will be to Monique Mojica, *Princess Pocahontas and the Blue Spots* (Toronto: Women's Press, 1991).

62 Monique Mojica, "Chocolate Woman Dreams the Milky Way," in *Collective Creation, Collaboration and Devising*, ed. Bruce Barton, Vol. 12 of *Critical Perspectives on Canadian Theatre in English*, (Toronto: Playwrights Canada Press, 2009), 167–181. In her brief discussion of the piece, Mojica refers to it as *Un(tit)led* and provides an excerpt.

63 Janice Hladki, "Negotiating Drama Practices: Struggles in Racialized Relations of Theatre Production and Theatre Research," in *How Theatre Educates: Convergences and Counterpoints*, eds. Kathleen Gallagher and David Booth (Toronto: University of Toronto Press, 2003), 144–161. In her article, Hladki identifies the work as *Onions, Strawberries, and Corn*.

64 For further discussion on the play and other examples of Aboriginal women's theatre, see Shelley Scott, "Embodiment as a Healing Process:

Native Women and Performance," in *Native American Performance and Representation*, ed. S.E. Wilmer (Tucson: Arizona University Press, 2009).

65 At least according to Jon Kaplan, "Spiderwoman's Struggle," *NOW*, 1–7 July 1982, 12. Mojica has also written about the process of creating the play, and about the importance of her long-term working relationship with Muriel Miguel. See Monique Mojica, "Chocolate Woman Dreams the Milky Way," 176.

66 Mojica played: Princess Buttered-on-Both-Sides; Contemporary Woman #1; Malinche; Storybook Pocahontas; Pocahontas/Lady Rebecca/ Matoaka; Deity/Woman of the Puna/Virgin; Marie/ Margaret/Madelaine; Cigar Store Squaw; and Spirit Animal. Alejandra Nunez played: the Host; the Blue Spots; Contemporary Woman #2; Troubadour; Ceremony; the Man; Spirit-Sister; and the Musician.

67 Mojica, *Princess Pocahontas and the Blue Spots*, 14.

68 Ric Knowles, *The Theatre of Form and the Production of Meaning: Contemporary Canadian Dramaturgies* (Toronto: ECW Press, 1999), 208.

69 Mojica, *Princess Pocahontas and the Blue Spots*, 35.

70 Ibid., 60.

71 Knowles, *The Theatre of Form and the Production of Meaning*, 208.

72 "*Dryland* inaugurates new studio theatre," *Night Talk* vol. 4 no. 2 (Winter 1993): 1.

73 Monique Mojica, "Of Borders, Identity and Cultural Icons: A Rant," *Canadian Theatre Review* 125 (Winter 2006): 35–40.

74 Mojica, "Chocolate Woman Dreams the Milky Way," 172–173.

75 Monique Mojica, "Stories From the Body: Blood Memory and Organic Texts," *alt.theatre: Cultural Diversity and the Stage* vol. 4 nos. 2 and 3 (May 2006): 16.

76 Ibid., 17.

77 Ibid., 20.

78 Kelley Jo Burke has jokingly referred to herself, in the Nightwood newsletter, as "the only radical feminist in Saskatchewan." One might interpret this to be a statement of affiliation with cultural feminism, or perhaps radical is here being used in the sense of committed or fervent. In any case, a materialist, or at least a problematized, reading of her play is still possible.

79 Jill Lawless, "Deft performer unravels fairy tales' romantic web," *NOW*, October 1993, 28.

80 Donna Haraway, *Simians, Cyborgs, and Women: The Reinvention of Nature* (New York: Routledge, 1991), 82.

81 Carolynne Larrington, *The Feminist Companion to Mythology* (London: Pandora Press, 1992), xi.

82 Jane Caputi, "Psychic Activism: Feminist Mythmaking," in Larrington, *The Feminist Companion to Mythology*, 425.

83 Ibid., 426.

84 Lena B. Ross, *To Speak or Be Silent: The Paradox of Disobedience in the Lives of Women* (Wilmette, Il.: Chiron Publications, 1993), xii.

85 Kate Lushington, interview with author, Toronto, 9 June 1996. Lushington remarked that although the character had not been written as someone from the West Indies, both Alison Sealy-Smith (in workshops) and, independently, Djanet Sears in rehearsal, discovered the accent fit the character. Lushington speculated that it might be related to the consciousness of class issues specific to colonized societies.

86 Yvonne Hodkinson, *Female Parts: The Art and Politics of Women Playwrights* (Montreal: Black Rose Books, 1991), 134.

87 Diane Purkiss, "Women's Rewriting of Myth," in Larrington, *The Feminist Companion to Mythology*, 444.

88 Ibid., 448.

89 Kelley-Jo Burke, *Charming and Rose: True Love*, in *Amazing Plays: 3 from the '92 Winnipeg Fringe* (Winnipeg: Blizzard Publishing, 1992), 35.

90 Ibid., 33.

91 Linda Williams,"When the Woman Looks," in *Re-Vision: Essays in Feminist Film Criticism*, eds. Mary Ann Doane, Patricia Mellencamp, and Linda Williams (Los Angeles: University Publications of America, Inc./ American Film Institute, 1984), 87–88.

92 Ibid., 87.

93 Haraway, *Simians, Cyborgs, and Women*, 155.

94 Ibid., 135.

95 Lynda Hill, "Festival is proud of the feminist label," *Annex Town Crier*, December 1991, 3.

96 Kate Lushington, interview with author, 9 June 1996. "When you find yourself realizing that every new idea someone has tried: 'Well, we did that in 1980, but it didn't work because…!' [laughs] There are new things, but when you find that happening you've got to move on, which I find very easy. I was in mourning before I left, but not after. I needed

to be gone. I think Nightwood is great, but I don't think, 'they should do this or that.' So, you know, it's not part of me now."

97 Mary Lou Zeitoun, "Sex and the working theatre girls," *eye*, 14 October 1993, 24.

CHAPTER THREE

1 Sky Gilbert, telephone interview with author, 1996.

2 Catherine Glen, "On the Edge: Revisioning Nightwood," *Canadian Theatre Review* 82 (Spring 1995): 37.

3 In 2003, Palmer and MacDonald were married and adopted a daughter.

4 Alisa Palmer, interview with author, Toronto, 7 March 1996.

5 Leslie Lester, interview with author, Toronto, 23 January 1996.

6 Diane Roberts, interview with author, Toronto, 7 February 1996.

7 1992 mandate statement, provided as part of the application package to candidates for the position of artistic director.

8 Curated by Soraya Peerbaye, Alisa Palmer, and Sandra Laronde in association with Native Women in the Arts and Equity Showcase Theatre.

9 Leslie Lester, interview with author, Toronto, 23 January 1996.

10 Sessle, Erica. "Nightwood focuses on a diverse female aesthetic," *The Varsity*, March 1995, 11.

11 Alisa Palmer, Leslie Lester, and Diane Roberts, "The first big word from the New Leadership Team," *Nighttalk*, Fall 1994, n.p.

12 Quoted in Soraya Peerbaye, "Look to the Lady: Re-examining Women's Theatre," *Canadian Theatre Review* 84 (Fall 1995): 24.

13 Ibid., 23.

14 The cast was Barbara Barnes-Hopkins, Jeff Jones, Dawn Roach, Alison Sealy-Smith, and Nigel Shawn Williams. There was also a duo providing live musical accompaniment. The assistant director was Maxine Bailey, dramaturgy was by Kate Lushington and Diane Roberts, and ahdri zhina mandiela was listed as a resource artist.

15 Held at Hart House at the University of Toronto. Alex Bulmer was joined by panellists Lynn Fernie, Brigitte Gall, Nalo Hopkinson, and Mirah Soleil-Ross.

16 Alex Bulmer, "Playwright's Note, Smudge," *Canadian Theatre Review* 108 (Fall 2001): 53.

17 Bulmer, "Smudge," 61.

18 *Canadian Theatre Review* 108 (Fall 2001): 53–67.

19 Jon Kaplan, "Smudge has clarity," *NOW*, 30 November–6 December 2000, n.p.

20 Elisa Kukla, "Lifting the blind," *eye*, 23 November 2000, 50.

21 For further discussion of the play, see Shelley Scott, "*Finding Regina, Third Wave Feminism, and Regional Identity*" in the forthcoming collection *West-Words*, ed. Moira Day, published by Prairie Forum.

22 Other plays by Sperling include the one-person shows *The Rise and Fall of Vella Dean, The Golden Mile,* and *Sheboobie*. Most recently, she wrote *The Guilty Play Room* with Teresa Pavlinek and premiered it at the 2004 "Hysteria Festival." Most of her work has been done at the "Fringe" or other festivals. After leaving Regina, she attended university at York and Concordia.

23 Shoshana Sperling quoted in *Nightwood Theatre Newsletter*, Spring 2003, 1.

24 Shoshana Sperling, *Finding Regina* (Winnipeg: Scirocco Drama, 2003), 5.

25 Sperling quoted in *Nightwood Theatre Newsletter*, 1.

26 Glenn Sumi, "Shoshana Sperling: Funny Girl Plays with her Regina," *NOW* vol. 22 no. 25, 20–26 February 2003, 58.

27 Sperling, *Finding Regina*, 22.

28 Ibid., 27.

29 Ibid., 28.

30 Ibid., 38.

31 Ibid.

32 Held at the Tarragon Theatre Extra Space, the discussion featured Marjorie Chan, Susan Eng, Avvy Go, Shirley Hoy, Brenda Joy Lem, Vivienne Poy, and Kristyn Wong-Tam.

33 Marjorie Chan, *China Doll* (Winnipeg: Scirocco, 2004), 24.

34 Ibid., 86–87.

35 Kelly Thornton, interview with author, 28 May 2002.

36 See Chapter Four for more on youth mentorships.

37 *Cast Iron* was also done at the 2002 Toronto "Fringe," produced by Codrington's own company, Back Row Theatre. It was part of the 2004 Banff playRites Colony, and the "CrossCurrents Festival" at the Factory Theatre in 2004. See the Chronology for further information on this and other productions mentioned.

38 Monica Esteves, interview with author, Toronto, 23 May 2006.

39 In conversation, this was compared to the Canadian Stage budget of almost twelve million dollars.

40 For further discussion on the use of the Bajan dialect and critical reception to the play, see Michelle MacArthur, "Patrolling Our Borders: Critical Reception of Lisa Codrington's *Cast Iron*," *alt.theatre: Cultural Diversity and the Stage*, vol. 6 no. 3 (March 2009): 24–33.

41 Kelly Thornton, interview with author, Toronto, 23 May 2006.

42 For further discussion of the play, see Shelley Scott, "Sickness and Sexuality: Feminism and the Female Body in *Age of Arousal* and *Chronic*," forthcoming in *Theatre Research in Canada* 31.1 (2010).

43 Linda Griffiths, "Playwright's Note," *Age of Arousal* (Toronto: Coach House Books, 2007), 12.

44 Ibid., 9.

45 Griffiths, "Production," *Age of Arousal* (Toronto: Coach House Books, 2007), 13.

46 Layne Coleman, "Foreword," *Age of Arousal* (Toronto: Coach House Books, 2007), 6.

47 Ibid., 6–7.

48 Griffiths, "A Flagrantly Weird Age: A reaction to research, time travel and the history of the suffragettes," 134. Strangely, Griffiths misidentifies these feminist scholars as belonging to the First Wave.

49 Griffiths "Playwright's Note," 8.

50 Griffiths, *Age of Arousal*, 93.

51 Ibid., 113.

52 Ibid., 122.

53 Ibid., 111.

54 Ibid., 50.

55 Griffiths, "A Flagrantly Weird Age," 166.

56 Ibid., 145.

57 Monica Esteves, Nightwood *Juicy News* email newsletter, vol. 2, issue 2, 11 March 2008, n.p.

58 Michael McKinnie, *City Stages: Urban Space in a Global City* (Toronto: University of Toronto Press, 2007), 120.

59 Ibid., 131.

60 Ibid., 128.

61 21 March 2008 letter.

62 7 December 2007 letter.

63 Nightwood Theatre Artistic and Financial Mid-Season Review, 2008, 3.

Chapter Four

1   Phyllis Mael with Rosemary Curb and Beverley Byers-Pevitts, "The First Decade of Feminist Theatre in America," *Catalogue of Feminist Theatre: Chrysalis; A Magazine of Women's Culture*, no. 10 (April 1980): 51.

2   Mael, "The First Decade of Feminist Theatre in America," 52.

3   Ibid., 63.

4   In Toronto, for example, there was a lesbian theatre company called Atthis. Its founder, Keltie Creed, also worked on Nightwood's 1986 production of *The Edge of the Earth is Too Near, Violette Leduc* by Jovette Marchessault.

5   Curb, "The First Decade of Feminist Theatre in America," 64.

6   Ibid.

7   Dinah Luise Leavitt, *Feminist Theatre Groups* (Jefferson, N.C: McFarland & Company Inc., 1980), 60–61.

8   Curb, "The First Decade of Feminist Theatre in America," 65.

9   This is a trait held in common with other collective creators of the time. See, for example, Denis W. Johnston, *Up the Mainstream: The Rise of Toronto's Alternative Theatres* (Toronto, Buffalo, London: University of Toronto Press, 1991), 26; Johnston describes the making of *The Farm Show*, the most famous of all Canadian collective creations.

10 Curb, "The First Decade of Feminist Theatre in America," 65.

11 Lizbeth Goodman, *Contemporary Feminist Theatres: To Each Her Own* (New York: Routledge, 1993), 63.

12 Goodman, *Contemporary Feminist Theatres*, 67.

13 For discussion of these categories, see also Gayle Austin, *Feminist Theories for Dramatic Criticism* (Ann Arbor: The University of Michigan Press, 1990); Jill Dolan, *The Feminist Spectator as Critic* (Ann Arbor: The University of Michigan Press, 1988); and Alison M. Jagger, *Feminist Politics and Human Nature* (Totawa, NJ: Rowman and Allanheld, 1983). A good example of someone who problematizes the categories is Shannon Bell, *Reading, Writing and Rewriting the Prostitute Body* (Bloomington and Indianapolis: Indiana University Press, 1994).

14 Austin, *Feminist Theories for Dramatic Criticism*, 4.

15 Heather Jones, "Connecting Issues: Theorizing English-Canadian

Women's Drama," in *Women on the Canadian Stage: The Legacy of Hrotsvit*, ed. Rita Much (Winnipeg: Blizzard Publishing, 1992), 86.

16 Kate Lushington quoted in Nigel Hunt, "Bringing the Heroine Back to Life," *Performing Arts* (March/Spring 1990): 27.

17 Janice Bryan quoted in Martha J. Bailey, "Editor's Column," *Queens Quarterly* 96/1 (Spring 1989): 219.

18 Mary Vingoe quoted in Myrna Wyatt Selkirk, "Cultural Diversity and the Magnetic North Theatre Festival: A Chat with Mary Vingoe, Artistic Director of the Magnetic North Theatre Festival," *alt.theatre: Cultural Diversity and the Stage*, vol. 5 no. 1 (February 2007): 12.

19 Nightwood Theatre, "Notes from the Front Lines," *Canadian Theatre Review* 43 (Summer 1985): 45.

20 Meredith Levine, "Feminist Theatre — Toronto 87," *Theatrum: A Theatre Journal* (Spring 1987): 6.

21 Sue-Ellen Case, *Feminism and Theatre* (London: MacMillan Publishers Ltd., 1988), 4.

22 Julia Miles, "Introduction," *The Women's Project* 2 (New York: Performing Arts Journal Publications, 1984), 10.

23 Ibid.

24 Judith Butler, "Performative Acts and Gender Constitution: An Essay in Phenomenology and Feminist Theory," in *Performing Feminisms: Feminist Critical Theory and Feminism*, ed. Sue-Ellen Case (Baltimore and London: The Johns Hopkins University Press, 1990), 281.

25 Leavitt, *Feminist Theatre Groups*, 101.

26 Charlotte Canning, *Feminist Theaters in the U.S.A.: Staging Women's Experience* (London and New York: Routledge, 1996), 60.

27 Ibid., 66.

28 Ibid.

29 Dolan, *The Feminist Spectator as Critic*, 10.

30 Austin, *Feminist Theories for Dramatic Criticism*, 15–16.

31 In *Cloud Nine*, the second act takes place one hundred years after the first act, but for the characters only twenty-five years have passed. In *Top Girls*, women from different countries and time periods share a dinner party.

32 Jill Dolan, "Breaking the Code," in *Presence and Desire* (Ann Arbor: The University of Michigan Press, 1993), 141.

33 Linda Hutcheon, *The Politics of Postmodernism* (London and New York: Routledge, 1989), 19–20.

34 Ibid., 10.

35 American Third Wave feminist magazines *Bust* and *Bitch* provide a wealth of examples.

36 Bell, *Reading, Writing and Rewriting the Prostitute Body*, 137.

37 Hutcheon, *The Politics of Postmodernism*, 167.

38 Suzanna Danuta Walters, *Material Girls: Making Sense of Feminist Cultural Theory* (Berkeley: University of California Press, 1995), 117. The most commonly cited of these conservative American post-feminists are Katie Roiphe, Naomi Wolf, and Camille Paglia.

39 Sarah Gamble, ed., *The Routledge Companion to Feminism and Postfeminism* (London and New York: Routledge, 2001), 298.

40 Sarah Gillis and Rebecca Munford, "Genealogies and Generations: The Politics and Praxis of Third Wave Feminism," *Women's History Review* vol. 13 no. 2 (2004): 168.

41 Leslie Heywood and Jennifer Drake, *Third Wave Agenda: Being Feminist, Doing Feminism* (Minneapolis: University of Minnesota Press, 1997), 3.

42 Gamble, *The Routledge Companion to Feminism and Postfeminism*, 49.

43 Ibid., 298.

44 Ibid., 327.

45 Ibid., 298.

46 Heywood and Drake, *Third Wave Agenda*, 7.

47 Lisa Rubin and Carol Nemeroff, "Feminism's Third Wave: Surfing to Oblivion?" in *The Next Generation: Third Wave Feminism Psychotherapy*, ed. Ellyn Kaschak (New York: The Haworth Press, Inc., 2001), 98.

48 Cindy Bruns and Colleen Trimble, "Rising Tide: Taking our Place as Young Feminist Pyschologists," in *The Next Generation: Third Wave Feminism Psychotherapy*, ed. Ellyn Kaschak (New York: The Haworth Press, Inc., 2001), 33.

49 Sherin Saadallah, "Muslim Feminism in the Third Wave: A Reflective Inquiry," in *Third Wave Feminism: A Critical Exploration*, eds. Stacy Gillis, Gillian Howie, and Rebecca Munford (Hampshire and New York: Palgrave MacMillan, 2004), 216.

50 Gillis and Munford, "Genealogies and Generations," 172.

51 Even the name Busting Out! references the Third Wave publication *Bust* magazine.

52 Heywood and Drake, *Third Wave Agenda*, 4.

53 Goodman, *Contemporary Feminist Theatres*, 3.

54 Rina Fraticelli, "Any Black Crippled Woman Can!" *Room of One's Own* vol. 8 no. 2, 15–16.

55 Ibid., 17.

Bibliography

Ann, Martha, and Dorothy Myers, eds. *Goddesses in World Mythology*. Santa Barbara: ABC–Clio Inc., 1993.

Anna Project, The. "Fragments, Afterthoughts." *Canadian Theatre Review* 43 (Summer 1985): 167–173.

———. "This is For You, Anna: A spectacle of revenge." *Canadian Theatre Review* 43 (Summer 1985): 127–166.

Austin, Gayle. *Feminist Theories for Dramatic Criticism*. Ann Arbor: The University of Michigan Press, 1990.

Bailey, Martha J. "Editor's Column." *Queens Quarterly* 96/1 (Spring 1989): 219.

Barton, Bruce. "Introduction: Devising the Creative Body." In *Collective Creation, Collaboration and Devising*, edited by Bruce Barton, vii–xxvii. Vol. 12 of *Critical Perspectives on Canadian Theatre in English*. Toronto: Playwrights Canada Press, 2009.

Bassnett-McGuire, Susan E. "Towards a Theory of Women's Theatre." In *Semiotics of Drama and Theatre*, edited by Herta Schmid and Aloysius Van Kestern, 445–463. Vol. 10 of *Linguistic and Literary Studies in Eastern Europe*. Amsterdam/Philadelphia: John Benjamins Publishing Co., 1984.

Baumgardner, Jennifer, and Amy Richards. *Manifesta: Young Women, Feminism and the Future*. New York: Farrar, Straus and Giroux, 2000.

Bell, Brandi Leigh-Ann. "Riding the Third Wave: Women-Produced Zines and Feminisms." *Resources for Feminist Research* vol. 29 nos. 3 and 4 (Fall 2002): 187–198.

Bell, Shannon. *Reading, Writing and Rewriting the Prostitute Body*. Bloomington and Indianapolis: Indiana University Press, 1994.

Belsey, Catherine. *Critical Practice*. New York: Methuen and Co., 1980.

Bennett, Susan. *Theatre Audiences*. London and New York: Routledge, 1990.

Bennett, Susan, and Alexandria Patience. "Bad Girls Looking for Money —Maenad Making Feminist Theatre in Alberta." *Canadian Theatre Review* 82 (Spring 1995): 10–13.

Benson, Eugene, and L.W. Conolly. *English Canadian Theatre: Perspectives on Canadian Culture*. Toronto: Oxford University Press, 1987.

Bishop, André. Foreword to *The Heidi Chronicles and Other Plays*, by Wendy Wasserstein. New York: Harcourt Brace Jovanovich, 1990.

Boni, Franco, ed. *Rhubarb-o-rama!: Plays and Playwrights from the Rhubarb! Festival*. Winnipeg: Blizzard, 1998.

Braithwaite, Diana. *Martha and Elvira*. Toronto: Sister Vision Press, 1993.

Breslauer, Jan, and Helene Keyssar. "Making Magic Public: Megan Terry's Traveling Family Circus." In Hart, *Making a Spectacle*, 169–180.

Brighton, Pam. "Directions." In *Women and Theatre: Calling the Shots*, edited by Susan Todd, 47–61. London: Faber and Faber, 1984.

Brooks, Ann. *Postfeminisms: Feminism, Cultural Theory and Cultural Forms*. London and New York: Routledge, 1997.

Bruns, Cindy M., and Colleen Trimble. "Rising Tide: Taking our Place as Young Feminist Psychologists." In Kaschak, *The Next Generation*, 19–36.

Bulmer, Alex. "Smudge." *Canadian Theatre Review* 108 (Fall 2001): 53–67.

Burke, Kelley Jo. "Charming and Rose: True Love." In *Amazing Plays: 3 from the '92 Winnipeg Fringe*, 31–62. Winnipeg: Blizzard Publishing, 1992.

Burnett, Linda. "'Redescribing a World': Towards a Theory of Shakespearean Adaptation in Canada." *Canadian Theatre Review* 111 (Summer 2002): 5–9.

Burton, Rebecca. "Adding It Up: (En)Gendering (and Racializing) Canadian Theatre." *alt.theatre: Cultural Diversity and the Stage* vol. 5 no. 1 (February 2007): 6–8.

Butler, Judith. *Gender Trouble: Feminism and the Subversion of Identity*. New York: Routledge, 1989.

———. "Performative Acts and Gender Constitution: An Essay in Phenomenology and Feminist Theory." In Case, *Performing Feminisms*, 270–282.

Canning, Charlotte. *Feminist Theaters in the U.S.A.: Staging Women's Experience*. London and New York: Routledge, 1996.

Caputi, Jane. "Psychic Activism: Feminist Mythmaking." In Larrington, *The Feminist Companion to Mythology*, 425–440.

Carson, Fiona. "Feminism and the Body." In Gamble, *The Routledge Companion to Feminism and Postfeminism*, 117–128.

Case, Sue-Ellen. *Feminism and Theatre*. London: MacMillan Publishers Ltd., 1988.

———, ed. *Performing Feminisms: Feminist Critical Theory and Feminism*. Baltimore and London: The Johns Hopkins University Press, 1990.

Chan, Marjorie. *China Doll*. Winnipeg: Scirocco, 2004.

Churchill, Caryl. Introduction to *Vinegar Tom*. In *Plays: One*. London: Methuen Drama, 1985.

Cixous, Hélène. "The Laugh of the Medusa." Translated by Keith Cohen and Paula Cohen. *Signs* I (1976): 880.

Codrington, Lisa. *Cast Iron*. Toronto: Playwrights Canada Press, 2007.

Cole, Susan G. "Ten Years and Five Minutes: Nightwood Celebrates a Decade of Feminist Theatre." *FUSE*, Spring 1990, 12–15.

———. "A Very Fertile Imagination: Interview." *Night Talk* newsletter vol. 2 no. 2 (Winter 1991): 1, 3.

Coleman, Layne. Foreword to *Age of Arousal*, by Linda Griffiths, 6–7. Toronto: Coach House Books, 2007.

Curb, Rosemary, with Phyllis Mael and Beverley Byers-Pevitts. "The First Decade of Feminist Theatre in America." *Catalogue of Feminist Theatre: Chrysalis: A Magazine of Women's Culture* 10 (April 1980): 51–75.

Daniels, Rebecca. *Women Stage Directors Speak*. Excerpted in "Gender, Creativity & Power," *American Theatre* vol. 15 no. 7 (September 1998): 30–31, 80–81.

Davey, Frank. "Toward the Ends of Regionalism." In Riegel and Wyile, *A Sense of Place*, 1–17.

de Lauretis, Teresa. *Alice Doesn't: Feminism, Semiotics, Cinema*. Bloomington: Indiana University Press, 1984.

———. *Technologies of Gender: Essays on Theory, Film and Fiction*. Bloomington: Indiana University Press, 1987.

Diamond, Elin. "(In)Visible Bodies in Churchill's Theater." In Hart, *Making a Spectacle*, 259–281.

———. "Mimesis, Mimicry and the 'True-Real.'" In Hart and Phelan, *Acting Out*, 363–382.

DiCenzo, Maria. "Review of Fair Play." *Theatre History in Canada* vol. 12 no. 2 (Fall 1991): 219.

Dickinson, Peter. "Duets, Duologues, and Black Diasporic Theatre: Djanet Sears, William Shakespeare, and Others." *Modern Drama* vol. XLV no. 2 (Summer 2002): 188–208.

Dolan, Jill. "Breaking the Code." In *Presence and Desire*, 135–150. Ann Arbor: The University of Michigan Press, 1993.

———. *The Feminist Spectator as Critic*. Ann Arbor: The University of Michigan Press, 1988.

Edwards, Justin D., and Douglas Ivison. "Introduction: Writing Canadian Cities" and "Epilogue." In *Downtown Canada: Writing Canadian Cities*, edited by Edwards and Ivison, 3–13 and 197–208. Toronto: University of Toronto Press, 2005.

Elam, Keir. *The Semiotics of Theatre and Drama*. London and New York: Methuen, 1980.

Endres, Robin. "Introduction." In *Eight Men Speak and Other Plays from the Canadian Workers' Theatre*, xi–xxxvi. Toronto: New Hogtown Press, 1976.

Feindel, Janet. *A Particular Class of Women*. Vancouver: Lazara Publications, 1988.

Fenton, Natalie. "Feminism and Popular Culture." In Gamble, *The Routledge Companion to Feminism and Postfeminism*, 104–116.

Feral, Josette. "Writing and Displacement: Women in Theatre." Translated by Barbara Kerslake. *Drama* vol. XXVII no. 4 (Dec. 1984): 549–563.

Filewod, Alan. *Collective Encounters: Documentary Theatre in English Canada*. Toronto, Buffalo, London: University of Toronto Press, 1987.

———. "Erasing Historical Difference: The Alternative Orthodoxy in Canadian Theatre." *The Theatre Journal* vol. 42 no. 2 (May 1989): 201–210.

———. "The Interactive Documentary in Canada: Catalyst Theatre's *It's About Time*." *Theatre History in Canada* vol. 6 no. 2 (Fall 1985): 133–147.

Forsyth, Louise H. "Feminist Theatre." In *Oxford Companion to Canadian Theatre*, 206. Toronto: Oxford University Press, 1989.

———. "Stripping Off Patriarchal Trappings—What Tools Remain for Making Theatre?" *alt.theatre: Cultural Diversity and the Stage* vol. 6 no. 3 (March 2009): 8–13.

Forte, Jeanie. "Women's Performance Art: Feminism and Postmodernism." In Case, *Performing Feminisms*, 251–269.

Fortier, Mark. "Shakespeare with a Difference: Genderbending and Genrebending in *Goodnight Desdemona*." *Canadian Theatre Review* 59 (Summer 1989): 47–51.

Fox, Marcia R. Introduction to *The Odd Women*, by George Gissing. New York: Norton Library, 1977.

Fraticelli, Rina. *The Status of Women in the Canadian Theatre*. A Report prepared for Status of Women Canada, June 1982. Published as "Any Black Crippled Woman Can!" *Room of One's Own* vol. 8 no. 2: 7–18.

Freedman, Barbara. "Frame-Up: Feminism, Psychoanalysis, Theatre." In Case, *Performing Feminisms*, 54–76.

Gallagher, Kathleen. "Dramatic Arenas for Ethical Stories." *Resources for Feminist Research* vol. 29 nos. 3 and 4 (Fall 2002): 167–176.

Gamble, Sarah, Ed. *The Routledge Companion to Feminism and Postfeminism*. London and New York: Routledge, 2001.

Gilbert, Sky. "Inside the Rhubarb! Festival." *Canadian Theatre Review* 49 (Winter 1986): 40–43.

Gillis, Stacy, and Rebecca Munford. "Genealogies and Generations: The Politics and Praxis of Third Wave Feminism." *Women's History Review* vol. 13 no. 2 (2004): 165–182.

Gillis, Stacy, Gillian Howie, and Rebecca Munford, eds. *Third Wave Feminism: A Critical Exploration*. Hampshire and New York: Palgrave MacMillan, 2004.

Gilman, Charlotte Perkins (Stetson). *The Yellow Wallpaper*. Old Westbury, New York: The Feminist Press, 1973.

Glen, Catherine. "On the Edge: Revisioning Nightwood." *Canadian Theatre Review* 82 (Spring 1995): 36–39.

Godard, Barbara. "Between Repetition and Rehearsal: Conditions of (Women's) Theatre in Canada in a Space of Reproduction." *Theatre Research in Canada* vol. 13 nos. 1 and 2 (Spring/Fall 1992): 18–33.

———. Introduction to *Lesbian Triptych*, by Jovette Marchessault. Translated by Yvonne M. Klein. Toronto: Women's Press, 1985.

Gold, Sylviane. "The Possession of Julie Taymor." *American Theatre* vol. 15 no. 7 (September 1998): 20–25.

Goodman, Lizbeth. *Contemporary Feminist Theatres: To Each Her Own*. New York: Routledge, 1993.

Grant, Cynthia. "Still 'Activist' after All These Years?" *Canadian Theatre Review* 117 (Winter 2004): 14–16.

Grant, Cynthia, Susan Seagrove, and Peggy Sample. "Penelope." *Canadian Theatre Review* 78 (Spring 1994): 42–58.

Grant, Diane. *What Glorious Times They Had: a satire*. Toronto: Simon and Pierre Publishing Co. Ltd.: Can Play Series, 1974.

Graves Miller, Judith. "Contemporary Women's Voices in French Theatre." *Modern Drama* vol. XXVII no. 1 (March 1989): 5–23.

Griffiths, Linda. *Age of Arousal*. Toronto: Coach House Books, 2007.

———. "Playwrights Note," "Production," "A Flagrantly Weird Age: A reaction to research, time travel and the history of the suffragettes." In Griffiths, *Age of Arousal*, 8–12, 13–22, 136–168.

Haar, Sandra. "Breeding Ground: Dyke sensibility weeded out of play's production." *RITES*, April 1991, 15.

Hadfield, D.A. *Re: Producing Women's Dramatic History: The Politics of Playing in Toronto*. Vancouver: Talonbooks, 2007.

Haraway, Donna. *Simians, Cyborgs, and Women: The Reinvention of Nature*. New York: Routledge, 1991.

Hart, Lynda, ed. *Making a Spectacle: Feminist Essays on Contemporary Women's Theatre*. Ann Arbor: University of Michigan, 1989.

Hart, Lynda, and Peggy Phelan, eds. *Acting Out: Feminist Performances*. Ann Arbor: University of Michigan Press, 1993.

Hengen, Shannon. "Towards a Feminist Comedy." *Canadian Literature* 146 (Autumn 1995): 97–109.

Heywood, Leslie, and Jennifer Drake. *Third Wave Agenda: Being Feminist, Doing Feminism*. Minneapolis: University of Minnesota Press, 1997.

Hladki, Janice. "Negotiating Drama Practices: Struggles in Racialized
    Relations of Theatre Production and Theatre Research." In *How
    Theatre Educates: Convergences and Counterpoints*, edited by Kathleen
    Gallagher and David Booth, 144–161. Toronto: University of Toronto
    Press, 2003.

Hodkinson, Yvonne. *Female Parts: The Art and Politics of Women Playwrights.*
    Montreal: Black Rose Books, 1991.

Hollingsworth, Margaret. "War Babies." In *Willful Acts.* Toronto: Coach
    House Press, 1985.

hooks, bell. *Black Looks: Race and Representation.* Boston: South End Press,
    1992.

Horne, Sharon, Susan Mathews, Pam Detrie, Mary Burke, and Becky
    Cook. "Look it up Under 'F': Dialogues of Emerging and
    Experienced Feminists." In Kaschak, *The Next Generation*, 5–18.

Houppert, Karen. "Ruth Maleczech: Her Life in Art." *American Theatre* vol.
    15 no. 7 (September 1998): 72–73, 86–87.

Hunt, Nigel. "Bringing the Heroine Back to Life." *Performing Arts* (March/
    Spring 1990): 27.

Hutcheon, Linda. "'Circling the Downspout of Empire': Post-Colonialism
    and Postmodernism." In *Unhomely States: Theorizing English-Canadian
    Postcolonialism*, edited by Cynthia Sugars, 71–93. Mississauga:
    Broadview Press, 2004.

———. *The Politics of Postmodernism.* London and New York: Routledge, 1989.

Ives, L. Patricia. "The Very Best Bad Girls Create…" *Canadian Theatre
    Review* 50 (Spring 1987): 30–33.

Jagger, Alison M. *Feminist Politics and Human Nature.* Totawa, NJ: Rowman
    and Allanheld, 1983.

Johnston, Denis W. *Up the Mainstream: The Rise of Toronto's Alternative
    Theatres.* Toronto, Buffalo, London: University of Toronto Press,
    1991.

Jones, Heather. "Connecting Issues: Theorizing English-Canadian
    Women's Drama." In Much, *Women on the Canadian Stage*, 81–91.

Kamen, Paula. *Her Way: Young Women Remake the Sexual Revolution.* New
    York: New York University Press, 2000.

Kaplan, E. Anne. *Women and Film: Both Sides of the Camera.* New York:
    Methuen, 1983.

Kaplan, Jon. "Actors make Rhubarb." *NOW,* November 1982, n.p.

———. "Cynthia Grant Builds Images." *NOW,* August 1982, 13.

———. "Kate Lushington: Feminism fuels director's vision for fertile
    comedy." *NOW,* 31 January–6 February 1991, 22.

———. "Renders goes solo in noisy kids' show." *NOW,* 17–23 December
    1987, 19.

Kaschak, Ellyn, Ed. *The Next Generation: Third Wave Feminism Psychotherapy.* New York: The Haworth Press, Inc., 2001.

Keeney Smith, Patricia. "Living with Risk." *Canadian Theatre Review* 38 (Fall 1983): 34–43.

Knowles, Ric. *The Theatre of Form and the Production of Meaning: Contemporary Canadian Dramaturgies* (Toronto: ECW Press, 1999).

Knowles, Richard Paul. "Othello in Three Times." In *Shakespeare in Canada: A World Elsewhere?* edited by Diana Brydon and Irena R. Makaryk, 371–394. Toronto: University of Toronto Press, 2002.

——. "Reading Material: Transfers, Remounts, and the Production of Meaning in Contemporary Toronto Drama and Theatre." *Essays on Canadian Writing* nos. 51–52 (Winter 1993–Spring 1994): 258–295.

Kristeva, Julia. "Woman Can Never Be Defined." In *New French Feminisms,* edited by Elaine Marks and Isabella de Courtivron, 137. New York: Schocken Books, 1981.

Lamont, Rosette C. "Introduction." In *Women on the Verge: Seven Avant Garde Plays,* edited by Rosette C. Lamont. New York: Applause Theatre Books, 1993.

Larrington, Carolynne, ed. *The Feminist Companion to Mythology.* London: Pandora Press, 1992.

Lavery, Bryony. "But Will Men Like It? Or living as a feminist writer without committing murder." In *Women and Theatre: Calling the Shots,* edited by Susan Todd, 24–32. London: Faber and Faber, 1984.

Leavitt, Dinah Luise. *Feminist Theatre Groups.* Jefferson, N.C: McFarland & Company Inc., 1980.

Lesnick, Harry, ed. "Burning City Women." In *Guerilla Street Theatre.* New York: Avon Books, 1973.

Levine, Meredith. "Feminist Theatre—Toronto 87." *Theatrum: A Theatre Journal* (Spring 1987): 5–10.

Lushington, Kate. "The Changing Body of Women's Work." *Broadside* (August/September 1989): 20–21.

——. "Fear of Feminism." *Canadian Theatre Review* 43 (Summer 1985): 5–11.

——. "The Possibility and the Habit." *FUSE,* Summer 1983, 62–63.

MacArthur, Michelle. "Patrolling Our Borders: Critical Reception of Lisa Codrington's *Cast Iron.*" *alt.theatre: Cultural Diversity and the Stage* vol. 6 no. 3 (March 2009): 24–33.

MacDonald, Ann-Marie. *Good Night Desdemona (Good Morning Juliet).* Toronto: Coach House Press, 1990.

MacDonald, Ann-Marie, and Kathleen Gallagher. "Intellectual Passions, Feminist Commitments, and Divine Comedies: A Dialogue with Ann-Marie MacDonald." In *How Theatre Educates: Convergences and*

Counterpoints, edited by Kathleen Gallagher and David Booth, 247–267. Toronto: University of Toronto Press, 2003.

Mael, Phyllis, with Rosemary Curb and Beverley Byers-Pevitts. "The First Decade of Feminist Theatre in America." *Catalogue of Feminist Theatre: Chrysalis; A Magazine of Women's Culture* 10 (April 1980): 51–75.

mandiela, ahdri zhina. *dark diaspora... in DUB.* Toronto: Sister Vision Press, 1991.

Martin, David. "'Regionalist' Fiction and the Problem of Cultural Knowledge." In Riegel and Wyile, *A Sense of Place,* 35–50

McKay, Ellen. "The Spectre of Straight Shakespeare." *Canadian Theatre Review* 111 (Summer 2002): 10–14.

McKinnie, Michael. *City Stages: Urban Space in a Global City.* Toronto: University of Toronto Press, 2007.

McNay, Lois. *Foucault and Feminism.* Cambridge: Polity Press, 1992.

Miles, Julia. "Introduction." In *The Women's Project: Seven New Plays by Women,* edited by Julia Miles. New York: Performing Arts Journal Publications and American Place Theatre, 1980.

———. "Introduction." In *The Women's Project* 2. New York: Performing Arts Journal Publications, 1984.

———. *Womenswork: 5 New Plays from the Women's Project.* New York: Applause Books, 1989.

———. "Year of the Woman?" *American Theatre* vol. 15 no. 7 (September 1998): 19.

Moi, Toril. *Sexual/Textual Politics: Feminist Literary Theory.* London: Methuen, 1985.

Mojica, Monique. "Chocolate Woman dreams the Milky Way." In Barton, *Collective Creation, Collaboration and Devising,* 167–181.

———. *Princess Pocahontas and the Blue Spots.* Toronto: Women's Press, 1991.

———. "Stories From the Body: Blood Memory and Organic Texts." *alt. theatre: Cultural Diversity and the Stage* vol. 4 nos. 2 and 3 (May 2006): 16–20.

Much, Rita. "Introduction." In *New Canadian Drama* 6, vii–xii. Ottawa: Borealis Press, 1993.

———, ed. *Women on the Canadian Stage: The Legacy of Hrotsvit.* Winnipeg: Blizzard Publishing, 1992.

Much, Rita, and Judith Rudakoff, eds. *Fair Play: Twelve Women Speak; Conversations with Canadian Playwrights.* Toronto: Simon and Pierre, 1990.

Mulvey, Laura. "Visual Pleasure and Narrative Cinema." In *Film Theory and Criticism,* edited by Gerald Mast, Marshall Cohen, and Leo Braudy. New York and Oxford: Oxford University Press, 1992.

New, W.H. *Land Sliding: Imagining Space, Presence, and Power in Canadian Writing.* Toronto: University of Toronto Press, 1997.

Nightwood Theatre. "Notes from the Front Lines." *Canadian Theatre Review* 43 (Summer 1985): 44–51.

Novy, Marianne. "Saving Desdemona and/or Ourselves: Plays by Ann-Marie MacDonald and Paula Vogel." In *Transforming Shakespeare: Contemporary Women's Re-visions in Literature and Performance,* edited by Marianne Novy, 67–85. New York: St. Martin's Press, 1999.

Palmer, Alisa. Nightwood Theatre newsletter, Spring 1997, n.p.

Peerbaye, Soraya. "Look to the Lady: Re-examining Women's Theatre." *Canadian Theatre Review* 84 (Fall 1995): 22–25.

Phelan, Peggy. *Unmarked: The Politics of Performance.* London and New York: Routledge, 1993.

Phoca, Sophia, and Rebecca Wright. *Introducing Postfeminism.* New York: Totem Books, 1999.

Porter, Laurin R. "Shakespeare's Sisters: Desdemona, Juliet and Constance Ledbelly in *Goodnight Desdemona (Good Morning Juliet).*" *Modern Drama* vol. XXXVIII no. 3 (Fall 1995): 362–377.

Porter, McKenzie. "Ida: postgraduate study in wasted intelligence." *Toronto Star,* 26 October 1979, 101.

Porter, Natalie, Dalia G. Ducker, Holley E. Ferrell, and Laura Helton. "Exploring the Rift: An Intergenerational Dialogue About Feminism." In Kaschak, *The Next Generation,* 57–78.

Posner, Michael. "In search of a little play equity." *Globe and Mail,* 8 August 2009, R7.

Pribram, E. Deidre, ed. *Female Spectators: Looking at Film and Television.* London and New York: Verso, 1988.

Pryse, Marjorie. "Writing Out of the Gap: Regionalism, Resistance, and Relational Reading." In Riegel and Wyile, *A Sense of Place,* 19–34.

Purkiss, Diane. "Women's Rewriting of Myth." In Larrington, *The Feminist Companion to Mythology,* 441–455.

Reinelt, Janelle. "Feminist Theory and the Problem of Performance." *Modern Drama* 32 (March 1989): 48–51.

Renders, Kim. "Letter to the Editor." *Canadian Theatre Review* 119 (Summer 2005): 4.

Rewa, Natalie. "Baṇuta Rubess: New Languages for Performance." *Tessera* vol. 11 (Winter 1991): 82–91.

Riegel, Christian, and Herb Wyile, eds. *A Sense of Place: Re-evaluating Regionalism in Canadian and American Writing.* Edmonton: The University of Alberta Press, 1998.

Riis, Sharon. *The True Story of Ida Johnson.* The Women's Press: Toronto, 1976.

Roberts, Diane. "Dramaturgy: A Nightwood Conversation." *Canadian Theatre Review* 87 (Summer 1996): 22–24.

Ross, Lena B., ed. *To Speak or Be Silent: The Paradox of Disobedience in the Lives of Women*. Wilmette, Il.: Chiron Publications, 1993.

Rozett, Martha Tuck. *Talking Back to Shakespeare*. Newark: University of Delaware Press, 1994.

Rubess, Baṇuta. *Pope Joan: a non-historical comedy*. Toronto: Playwrights Union, 1984.

Rubess, Baṇuta, with Peggy Christopherson, Ann-Marie MacDonald, Mary Marzo, Kim Renders, and Maureen White. *Smoke Damage: A story of the witch hunts*. Toronto: Playwrights Canada, 1985.

Rubin, Lisa and Carol Nemeroff. "Feminism's Third Wave: Surfing to Oblivion?" In Kaschak, *The Next Generation*, 91–104.

Saadallah, Sherin. "Muslim Feminism in the Third Wave: A Reflective Inquiry." In Gillis, Howie, and Munford, *Third Wave Feminism: A Critical Exploration*, 216–226.

Scott, Shelley. "Enacting *This is For You, Anna*." *Canadian Theatre Review* 121 (Winter 2005): 41–45.

Sears, Djanet. *Afrika Solo*. Toronto: Sister Vision Press, 1990.

Sears, Djanet, and Alison Sealy-Smith with Ric Knowles. "The Nike Method." *Canadian Theatre Review* 97 (Winter 1998): 24–30.

Sheehan, Nick. "Theatre Centre's collective core." *NOW*, 15–21 March 1984, 7.

Shiller, Romy. "Drag King Invasion: Taking Back the Throne." *Canadian Theatre Review* 86 (Spring 1996): 24–28.

Showalter, Elaine. *Sexual Anarchy: Gender and Culture at the Fin de Siècle*. New York: Viking, 1990.

Sidnell, Michael J. "Used Words." *Canadian Theatre Review* 75 (Summer 1993): 4–7.

Snyder, Laurel, and Lisa Miya-Jervis, Donna Jean Troka, Audrey Bilger, Jeanne Fury, Tara Bracco, Ayun Halliday. "Now Showing! Broad Way: Starring the ultratalented women making great theater down the street from you." *Bitch: Feminist Response to Pop Culture* no. 17, Summer 2002, 34–43, 95.

Sperling, Shoshana. *Finding Regina*. Winnipeg: Scirocco Drama, 2003.

Spiers, John and Pierre Coustillas. *The Rediscovery of George Gissing: A Reader's Guide*. London: National Book League, 1971.

Sumi, Glenn. "Shoshana Sperling: Funny Girl Plays with her Regina." *NOW* vol. 22 no. 25, 20–26 February 2003, 58.

Vingoe, Mary. Letter to Nathan H. Gilbert, Executive Administrator, Laidlaw Foundation, 1 March 1984.

Volker, Francine. "Running a Redlight." *Theatrum* (April/May 1989): 29, 52.

Wagner, Jane. *The Search for Signs of Intelligent Life in the Universe*. New York: Harper and Row, 1986.

Wagner, Vit. "A Shallow Look at Sexual Politics." *Toronto Star,* 7 February 1991, B5.

Wallace, Robert. *Producing Marginality: Theatre and Criticism in Canada*. Saskatoon: Fifth House Publishers, 1990.

Walling, Savannah. "Survival Techniques: Forces on the Artists/Artists on the Forces." *Canadian Theatre Review* 88 (Fall 1996): 11–17.

Walters, Suzanna Danuta. *Material Girls: Making Sense of Feminist Cultural Theory*. Berkeley: University of California Press, 1995.

Wandor, Michelene. *Post-War British Drama: Look Back in Gender*. London and New York: Routledge, 2001.

Williams, Jay. *Stage Left: An Engrossing Account of the Radical Theatre Movement in America*. New York: Scribner, 1974.

Williams, Linda. "When the Woman Looks." In *Re-Vision: Essays in Feminist Film Criticism*, edited by Mary Ann Doane, Patricia Mellencamp, and Linda Williams. Los Angeles: University Publications of America, Inc./American Film Institute, 1984.

Wilson, Ann. "Critical Revisions: Ann-Marie MacDonald's *Goodnight Desdemona (Good Morning Juliet)*." In Much, *Women on the Canadian Stage*, 1–12.

———. "The Politics of the Script." *Canadian Theatre Review* 43 (Summer 1985): 174–179.

Wyatt Selkirk, Myrna. "Cultural Diversity and the Magnetic North Theatre Festival: A Chat with Mary Vingoe, Artistic Director of the Magnetic North Theatre Festival." *alt.theatre: Cultural Diversity and the Stage* vol. 5 no. 1 (February 2007): 12–14.

Wyile, Herb, Christian Riegel, Karen Overbye, and Don Perkins. "Introduction: Regionalism Revisited." In Riegel and Wyile, *A Sense of Place*, ix–xiv.

Zimmerman, Cynthia. *Playwriting Women: Female Voices in English Canada*. Toronto: Simon and Pierre, 1994.

Index

Note: **Bold** numbers indicate pictures.

D

E

F

Marquis Book Printing Inc.

Québec, Canada

2010